Das Reich ohne Mitte

The Empire Without a Center

Thomas D. Trummer
Hrsg. / Ed.

VERLAG FÜR MODERNE KUNST

Inhalt
Content

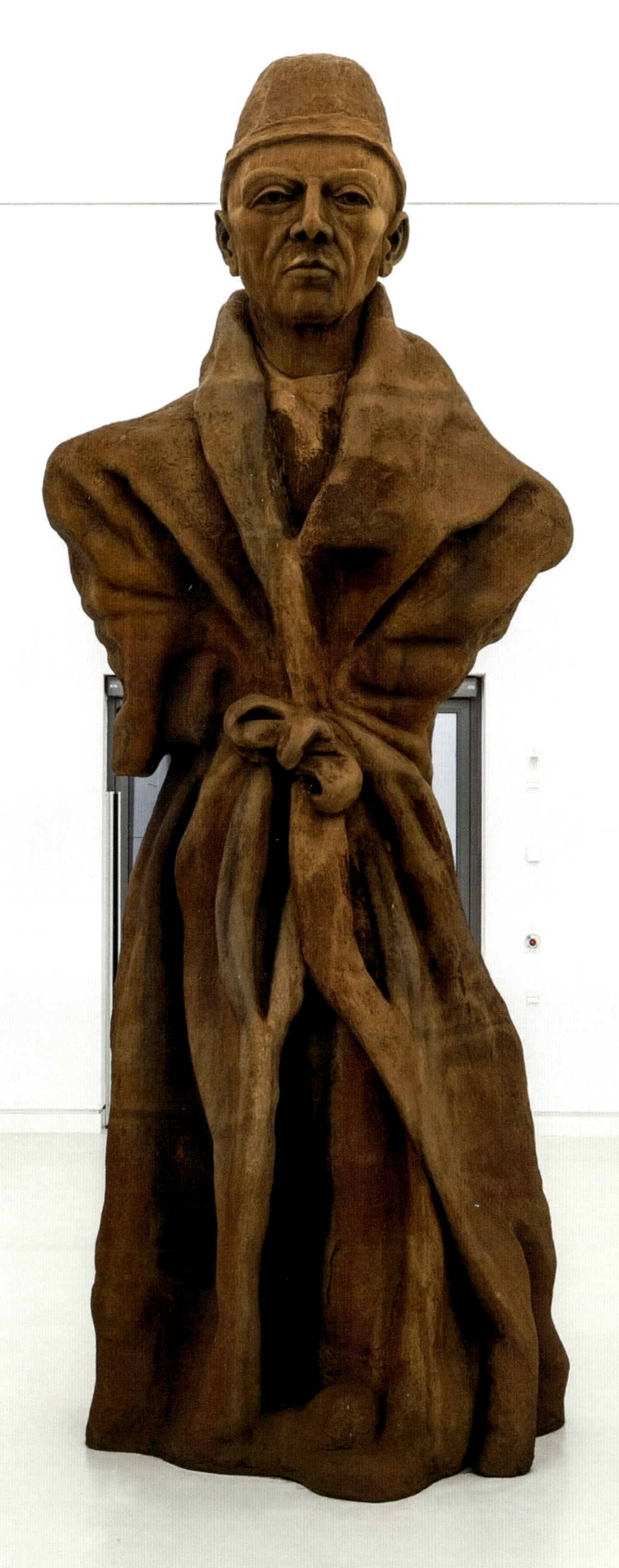

Einleitung
Introduction

Thomas D. Trummer

Wie stellt sich der Staat selbst dar, welches Bild findet er für sich, und vor allem welche Statuen? Denn in den Statuen begegnet der Staat seinen Bürger/innen. Er stellt sich auf und an die besten Plätze. Öffentliche Statuen sind selten bescheiden. Es sind Herrschaftsbekundungen oder Huldigungen, Siegeszeichen oder pompöse Weihestätten. Statuen sind Machtdemonstrationen. Sie setzen sich an Boulevards und Sternkreuzungen, sie strahlen herab von Höhenzügen oder stellen sich an urbane oder landschaftliche Prägepunkte. Es geht um Beständigkeit, um Zeitlosigkeit und großen Maßstab, ja und – um einen Auftrag. Statuen, die politisch beauftragt werden, tragen eine Botschaft, sie sind Statements, Stellungnahmen im wörtlichen Sinn.

Eine plastische Stellungnahme ist die Darstellung der *Germania* auf dem Niederwald in der Nähe von Rüdesheim allemal (Kat. 04 ff). Misst man den Sockel mit, ist die Statue über 30 Meter hoch. Sie wird unmittelbar nach dem Deutsch-Französischen Krieg 1870/1871 in Auftrag gegeben und befindet sich nur wenige Kilometer entfernt von Mainz. Die Personifikation Deutschlands ist rundum sichtbar auf einer bewaldeten Anhöhe über dem Rhein. Dargestellt ist eine Frau als Allegorie Deutschlands. Die Figur sitzt auf einem Thron, der von grimmigen Adlern bewacht wird. In der linken Hand hält sie ein Schwert, mit der Rechten bekrönt sie sich. Das wallende Haar gleitet die Brust herab. Die üppigen Symbole sind Kennzeichen des Historismus. Auch die Durchmengung geschichtlicher Stile und Zitate ist ein Merkmal dieser Epoche. Die Gestalt der *Germania* und ihre Gesichtszüge sind zum Beispiel von der Antike inspiriert. Wappen, Brustpanzer und Siegeszeichen erinnern an mittelalterliche Panzer und Rüstungen. Auch andere Elemente verweisen auf historische Bezüge. Alle diese Merkmale dienen jedoch der Rechtfertigung der Gegenwart: der Errichtung des deutschen Kaiserreichs nach erfolgreichem Feldzug. Diesen Bezug stellt das Programm der Statue unverhohlen dar. Unter dem Standbild der *Germania* ist ein Relief mit vielen Köpfen und Körpern zu sehen. Es zeigt Kaiser Wilhelm in der Mitte reitend, umgeben von seinem militärischen Gefolge. Alle dargestellten Personen sind identifizierbar. Als Zeugen beglaubigen sie die Apotheose, zugleich sind sie Würdenträger und faktische historische Gründer. Dazu kommen noch andere, idealere Zeugen. An den Ecken stehen die beiden allegorischen Figuren von Krieg und Friede, an den Seitenflächen des Sockels sind die Orte der Schlachten gelistet. Nirgendwo wird Bescheidenheit ruchbar. Im Gegenteil, die monumentale Anlage wirkt wie ein pompöses Theaterprospekt. Die Skulptur ist ein Huldigungsmonument hoch erhaben auf einem Hügel. Sie verhält sich wie eine laut tönende Kundgebung. Sie ruft jedes mögliche Medium sichtbarer Verlautbarung auf: Bilder, Texte, Embleme, Gesten und Attribute.

How does a nation present itself, what imagery does it use for this purpose, and especially, which statues? Because it is through statues, erected at the most prominent locations, that a nation addresses its citizens. Public statues are rarely of a modest nature. They demonstrate authority or pay tribute, symbols of victory and pompous places of worship. Statues are demonstrations of power. They mark boulevards and squares; they stare down from high above, gracing mountain ranges as well as urban and scenic points of interest. Statues emit a sense of stability, timelessness and magnitude — and yes, a mission. Statues commissioned within a political content bear a message; they serve as statements.

One such sculptural statement is the monument of *Germania* on the Niederwald near Rüdesheim (cat. 04 ff). With its base, the statue is more than 30 meters tall. It was commissioned directly following the Franco-Prussian War of 1870 – 71 and is located just a few kilometres outside of Mainz. This personification of Germany was erected on a forested hill overlooking the Rhine and is visible from any angle. The female figure represented in the sculpture is an allegory of the nation of Germany. Seated on a throne and guarded by fierce eagles, she holds a sword in her left hand, and crowns herself with her right. Her long wavy hair flows over her breast. Such profuse symbols are characteristic of historicism, while the mixture of historical styles and quotations is a particular trait of this epoch. The statue of *Germania* and her facial features are, for instance, inspired by the art of classical antiquity. Her coat of arms, breastplate, and trophy are reminiscent of medieval armours and weaponries, and other elements are indicative of historical references. All of these features, however, solely serve as a justification for the present: the establishment of the German Empire following its triumphant victory. The entire make-up of the statue is a blatant reference to this. Beneath the figure of *Germania* is a relief depicting numerous heads and bodies. It shows Emperor Wilhelm in the centre on horseback, surrounded by his commanders and soldiers. All the people depicted in the relief can be identified. As witnesses, they affirm the apotheosis, but they are also dignitaries founded in historical fact. Added to this are other, more idealistic onlookers. The corners are adorned with two allegorical figures symbolising war and peace; the areas on the side of the base list the places the battles had taken place. There are no expressions of modesty here. Quite the contrary, this monumental work comes across as a pompous theatrical backdrop. The sculpture is a homage situated high above a hilltop, a boisterous declaration. It invokes every possible medium of visible proclamation: imagery, text, emblems, gestures, and power.

It is worth mentioning that the monument, which was inaugurated in 1883 in the presence of the Emperor and within the framework of

Es ist wert, erwähnt zu werden, dass das Denkmal, das 1883 unter Anwesenheit des Kaisers und im Rahmen eines umfangreichen Zeremonienprotokolls eröffnet wird, eigentlich aus einem Lied hervorgeht: *Die Wacht am Rhein*. Die Skulptur ist eine Art erstarrter Gesang. Das Soldatenlied, dessen Text bereits um 1840 verfasst wird, wird zuerst bei Sängerwettbewerben vorgetragen. Es erfreut sich bei folkloristischen Chören großer Beliebtheit. Anlässlich Wilhelms Silberhochzeit erhält das Lied staatliche preußische Würde. Sein späterer Status im Kaiserreich kommt dem Rang einer informellen Hymne gleich. Am Niederwald wird das Lied angestimmt. Es wird bei der Grundsteinlegung gesungen und bei der feierlichen Enthüllung im Jahr 1883 (Kat. 06). Auch in nachfolgender Geschichte bleibt *Die Wacht am Rhein* populär. Sie wird immer dann skandiert, wenn es darum geht, dem „Erbfeind" Frankreich die Stirn zu bieten. Deshalb ist der Text entschlossen und kriegerisch. Dazu kommen lautmalerische Akzente. Scharfe Konsonanten und kantige Verse erinnern an Kampf und Waffenstreit. „Es braust ein Ruf wie Donnerhall, wie Schwertgeklirr und Wogenprall". (Kat. 30) Wellenförmig ist gleichfalls die emotionale Dynamik des Liedes. Der Refrain versucht, die Erregung zu beruhigen. Er wendet sich an die bangenden Menschen hinter der Front. „Lieb Vaterland magst ruhig sein, fest steht und treu die Wacht am Rhein". Bezeichnenderweise sind die Strophen des Liedes unter dem Kaiser in Stein gemeißelt.

Die markige Sprache und der Sieg über Frankreich sind nur zwei Gründe, warum Lied, Text und Statue allgemein bekannt werden. Dazu kommen noch Zirkulation und Verbreitung. Die Statue erhält eine Reichweite über ihre Sichtbarkeitsgrenzen hinaus. Dies wird durch Reproduktionen ermöglicht, die von ihr in vielen Bildern angefertigt werden. Das 19. Jahrhundert ist das Zeitalter national gesinnter Vervielfältigung. Die Propagandamaschinerie des Wilhelminismus sorgt für die Vermehrung und auch allgemeine Leitbilder der Erziehung. Die Figur wird dadurch zu einem begehrten und weithin bekannten Sujet. Dies lässt sich gut an der Konjunktur der Bildreproduktion nachweisen. In der Ausstellung sind zahlreiche Postkarten zu sehen, die im Zuge der Errichtung, der Eröffnung und danach entstehen (Kat. 07, 11 – 14, 19, 20). Die *Germania* wird als nationale Weihestätte gefeiert. Dazu wird sie zum Sinnbild deutscher Selbstdarstellung. Auch Perioden des Niedergangs werden an ihrem Schicksal dokumentiert. Eine Postkarte zeigt Reich und Allegorie erniedrigt (Kat. 11). Nach dem Ersten Weltkrieg sitzt *Germania* vor ihrem eigenen Sockel, die linksrheinischen Gebiete mussten entmilitarisiert werden. Andere Karten belegen neuerliche Erregung und Widerstandslust. Bei der Saarkundgebung der Nationalsozialisten wird die Statue in den Mittelpunkt gesetzt (Kat. 20). Das Gelände wird zur Beflaggung genutzt. Bis

extensive ceremonial protocol, is actually based on a song, "Die Wacht am Rhein" (Watch on the Rhine). The sculpture is thus a sort of song set in stone. The patriotic hymn, whose lyrics had been penned in 1840, was initially performed during *Song festivals* events. It was extremely popular among folklore choirs, and was performed on the occasion of Wilhelm's silver wedding anniversary, where it attained a sense of national Prussian honour. Its later status in the Empire was that of an informal hymn. On Niederwald, the monument embodies this song. It was sung during the laying of its foundation stone, as well as on the occasion of its festive inauguration in the year 1883 (cat. 06). In the years to follow, the song retained its popularity. It was sung on occasions that involved a display of defiance toward "arch enemy" France, which is why the lyrics themselves are unflinching and bellicose. It is further characterised by onomatopoetic accents. Sharp consonants and coarse verses are reminiscent of battle and armed conflict. "The cry resounds like thunder's peal, like crashing waves and clang of steel." (cat. 30) The emotional dynamics of the song are also equally undulating. The refrain attempts to appease the uproar, addressing the fearful populace behind the front. "Dear Fatherland, no fear be thine, Firm and True stands the Watch, the Watch at the Rhine." Unsurprisingly, these are the verses engraved in stone beneath the Emperor.

The pithy use of language and the victory over France are merely two reasons for the general popularity of the song, its lyrics, and the statue. Further reasons are circulation and distribution. The statue has a reach that far surpasses its limits of visibility, achieved by numerous reproductions. The 19th century was an era of patriotic reproduction; the propaganda machine of the Wilhelmine period also ensured its distribution for additional general educational purposes. This turned the figure into a much sought-after and popular subject, which is confirmed by the extent to which the image was reproduced. The exhibition shows several postcards which were created during the course of its construction, inauguration, and afterwards (cat. 07, 11 – 14, 19, 20). *Germania* is celebrated as a national shrine, making her a symbol of German self-expression. Periods of defeat are also documented in her fate. One postcard illustrates the German Reich and its symbolic debasement (cat. 11). After the First World War, when the territories on the left bank of the Rhine had to be demilitarised, *Germania* is shown seated before her own pedestal. Other cards document the excitement of new things to come and a zest for resistance. During the Saar manifestations of the National Socialists, the statue has a central position (cat. 20). The perimeter is used for the display of banners. References and quotations made in relation to this event are still being made to this day, extending up to Johannes Mario Simmel, a writer who uses the refrain of the lyrics for a title of an espionage tale that takes place during the period of the

heute dauert die Kette der Referenzen und Bezugnahmen an. Sie reicht bis zu Johannes Mario Simmel, der im Kalten Krieg einer Spionage-Geschichte den Titel des Refrains gibt (Kat. 16). Auch Udo Jürgens schreibt 1970 einen Schlager, der sich „Lieb Vaterland" nennt (Kat. 28). Im Sinne der 68er Generation geraten die altbackenen Funktionäre und Bonzen der Wirtschaftswunderzeit ins Visier. Diese Referenzen, von denen unzählbare im Umlauf sind, sind mehr als nur Fußnoten einer bis heute wirkenden Geschichte. Es sind mediale Übertragungen. Sie verbreiten sich durch Übersetzungen, in denen ein Ausdrucksträger einen anderen ersetzt. So ist die Geschichte der *Germania* selbst eine Geschichte medialer Substituierung. Ihr Sinnbild wird durch die Kunstgattungen weitergereicht. Aus einem ursprünglich politischen Gedicht entsteht ein populäres Lied, aus dem Lied wird eine Statue. Die Statue stützt die nationale Ideologie und die Rheinromantik, diese wiederum bewirkt eine Flut von Postkarten. Die Postkartensujets sorgen für die bis heute andauernde touristische Anziehung, die ihrerseits an die Anfänge erinnert. Auch moderne Medien treiben diesen Staffellauf weiter. Ab den 1970er und 1980er Jahren kommen Fernsehbeiträge hinzu. Das Fernsehen vereinigt Text, Bild und akustische Untermalung und aktualisiert demnach Eigenschaften, die schon im ursprünglichen Standbild in Rüdesheim angelegt waren. Einige dieser TV-Beiträge sind in der Ausstellung in Ausschnitten zu sehen. An diesen von öffentlichen Anstalten gedrehten Produktionen wird die Verquickung der Medien besonders deutlich. Schaulust und Erwartungshaltungen, Blickbedürfnisse und Geschichtsstereotypen werden gepflegt und weitergegeben. Damit greifen die jeweils neuesten Medien die Urbotschaft des Denkmals sinnverwandt und getreu auf. Schon die *Germania* war ja bemüht, Text, Bild und Botschaft rhetorisch zu verbreiten.

Auch wenn diese Fernsehbeiträge der Nachkriegszeit in demokratischem Geist verfasst sind und dem wilhelminischen Pomp kritisch gegenüberstehen, stehen sie dennoch in der Tradition der Bildverehrung und des Reproduktionsbegehrens. Das Fernsehen wirkt dabei als Nachfahre der bebilderten Postille des 19. Jahrhunderts. Die Geschichte der Postkarte ist übrigens eng mit dem Deutsch-Französischen Krieg verknüpft. Die so genannte „Correspondenzkarte", die zuvor in Österreich-Ungarn eingeführt wird, kommt noch während des zweiten Kriegsjahres in Gebrauch. Deutsche Soldaten haben freie Feldpost. Deren Kriegserlebnisse und die Statue sind daher eng verwoben. Bald danach entwickelt sich die für die *Germania* so wichtige Ansichtskarte. Weil im 19. Jahrhundert für die Anschrift eine Seite der Karte vorgesehen ist, bleibt für den Text ausschließlich die Bildseite. Daher sehen Ansichtskarten dieser Zeit im Binnenraum ihrer Motive freie Felder vor, um Nachrichten und Grüße aufzunehmen (Kat. 07). Das Sujet der Germania eignet sich dafür bestens, weil weite Landschaftsblicke Platz bieten oder Himmelsstreifen über der Statue Leerstellen zur Beschriftung freigeben.

Das Denkmal am Niederwald wird heute etwa von einer Million Besucher/innen im Jahr besichtigt. Viele sind Touristen aus dem benachbarten Frankreich, einige kommen sogar von anderen Kontinenten. Bedenkt man jedoch die akademische Ausführung des Werkes, scheint dieser Zuspruch kunsthistorisch kaum gerechtfertigt. Selten darf sich ein Kunstwerk in Deutschland solcher Aufmerksamkeit erfreuen. Das

Cold War (cat. 16). German singer and composer Udo Jürgens wrote a song in 1970 entitled *Lieb Vaterland* (Dear Fatherland) (cat. 28). Within the context of the Protests of 1968, focus is placed on the traditional functionaries and fat cats of the Wirtschaftswunder period. Such references, of which countless examples have been published, are mere footnotes to a history whose roots have extended to the events of current times. They are medial transmissions, disseminated through translations, one expression of which replaces the other. The history of *Germania* has thus itself become a history of transitional substitution. Her allegory is passed on through various genres; a popular song arises from a political poem and the song goes on to become a statue. The statue is a pillar of national ideology and the romance of the river Rhine, resulting in a torrent of postcards. To this day, the picture postcards have an appeal for tourists that is reminiscent of the early days. Modern media also continue to spread this symbolism. Television broadcasts started to be produced in the 1970s and 80s, combining words, imagery and acoustics, offering an entirely new take on the original properties of the statue in Rüdesheim. Some of these TV broadcasts are also shown in the exhibition. The interplay of the media becomes particularly apparent in such public institutions. Curiosity and expectation, the need to be seen, and historical stereotypes are nurtured and passed on, whereby state-of-the-art media faithfully takes on the original purpose of the statue. *Germania* herself was known for her ability to disseminate text, imagery, and statements to the masses.

Despite the fact that television broadcasts of the post-war era have been created in a democratic spirit and have been vigilantly critical of Wilhelmine pomp, they are nevertheless conceived in the tradition of symbolic worship and reproductive adoration. The role of television in this sense is that of a descendant of the illustrated tabloids of the 19th century. Incidentally, the history of the postcard is closely interlinked with the Franco-Prussian War. The so-called *Correspondence Card*, which had previously been introduced in Austria-Hungary, was still used during the second year of the war. German soldiers were afforded free army postal services. Their experiences of the war and the statue are therefore closely intertwined. Soon after, the illustrative postcard, which was to become a decisive element for *Germania*, was developed. As the front side of postcards of the 19th century was reserved for the address of the recipient, only the side bearing the image could be used to write text on. Thus postcards from this period had a blank field for writing within the postcard's image (cat. 07). The *Germania* motif was particularly suitable for this purpose as the wide landscape and horizon offered ample space for writing.

Today, the monument on Niederwald is frequented by some one million visitors every year. Many of the tourists visiting the statue hail from neighbouring France, while some come from different continents. However, considering the work's academic accomplishment, this popularity hardly seems art-historically justified. Rarely does a piece of German art attract so much attention. The work of art created by Johannes Schilling is the product of a competition that was uncritically dedicated to the contemporary aesthetic taste of that period. Schilling understood the principles of idealistic art. His contribution to the history of art from a contemporary perspective, however, is marginal. Added to this is the political message;

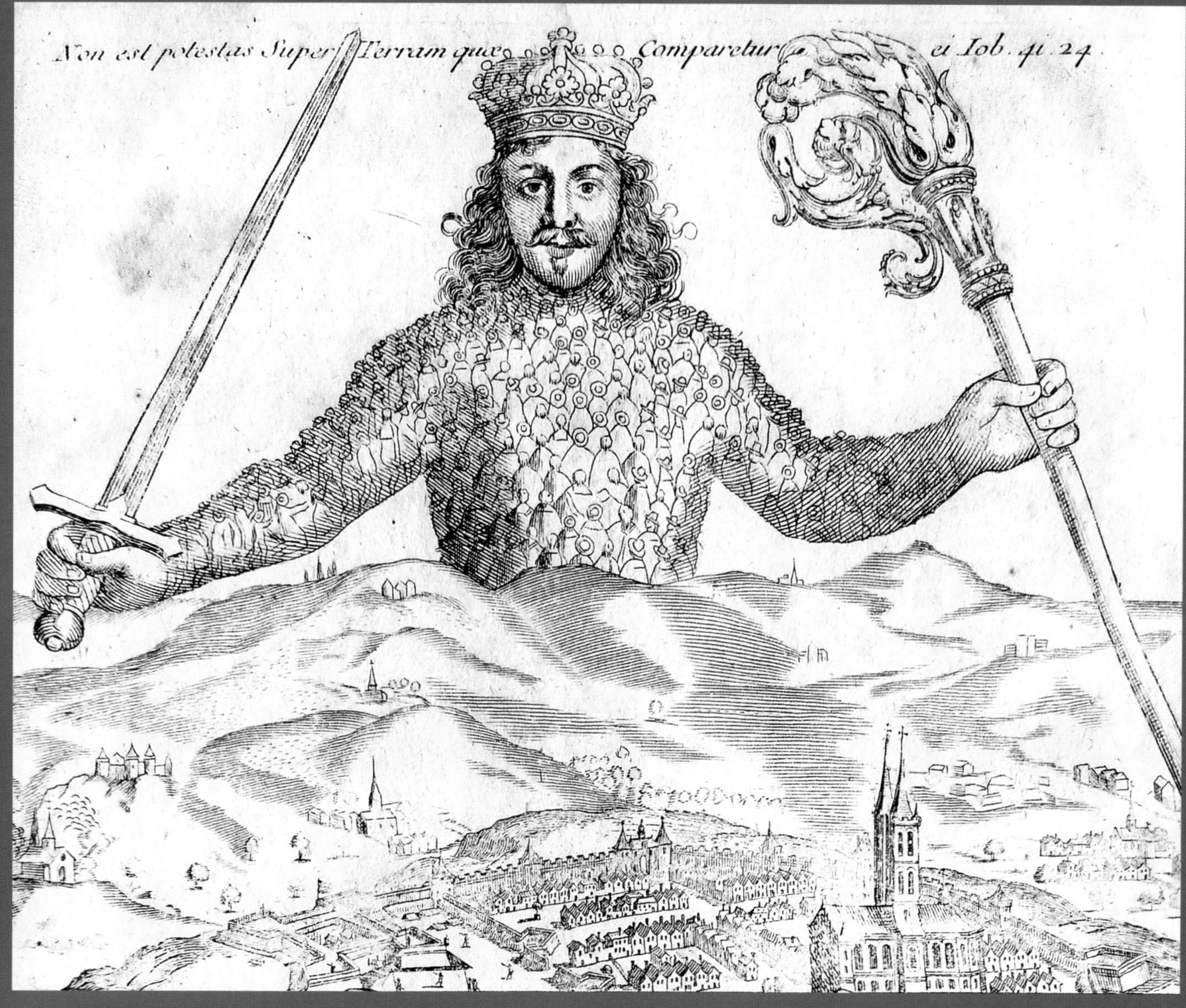

01.1

01

Thomas Hobbes
Leviathan
1651 Frontispiz von Abraham Bosse
Kupferstich/Copperplate engraving
24,1 × 15,7 cm
Niedersächsische Staats- und
Universitätsbibliothek Göttingen

01.1
Frontispiz/Frontispiece, Detail

01.2
Frontispiz/Frontispiece

Zur Mitte des 17. Jahrhunderts verfasst der
englische Philosoph Thomas Hobbes mit

Leviathan eines der wichtigsten Bücher politischer Philosophie. Zur Illustration seiner
Überlegungen zum staatlichen Recht als Ge-
meinschaftsvertrag lässt Hobbes von dem
niederländischen Stecher Abraham Bosse ein
Titelbild entwerfen. Das Frontispiz zeigt
Leviathan – ursprünglich ein apokalyptisches
Monster aus dem Alten Testament – in Hobbes' Auslegung jedoch ein bekrönter Friedensfürst, der über Land, Kultur und Menschen
regiert. Die Darstellung fasst die Grundge-
danken des Traktats zusammen. Im oberen
Teil des Bildes ist der bärtige Fürst mit den
Insignien der weltlichen und kirchlichen
Gewalt, Schwert und Krummstab, zu sehen.
Freundlich thront er hinter dem Horizont
mit dem Selbstverständnis eines jugend-
lichen Sonnengottes. Nicht unähnlich wird

Jahrhunderte später die *Germania* auf der
Hügelkette über Rüdesheim wachen. *Leviat-
hans* Herrschaft ist jedoch weniger kriegerisch und resolut, sondern auf der friedvollen
Gemeinschaft aller aufgebaut: sein Fürst ge-
bietet über Wiesen, Felder, Gehöfte und eine
Stadt, die über eine Kirche, zivile Häuser und
wie Mainz eine Zitadelle verfügt. Während
sich der obere Bildteil auf den Souverän konzentriert, besteht das untere Bildfeld aus Em-
blemen, die wie Schatullen angeordnet sind.
Die seitlichen Bildreihen nehmen die Gegenüberstellung von kirchlicher und staatlicher
Macht wieder auf, die Zeichen von Schwert
und Bischofsstab. Die Burg entspricht der
Kirche, die Krone der Mitra, die Kanone dem
Bannstrahl der Exkommunikation. Diese
korrespondierende Lesart setzt sich nach un-

ten fort. Die Kampfzeichen entsprechen den Waffen der Logik, die Schlacht links kommt der Disputation rechts unten gleich. Die Embleme rahmen das Mittelfeld ein, das durch einen verzierten Vorhang mit der Titelei hervortritt. Hobbes kündigt eine Abhandlung über „Matter, Forme and Power of a Common Wealth" an. Der Staat ist ein Gemeinwesen, ein gemeinschaftlicher Wert, der nach der Sache, der Form und seinen Gewalten erörtert wird. Sein Körper besteht aus der Vielzahl aller Bürger und doch fehlt ihm die Mitte. Der Vorhang ist Hinweis auf das Wechselspiel, auf sein Erscheinen und Verhüllen. *Leviathan* ist als metaphysische Seinsform der Welt enthoben, doch als Gigant und Gesetzeshüter stets gegenwärtig, die höchste Instanz „super terram" (auf Erden). /

During the mid-17th century, the English philosopher Thomas Hobbes published his *Leviathan*, one of the most predominant works of political philosophy. To illustrate his body of thought on political rights and his social contract, he commissioned Dutch engraver Abraham Bosse to design the frontispiece. This frontispiece displays *Leviathan* – originally an apocalyptic monster referenced in the Old Testament – in Hobbes's writings, however, he is a crowned Prince of Peace who rules over the land, culture and people. The image summarizes the basic principle of the treatise. The upper part of the image shows a bearded sovereign with the insignia of secular and religious violence, the sword and the crosier. He is seated on his throne with a friendly demeanour; behind him the horizon bears the self-conception of a youthful sun god. He is not unlike *Germania*, placed upon a hilltop overlooking Rüdesheim hundreds of years later. *Leviathan*'s sovereignty, however, is less belligerent and resolute, but rather established on the peaceful community of all: he rules over fields and meadows, homesteads and a city with a church, public institutions and, just like Mainz, a citadel. Whereas the upper part of the image focuses on the sovereign, the lower part consists of emblems arranged like caskets. The rows of images on the sides represent the contrasting powers of the church and the state, using the symbols of the sword and crosier. The castle represents the church, the crown the mitre, and the canon the thunderbolt of excommunication. This continues at the bottom. The signs of battle correspond to the weapons of logic; the battle at the right corresponds to the dispute at the lower left. The emblems represent a frame of the centre field, which protrudes through a decorative curtain with the title. Hobbes declares a treatise on the "Matter, Forme and Power of a Common Wealth". The state is a community, a common value that is based on its matter, form, and power. His body is made up of the plurality of all civilians, yet he has no centre. The curtain is a reference to the interplay of appearance and concealment. *Leviathan* is a metaphysical being not part of this world, yet always present as a giant and guardian of the law, the highest instance "super terram" (on earth).

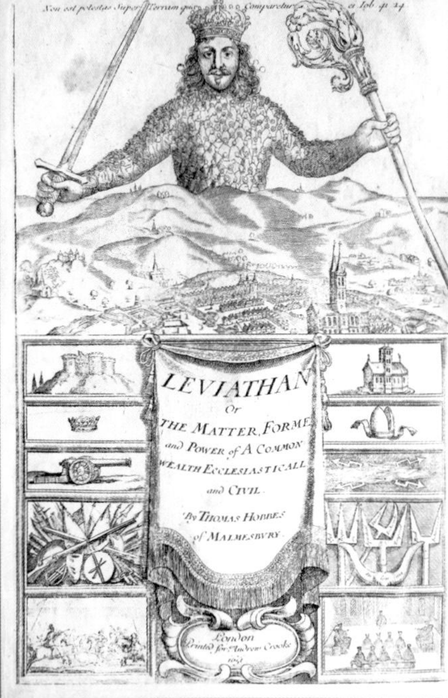

01.2

Werk von Johannes Schilling geht aus einem Wettbewerb hervor, der dem damaligen Zeitgeschmack unkritisch verpflichtet ist. Schilling versteht es, die Konventionen zu verbildlichen. Sein Beitrag für die Kunstgeschichte ist jedoch aus heutiger Beurteilung marginal. Dazu kommt die politische Botschaft. Das Statement der *Germania* ist keineswegs unproblematisch. Dies betrifft nicht nur die Art des Auftritts der staatlichen Selbstdarstellung, die hemmungsfreie und selbstherrliche Heroisierung der Nation, sondern auch den Anlass der Botschaft. Von heutigen Besucher/innen wird immer öfter vergessen, dass die Statue eigentlich eine aggressive, bellizistische Botschaft verkündet und sich diese Botschaft direkt und drohend an den Nachbarn richtet.

Doch der Feind ist auch Vorbild. Es gehört zu den bizarren Umkehrungen der Kriegsaggression zwischen den Nachbarn, dass die Figur der *Germania* eigentlich eine Prägung des Gegners übernimmt. Tatsächlich ist die *Germania* eine Nachahmung der französischen *Marianne*, die sich nach der Französischen Revolution als öffentliches Bildnis des Staates entwickelt (Kat. 21). Die Ausstellung in der Kunsthalle Mainz nimmt an dieser Stelle einen kunsthistorischen Faden auf, um zu belegen, wie das Herrscherbildnis, das ursprünglich den Staat repräsentiert, mit der Aufklärung ein neues Gepräge entwickelt. Vor der Französischen Revolution sind Staats- und Herrscherbildnis identisch. Aufklärung und Demokratisierung erzwingen jedoch einen Ersatz. In der *Marianne* wird er gefunden. Die *Marianne* ist eine Allegorie der nationalen Gemeinschaft, die den Übergang von Absolutismus zur Republik markiert. Sie ist nicht länger das Abbild einer bestimmten staatstragenden Person. Sie verlässt die Person und wird zur Personifikation. Die Ikonografie der *Marianne* entwickelt sich als Mischung der römischen *Libertas* und Jeanne d'Arc, also einer profanen Allegorie und einer christlichen Kämpferin. Sie nimmt damit weiters die Stilmischung von Antike und Mittelalter vorweg. Wie sich die weibliche Staatsallegorie ursprünglich aus der Herrschaftsdarstellung des Königsbilds entwickelt, das stellt sich in der Ausstellung an zwei besonders erwähnenswerten Stichen dar. Sie stammen vom Ende des 18. Jahrhunderts. Auf dem ersten Blatt ist Louis XVI. zu sehen (Kat. 03.1). Es stammt aus dem Jahr 1789, dem Revolutionsjahr, ist jedoch noch eindeutig im Geist des Absolutismus entworfen. Derselbe Künstler hat wenige Jahre danach seine Kupferplatte nochmals bearbeitet. Aus dem Jahr 1800 stammt das zweite Blatt (Kat. 03.2). Das Setting ist ähnlich. In der Bildmitte befindet sich ein Sockel, rundherum sind vielfältige allegorische Gestalten. Jedoch ist der König in der zweiten Darstellung ausradiert und statt ihm die Personifikation der Freiheit gesetzt. Freilich trägt sie die phrygische Mütze der Jakobiner. Die zwei Stiche sind wie ein kulturhistorisches Suchbild. Der Umsturz der politischen Systeme könnte nicht deutlicher werden, der Opportunismus mancher Künstler nicht weniger. Die Skulptur als Mittel wechselnder Herrschaftsapologie steht dabei im Zentrum. In Frankreich ist *Marianne* bis heute ein erfolgreiches Sinnbild geblieben. Viele prominente Schauspielerinnen lassen sich als *Marianne* abbilden, darunter Brigitte Bardot, Cathérine Deneuve und Sophie Marceau. In ihren bekanntesten Ausprägungen ist *Marianne* aber eine politische Figur. Sie ist Liberté, jugendlich und kämpferisch. Zum Beispiel in dem berühmten Bild von Eugène Delacroix: *Die Freiheit führt das Volk*

Germania's statement is by no means without complexity. This applies not only to the manner in which it exhibits nationalistic self-expression, its uninhibited and autocratic glorification of the nation, but also to the grounds for the message it imparts. Today's visitors often fail to remember that the statue is actually an aggressive, bellicose declaration directed unswervingly and imminently at its neighbour.

Yet the enemy is also an ideal. It is one of the bizarre reversals of confrontational aggression among neighbouring countries through which *Germania* actually assumes the role of the adversary. In fact, *Germania* is a reproduction of France's *Marianne*, which had become the public symbol of the nation following the French Revolution (cat. 21). This is exactly where the exhibition at the Kunsthalle Mainz picks up the art-historical threads, to demonstrate how the image of a ruler, which once represented the nation, has developed a new face. Prior to the French Revolution, the portrait of a nation and its ruler were identical. Enlightenment and democratization however called for an alternative, which was found in *Marianne*. *Marianne* is an allegory for national community, marking the transition from absolutism to a republic. She is no longer an effigy of a specific ruling person. She departs from the realm of the individual and becomes a personification. The iconography of *Marianne* is embodied in a mixture of the Roman *Libertas* and Joan of Arc, thus being a secular allegory of a Christian warrior. She also assumes a mixture of styles from antiquity and the Middle Ages. The exhibition illustrates how the female allegory of the state developed from the original expression of the image of the sovereign king as ruler, on the basis of two particularly memorable engravings, originating in the 18th century. The first depicts Louis XVI. (cat. 03.1) It dates back to the year 1789, the year of the Revolution, yet was clearly designed in the spirit of absolutism. Just a few years later, the same artist reprocessed his copperplate. The second originates from the year 1800 (cat. 03.2). The setting is similar: a pedestal is situated at the centre, surrounded by several allegorical figures. However, in this scene the king has been removed and in his place now stands the personification of liberty. Of course, she is wearing the Phrygian cap of the Jacobins. The second engraving is like a historico-cultural picture puzzle. The downfall of political systems could not be any clearer, or the opportunism of some artists. The sculpture as an apologia for changing power is the central focus of the motif. In France, *Marianne* has remained a successful allegory to this day. Many prominent actresses have portrayed *Marianne*, from Brigitte Bardot to Cathérine Deneuve and Sophie Marceau. In her most widely known manifestations, *Marianne* is portrayed as a political figure. She is Liberté: youthful, a fighter, as in the famous painting by Eugène Delacroix, *Liberty Leading the People* (1830) (cat. 17). Even back then, her breasts are bare and she displays a high degree of sexual appeal. Unlike her German counterpart, there are no songs written about her; yet "La Marseillaise", the French national anthem, is similarly popular and motivating. After all, it begins with the words "Allons enfants de la patrie". *Marianne* strives, *Germania* stands. The two anthems battled it out in the American production of *Casablanca* filmed in 1942 (cat. 15). A scene from this film is shown in the exhibition, where German Wehrmacht soldiers, all played by German-speaking immigrants, start singing *The Watch on*

von 1830 (Kat. 17). Schon dort ist sie topless und sexy. Sie wird zwar nicht direkt wie ihre deutsche Nachfolgerin besungen, aber die Marseillaise, die Französische Hymne, ist ähnlich populär und motivierend. Schließlich beginnt sie mit den Worten „Allons enfants de la patrie". *Marianne* strebt, die *Germania* steht. Der Wettstreit dieser beiden Lieder findet sich noch im 1942 gedrehten US-Film *Casablanca*. Ein Filmausschnitt ist in der Ausstellung zu sehen. Während dieser Szene beginnen die deutschen Wehrmachtssoldaten, durchwegs gespielt von deutschsprachigen Emigranten, die *Wacht am Rhein* anzustimmen. Sie haben sich in Rick's Café eingefunden, um nach einem tschechischen Widerstandskämpfer, Victor László, zu suchen. Rick, gespielt von Humphrey Bogart, wird in seiner Unterhaltung mit László von den grölenden Deutschen unterbrochen. László fordert die Kapelle auf, die Marseillaise anzustimmen, die letztlich die Deutschen übertönt. Die Szene, die den Krieg unter Nationen als Wettkampf der Lieder austrägt, wird in der deutschen Fassung des Films, die 1952 in die Kinos kommt, entfernt. Erst 1975 wird der Film in Deutschland in voller Länge ausgestrahlt.

Die Statue der *Germania* zieht viele Register des Ausdrucks: Skulpturen, Reliefs, Texte, Ton. Seit der Errichtung wuchern zudem Referenzen und Reproduktionen. Die Geschichte der Rezeptionen reicht vom Dokument der Grundsteinlegung über Johannes Mario Simmel und dem Schlagersänger Udo Jürgens bis in unserer Tage mit der Herstellung von Souvenirs und Nippes. Dass quer durch die Zeiten Botschaften und Medien aufeinander in vielfältiger Weise reagieren, das will die Regalwand im Zentrum der Ausstellung verständlich machen (Abb. S. 22, 23/44, 45/58, 59). In ihr sind Bücher, Bilder und Postkarten zu sehen, aber auch Urkunden, Poster, Kleinskulpturen und Andenken. Dabei sind alle Dokumente von hinten und vorne zu sehen, auch von der Seite bieten sich Einblicke. Diese Perspektiven belegen die vielfältige Geschichte, die sich hier versammelt und in einem Raum verdichtet wird, der wie ein Wikipedia-Eintrag zum Thema „staatstragende Skulpturen seit 1800" funktioniert. Das Regal ermöglicht zudem die Brücke zur Kultur der Moderne und Nachkriegszeit. Wie steht es mit der Republik, die in Deutschland eingeführt wird, etwa 150 Jahre nach der Republik in Frankreich und der Etablierung der *Marianne* als ihrer femininen Gestalt? Es sei vorausgeschickt, dass die Moderne dem Höhenstreben und der Selbsthuldigung ein Ende bereiten wird. Auch der unkritischen Selbstbelobigung. Doch was tritt an diese Stelle? Wie sehen die Alternativen der staatlichen Selbstdarstellung in der Gegenwart eigentlich aus?

Welche Kunst findet die Bundesrepublik nach der Germania als angemessene Repräsentantin ihrer Gemeinschaft? Dazu ist es notwendig, in die 1970er Jahre zu springen. In diesem Jahrzehnt kommt es zum ersten skulpturalen Großauftrag. Bundeskanzler Helmut Schmidt nimmt mit Henry Moore Kontakt auf, in der Absicht, den Innenhof des Bundeskanzleramtes aufzuwerten (Kat. 31 ff.). Moore kommt dieser Bitte des deutschen Kanzlers nach. Er liefert ein großformatiges Objekt aus polierter Bronze. Zwei rundlich weiche Volumen greifen wie negative Gegenstücke ineinander, berühren einander aber nicht. Eigentlich ist es ein zweiter Abguss einer ursprünglich erotisch konnotierten Komposition. Aus Gründen mangelhafter öffentlicher Akzeptanz wird die Skulptur zuerst geliehen

the Rhine. They enter Rick's Café looking for a Czech resistance fighter, Victor László. Rick, played by Humphrey Bogart, is talking to László when he is interrupted by bellowing Germans. László tells the band to play *La Marseillaise*, which ultimately drowns out the noise of the Germans. The scene, which portrays the battle among nations as a battle of songs, was removed from the German version of the film when it was released in 1952. It wasn't until 1975 that the film was shown in Germany in its original full length.

The statue *Germania* has several forms of expression: sculptures, reliefs, texts, sound. Since its completion, there have also been an abundance of references and reproductions. The history of the response to the statue dates from the laying of its foundation stone to Johannes Mario Simmel, the crooner Udo Jürgens, up to this very day, with the production of souvenirs and knick-knacks. The purpose of the wall of shelves in the centre of the exhibition is to illustrate the variety of ways in which messages and media have responded to one another throughout the ages (Ill. pp. 22, 23/44, 45/58, 59). The shelves contain books, images, and postcards, as well as official documents, posters, miniature sculptures, and souvenirs. All the documents can be seen from the front, the back, and the sides. These perspectives document the multifaceted history, collected and consolidated in one room, that functions like a kind of Wikipedia article on the subject of "nationalistic sculptures since 1800". The shelves also symbolize a bridge between the culture of modernity and the post-war period. And what of the republic that had been introduced in Germany, some 150 years after the republic in France, and the establishment of *Marianne* as its feminine embodiment? It goes without saying that modernity will put an end to narcissism and self-glorification — and to uncritical self-praise. Yet what comes in its stead? What are the alternatives to national self-expression in today's world?

Which art form can be found to suitably represent the Federal Republic after *Germania*? For this, we have to go to the 1970s. This is the decade in which the first major sculptural commission was granted, when Federal Chancellor Helmut Schmidt contacted Henry Moore, intending to upgrade the courtyard of the Federal Chancellery (cat. 31 ff). Moore complied with the request of the German Chancellor. He provided a large-sized object made of polished bronze: two round, soft volumes that reach into one another like negative counterparts, yet do not touch. It is actually a second cast of an original composition with an erotic connotation. Due to the lack of public acceptance, the sculpture was initially loaned (1979) and ultimately purchased ten years later by means of a Parliamentary resolution. A similar object, yet from another artist, was installed in front of the new Federal Chancellery in Berlin. As in Bonn, the artist chosen was not a German, which caused quite a stir in the tabloids and the art world. The sculpture was made by the Basque sculptor Eduardo Chillida and was bluntly entitled *Berlin* (1999) (cat. 46 ff). This time, however, a private patron paid for the commission. Here again, two forms give the impression of being interconnected; Chillida's work however is hard, bulky, and angular. He chooses rusted pliers supported by columns that meet in the air. The self-glorifying pathos of the Imperial era has been overcome. Obviously blatant messages are avoided, as is the histrionic interplay of various ex-

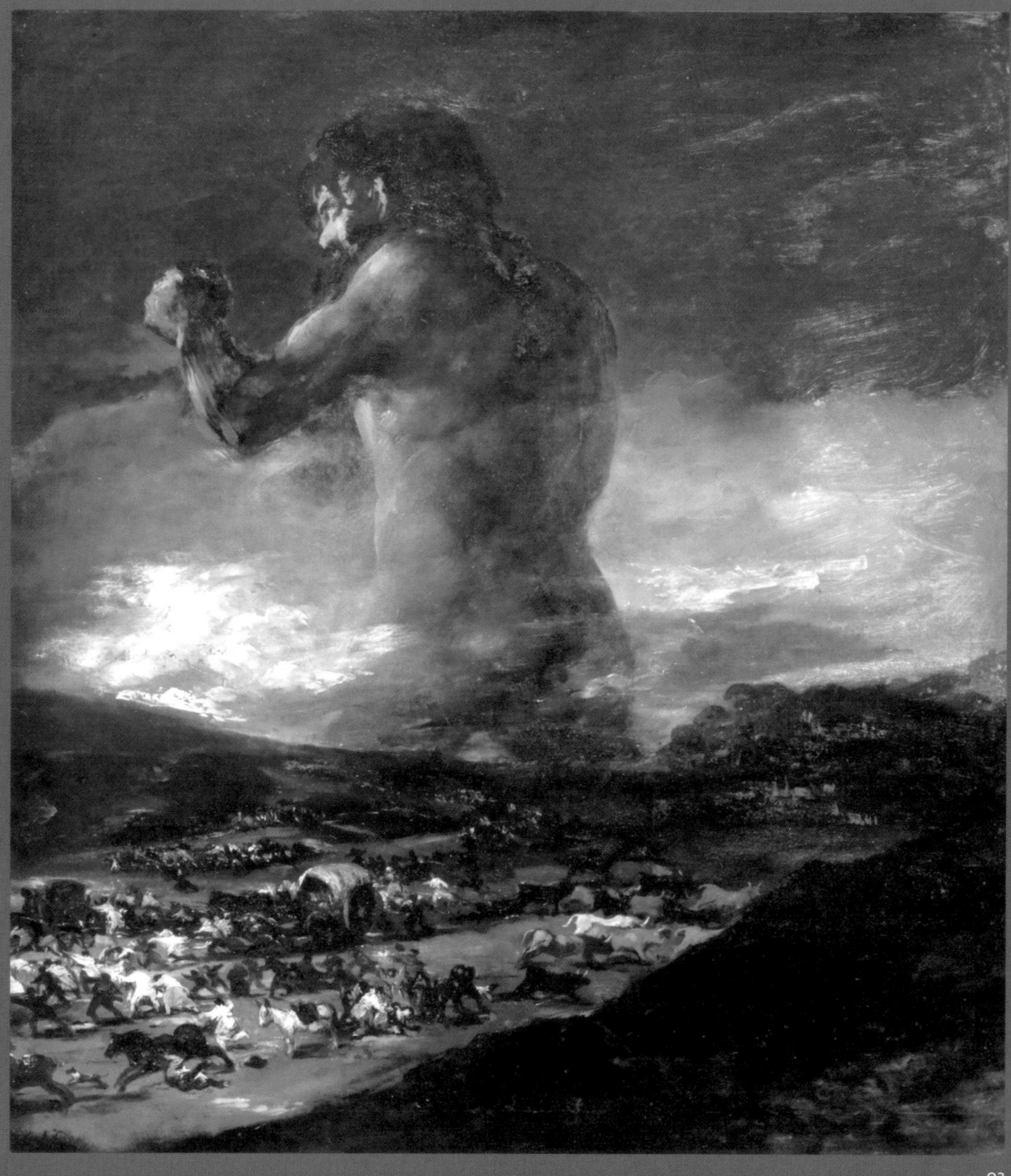

02

02

Francisco de Goya zugeschrieben
Der Koloss/The Colossus
1808–1812
Öl auf Leinwand/Oil on canvas
120 × 100 cm
Museo Nacional del Prado, Madrid

Die Parallelen zur Darstellung des *Leviathan* sind kaum zu übersehen. Doch in diesem Gemälde findet sich kein friedfertiger Fürst. Hinter einer Berglandschaft erscheint ein blutrünstiger Riese. Der Koloss mit schwarzem, zersaustem Haar entwächst der düsteren Landschaft wie ein böses Omen. Das Prinzip der Enthemmung, das Hobbes in den Menschen durch das Gesetz gebändigt betrachtet, ist zur alles beherrschenden, metaphysischen Größe aufgestiegen. Die Menschen flüchten panisch vor der übermenschlichen Grimasse. Pferde und Wagen stürzen nach vorn, Menschen hasten schutzlos ohne Hab und Gut. Verwundete werden notdürftig versorgt, Leichenberge säumen den Weg. Der Koloss hat die Fäuste kraftvoll geballt. Jedoch wendet er sich von den Erdenwesen ab und droht in Richtung des Horizontes. Sein Körper ist Ausdruck von gesetzloser Gewalt, Zerstörung und Angst./

One can hardly overlook the parallels to the representation of *Leviathan*. Yet there is no peaceful sovereign in this painting. A bloodthirsty giant appears behind the mountain range. The colossus with its black tousled hair protrudes from behind a sombre landscape like an evil omen. The principle of disinhibition, which Hobbes regards as restrained by laws, has ascended to an all-dominating, metaphysical variable. People flee in panic from the superhuman grimace. Horses and carriages topple, people flee unprotected and without any possessions. The injured are hastily tended to, heaps of corpses line the road. The colossus forcefully clenches its fists. However, it turns away from the terrestrial beings and threatens toward the horizon. Its body is an expression of lawless violence, destruction, and fear.

(1979), erst nach etwa zehn Jahren über einen Parlamentsbeschluss erworben. Ein ähnliches Objekt, jedoch von einem anderen Künstler, wird zwei Jahrzehnte später vor dem neuen Bundeskanzleramt in Berlin aufgestellt. Wie in Bonn kommt abermals kein Deutscher zum Zug, was in manchen Gazetten und Künstlerzirkeln für Aufregung sorgt. Die Skulptur stammt von dem baskischen Bildhauer Eduardo Chillida. (1999) Sie heißt schlicht *Berlin* (Kat. 46 ff.). Diesmal bezahlt ein privater Mäzen. Auch hier dringen zwei Formen ineinander, jedoch geraten sie bei Chillida hart, sperrig und kantig. Er wählt rostige Zangen, die, von Stelen getragen, einander in der Luft begegnen. Das selbsthuldigende Pathos der Kaiserzeit ist überwunden. Überdeutliche Botschaften werden vermieden, genauso wie das theatralische Zusammenspiel verschiedener Ausdruckselemente. An die Stelle treten abstrakte Formen. Sie sind prägnant und zeichenhaft. Diese Eigenschaft wird als staatstragend erachtet sowie die Tatsache, dass die Skulpturen ohne Sockel auf dem Grund ruhen. Das Herabsteigen der einzelnen elementaren Form ist gestaltprägend. In diesem Sinne ist auch eine Verschiebung der skulpturalen Energien zu deuten. Die beiden Skulpturen vor den Kanzlerämtern vermeiden Vertikalordnung und Höherstreben, wie dies im 19. Jahrhundert bei der *Germania* üblich war. Dagegen setzen sie auf eine Gegenüberstellung in der Waagrechte. Die Begegnung soll sinnfällig werden, widerstreitende oder sich wechselseitige ergänzende Prinzipien. Auf eine literarische Vorlage wird verzichtet, auch Kommentare und Ausdeutungen werden vermieden. Die Skulpturen sind pur, selbstbestimmt und archaisch. Zu den Charakteristika dieser Großobjekte zählt es, dass sie sich nicht in andere Sinndimensionen übertragen lassen. Transfer- oder Übersetzungsleistungen, ja Distributionen oder Vermehrungen würden die künstlerische Absicht, den Ethos der schlichten Setzung, korrumpieren. Die Skulpturen stehen für sich. Sie erweisen sich als aussagenresistent.

Nun ist interessant, dass gerade die Verweigerungshaltung diesen Typus an Skulptur für die politischen Auftraggeber geeigneter macht. Die Tatsache, dass sich diese Objekte äußerlichen Zuschreibungen gegenüber entziehen und sich gleichsam als Mangelwesen präsentieren, lässt sie für die schwere Aufgabe, die Werte der Gemeinschaft und des Staates darzustellen, geeigneter erscheinen. Die Allegorien der Republik sind bescheiden und stumm. Während nämlich die aristokratische Herrschaft des 19. Jahrhunderts viele Botschaften (Heimatgefühl, Stärke, Geschichtsbewusstsein etc.) vermitteln möchte, müssen demokratische Auftraggeber allumfassende homogenisierende Ideologien genauso vermeiden wie aufwändige und teure Inszenierungen. Darstellerisch bedeutet dies, dass eine Kultur der Unterbietung und Negation an die Kunst herangetragen wird. Um die Heterogenität des demokratischen Staatsgebildes zu bewahren, ist es nötig, bildhafte Offenbarungen zu unterbinden. An die Stelle tritt eine Ikonografie der Selbstnegation: Die beiden abstrakten Skulpturen bestimmen sich dadurch, was sie nicht sein wollen: sie sind nicht beredt, nicht ideologisch, nicht huldigend, nicht theatralisch, nicht übersetzbar etc.

Doch welche Folgen hat diese Entwicklung für die zeitgenössische Kunst? Die Ausstellung bemüht sich neben der historischen Herleitung des Themas besonders um die Frage, welche ästhetischen und politischen Auswirkungen die staatstragende Skulptur auf das freie, selbstbeauftragte

pressive elements. Abstract forms, concise and symbolic, are used in their stead. This characteristic is considered to symbolize the state, as is the fact that the sculptures are not set on pedestals, but rather rest on the ground. The descent of the individual basic form is integral. The displacement of the sculptural energy can also be interpreted in this vein. Both sculptures outside the Chancelleries avoid any vertical and upward-reaching arrangement, as was common practice in the 19th century with *Germania*. Instead, both pieces communicate a sense of confrontation in a horizontal arrangement, an evident encounter between conflicting or reciprocal principles. The works are not based on any literary model and do not comment or interpret. The sculptures are pure, self-determined, and archaic. One of the characteristics of these large-scale objects is that they cannot be transposed into other reflective dimensions. Transferral or translation, let alone distribution or reproduction, would corrupt the artistic intention, the ethos of the unpretentious setting. The sculptures stand alone. They resist statement.

It is interesting to note that this attitude of resistance is an aspect that particularly makes this type of sculpture more suitable for a political sponsor. The fact that these objects evade any form of exterior ascriptions and also express themselves as inadequate beings makes them appear more suitable to take on the difficult task of representing the values of community and of the nation. The allegories of the republic are modest and silent. Whereas the aristocratic authorities of the 19th century wanted to convey several messages (sense of home, strength, historical awareness, etc.), democratic commissioning bodies have to avoid comprehensively homogenizing ideologies, as well as extensive and costly production. From a representational perspective, this means that a culture of modesty and negation is being laid on artistic expression. To retain the heterogeneity of the principle of the democratic state, figurative manifestations have to be suppressed. In their place comes an iconography of self-negation. Both sculptures define themselves by what they do not want to be: they are non-eloquent, non-ideological, non-glorifying, non-theatrical, and non-translatable.

Yet what are the consequences of this for the development of contemporary art? Besides the historical inference of the theme, this exhibition particularly aims at answering the question as to what aesthetic and political consequences the nationalistic sculpture has on free, self-commissioned artistic expression. And what of the image of the state? How do artists approach the state commissioning bodies, their self-expression and self-representation? How do they comment on public sculpture? How do they interpret the history of modernity? How do they respond to the paradigm of resistive non-statement? The exhibition includes two exceptional pieces of work, sculptures by Thomas Schütte and Danh Vo, which form the closing brackets. Each has its own room, to allow for an historical excursion between them. Each sculpture does not celebrate the state; it shares it, particularly in a monumental format. And both works are based on a figurative likeness — meaning that they question the history of modernity while at the same time returning to its phases of foundation and formation, which also justifies the historical perspective.

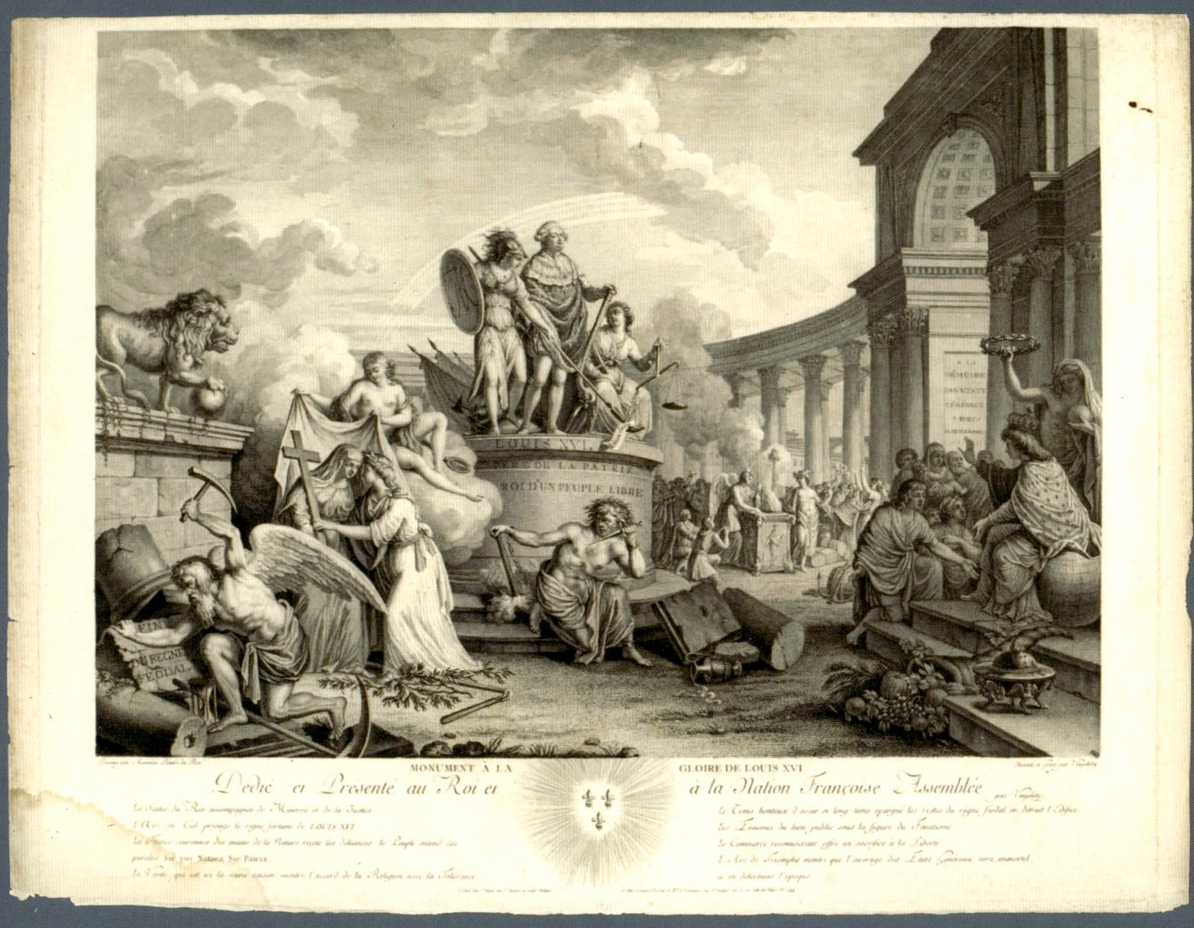

03.1

03

03.1
Nicolas-André Monsiau
Monument à la Gloire Louis XVI.,
1789
46,9 × 63,7 cm
Kupferstiche/Copperplate engraving
Musée de la Révolution française,
Vizille

03.2
Nicolas-André Monsiau
La Liberté triomphante, 1800
52,3 × 68,5 cm

Der Souverän gibt sich selbst ein Bild. In absolutistischen Systemen ist das Staatsbildnis dem Herrscherbildnis gleichzusetzen. Mit der französischen Revolution kommt es zu einer Entpersonifizierung des Staatskörpers. Die Heterogenität von Stimmen und Bürgern soll sich im Staatsbildnis zu erkennen geben. In Hobbes' doppelsinniger Gestalt vom Fürsten, dessen Körper aus seinen Bürgern besteht, kündigt sich diese Umdeutung an. Dieser bedeutsame Schritt wird jedoch nirgends deut-

licher als in den beiden Stichen des französischen Künstlers Nicolas-André Monsiau etwa 150 Jahre später. Die unterschiedlichen ikonografischen Programme vor und nach der Revolution werden in zwei Stichen augenscheinlich, die 1789 und 1800 entstehen. In der ersten Version, die Monsiau noch vor dem Ausbruch der Revolution im Jahr 1789 fertigt, findet sich der absolutistische Regent auf einem Sockel stehend. Der elegant gekleidete König Louis XVI. wird umgeben von Minerva, die an Rüstung, Speer und Schild zu erkennen ist, und einer weiteren allegorischen Frauengestalt, der römischen Göttin der Weisheit. Zu seiner Linken sitzt Justitia, die Gerechtigkeit, mit Waagschale und Schwert. Die Inschrift auf dem Sockel feiert den Regenten als „Vater des Vaterlandes" und „König des freien Volkes". Am Fuß des Sockels sitzt der blutrünstige Fanatismus. Er hält einen Dolch und eine Fackel und verkörpert die Feinde des Volkes, doch sind ihm Hand- und Fußfesseln angelegt. Der Blick fällt auf eine Gruppe von drei Frauen: Die Wahrheit sitzt auf einer Wolke, neben ihr der Spiegel. Sie lüftet das Tuch über der Religion, die als Nonne gekleidet ist und ein Kreuz im

Arm hält. Zu ihr neigt sich die Toleranz. In der linken Ecke des Werkes kniet die geflügelte Zeit. Am rechten Bildrand wird Frankreich von der Natur bekrönt. Das Füllhorn auf den Stufen verweist auf den Wohlstand des Landes. Im Hintergrund bringt der Handel der Freiheit ein Opfer dar. Die Inschrift im Triumphbogen erinnert an die Unsterblichkeit des Staates.

Doch diese tritt nicht ein. Louis XVI. wird nur wenig später gestürzt und geköpft. Monsiau passt sein Werk dem politischen Wandel an (Abb. 03.2). Die königstreue Huldigung wird opportunistisch in eine Apologie revolutionärer Ideen umgearbeitet. Dafür verwendet er dieselbe Kupferplatte ein zweites Mal. Er radiert die Stellen, die auf die Bourbonenherrschaft verweisen und ersetzt sie durch neue Bildformeln. Bereits die Unterschrift des Bildes ist eine andere: „Die triumphierende Freiheit." Auf dem Sockel steht nun nicht mehr der Monarch sondern La Liberté, die den Frieden nach Italien bringt. Zu ihren Füßen befindet sich wieder der Fanatismus mit Fackel und Dolch. Die Wahrheit enthüllt die Religion, die jedoch nunmehr ohne Kreuz abgebildet ist. Die ihr gegenüberstehende

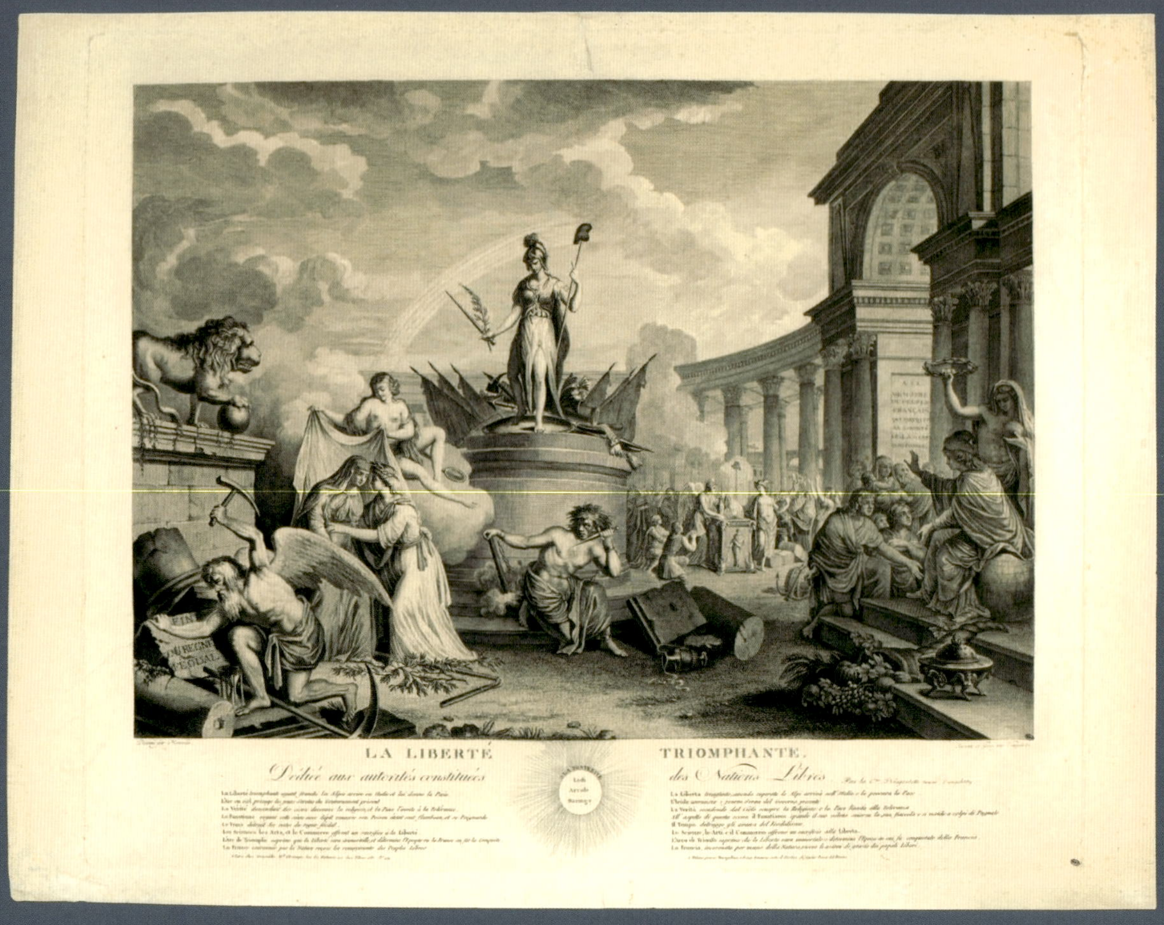

03.2

Allegorie wird als Frieden bezeichnet. Die Gestalt Frankreichs wird erneut von der Natur bekrönt, doch trägt sie keine Krone, sondern eine phrygische Mütze als Zeichen von Freiheitskampf und revolutionärer Gesinnung. Die Inschrift im Triumphbogen benennt das französische Volk, das sich am 14. Juli 1789 mit dem Sturm auf die Bastille die Freiheit erkämpft. / The sovereign creates his own image of himself. In absolute systems, the image of the state is identical to the image of its ruler. The French Revolution results in the depersonalisation of the state. The heterogeneity of voices and civilians should be reflected in the image of the state. This reinterpretation is reflected in the figure of the sovereign, whose body is made up of the people. Nowhere else is this decisive step more distinct than in the two engravings by French artist Nicolas-André Monsiau some 150 years later. The differing iconographical programmes before and after the Revolution are clearly evident in the two engravings produced in 1789 and 1800. The first version, which Monsiau made shortly before the onset of the Revolution in 1789, displays an absolutist regent standing upon a pedestal. The elegantly dressed King Louis XVI is surrounded by Minerva, who can be recognized by the armour, spear and shield, and a further allegorical female figure symbolizing the Roman goddess of wisdom. Justitia sits at his right, symbolizing justice with her scales and sword. The inscription on the pedestal celebrates the regent as the "Father of the Fatherland" and the "King of a free people". Fanaticism is seated at the base of the pedestal, holding a dagger and a torch, representing the enemy of the state. However, his hands and feet are shackled. The gaze falls on a group of three women: Truth is seated on a cloud, next to her a mirror. She lifts the cloth above Religion, who is dressed as a nun and holds a cross in her arms. Tolerance bends down towards her. A winged Father Time kneels in the left-hand corner of the piece. At the right edge of the image, France is being crowned by Nature. The horn of plenty on the steps is a reference to the country's wealth. In the background, the supporters of constitutional reform present offerings. The inscription on the triumphal arc is a reference to the immortality of the state.

However, this does not occur. It is not long before Louis XVI is overthrown and beheaded. Monsiau adapts his work to the political change (cat. 03.2). The faithful homage to the king is opportunistically turned into an apologia for revolutionist ideology. To this end, he makes use of the very same copperplate a second time. He removes the spaces that make any reference to the Bourbon dynasty, replacing them with new images. Even the inscription on the image is a different one: "The Triumph of Liberty". The monarch now no longer stands on the pedestal, but La Liberté, who brings peace to Italy. Fanaticism, bearing torch and dagger, is still at her feet. Truth reveals religion, which however is no longer portrayed with a cross. The allegory standing across is Peace. The figure of France is once again being crowned by Nature. However, she does not wear a crown, but rather a Phrygian cap as a sign of the struggle for freedom and revolutionary spirit. The inscription on the triumphal arch is a dedication to the people of France who fought for their freedom on 14 July 1789 while storming the Bastille.

Kunstschaffen hat. Wie steht es um das Bild des Staates? Wie verhalten sich Künstler/innen zur Auftraggeberschaft des Staates, seiner Selbstdarstellung und Selbstvermittlung? Wie kommentieren sie die öffentliche Skulptur? Wie interpretieren sie die Geschichte der Moderne? Wie reagieren sie auf das Paradigma der Aussagenresistenz? Die Ausstellung bringt zwei herausragende Werke. Es sind Skulpturen von Thomas Schütte und Danh Vo. Sie bilden die Klammer. Beiden ist jeweils ein Raum gewidmet, sodass der historische Exkurs zwischen ihnen steht. Beide Skulpturen feiern den Staat nicht, sondern geben ihn wieder, vor allem in einem monumentalen Format. Und beide Werke beziehen sich auf das figürliche Bildnis. Das heißt, sie hinterfragen die Geschichte der Moderne, gehen gleichsam auf ihre Gründungs- und Prägungsphasen zurück. Auch darum ist ein geschichtlicher Blick gerechtfertigt.

Im Eingangsraum empfängt die Besucher eine riesige männliche Skulptur von Thomas Schütte. Sie betitelt sich *Vater Staat* (Abb. S. 17 ff.). Die Figur ist in einen schweren Mantel gehüllt. Der Stoff fällt in wuchtigen Falten herab. Der Kopf des Mannes prägnant, sein Gesicht markig. Die Höhe erzwingt einen steilen Blick nach oben. *Vater Staat* ist weniger Staatsbild als eine Personifikation des Über-Ichs, ein hartgesottener Patriarch oder ein unbarmherziger Soldat, ein weiser Alter oder ein alternder Condottiere. Vielleicht ist er aber auch nur ein monumentaler Bildstock seiner eigenen Legende oder ein verwunschener Flaschengeist, gegossen und erstarrt in rotem Metall. Der *Vater Staat* blickt zurück in den Raum mit dem historischen Material. Sein Blick trifft auf ein Gipsmodell der *Germania*. Die Gegenüberstellung, die Schütte erdachte, ist dramaturgisch komponiert. *Vater Staat* trifft auf „Mutter Staat". Charakteristischerweise fehlen Schüttes Figur jedoch die erzählenden Attribute der Ahnin. Der Mann zeigt Fassung, aber keine großen Gesten oder sprechenden Zeichen. Es gibt kein Schwert, kein Zepter, keine Adler oder assistierenden Allegorien, keinen Krummstab und keine Krönung. Anders als Moore und Chillida, die dem staatlichen Auftrag durch abstrakte Kompositionen entsprechen, entscheidet sich Schütte für das menschliche Abbild. In seinem Werk kehrt das figürliche Menschenbild wieder. Während der Moderne problematisch geworden, erinnert es an die großen bildgebenden Statuen früherer Jahrhunderte. Dennoch verfällt Schütte nicht in die Theatralik des 19. Jahrhunderts, die Stilzitate des Historismus oder die skulpturale Prahlerei. *Vater Staat* ist auf merkwürdige Weise stumm und verhalten. Er übernimmt damit eine Eigenschaft der abstrakten Skulpturen der Moderne. Seine Verschwiegenheit entstammt jedoch nicht einer formalen Aussagenverweigerung, dem demokratiepolitisch induzierten Sinnbildentzug. Sie entsteht vielmehr aus der Haltung der Skulptur, einer psychologischen Verfasstheit und nicht zuletzt aus einer skulpturalen Setzung heraus, die sich zu Erhabenheit und Autoritätsbekundung entschließt. Schütte nimmt absichtsvoll die problematisch gewordenen Eigenschaften der Machtsymbolik auf. Tatsächlich blickt die Figur über alles streng hinweg. *Vater Staat* ist kein friedvoller Souverän wie etwa bei Hobbes, sondern ein angsteinflößendes, unberechenbares Monument. Doch Schütte vergisst nicht, diesen Eindruck zu brechen. Er verweigert ikonografische Zuordnungen. Entscheidend wird die Begegnung, das Aufeinandertreffen des skulpturalen Körpers mit dem lebendigen und beweglichen der

In the lobby, the visitor is greeted by a gigantic male sculpture made by Thomas Schütte. It is entitled *Vater Staat* (Father State) (Ill. p. 17f). The figure is dressed in heavy cloaks, with the material descending along the figure in massive folds. The head of the figure is laconic, his face pithy. Its height forces one to look steeply upward. *Vater Staat* is not so much a representation of the state as much as a representation of the Über-Ich, the super ego, a hardened patriarch or a merciless soldier, a wise elder or an ageing condottiere. Perhaps he is a monumental roadside shrine to his own legend or a cursed genie, cast and frozen in red metal. *Vater Staat* looks back into the room containing historical material, where his gaze falls on a plaster model of *Germania* in a dramaturgically staged confrontation: *Father State* meets "Mother State". Characteristically, Schütte's figure lacks the descriptive attributes of his predecessor. The man displays a sense of collectedness, yet without any major gestures or expressive symbols. There is no sword, no sceptre, no eagle or supporting allegories, no crosier and no coronation. Unlike Moore and Chillida, who responded to the governmental commission with abstract compositions, Schütte opts for a human effigy. The figurative conception of man returns in his work. Having become a problematic element in modernity, it is reminiscent of the large impressive statues of previous centuries. Yet Schütte does not lapse into the theatrics of the 19th century, the stylistic references of historicism or sculptural pomposity. *Vater Staat* is silent and restrained in some strange way. With this, he takes on a characteristic of the abstract sculptures of modernity. His reticence, however, cannot be ascribed to a formal refusal to communicate, the withdrawal from allegory induced by the philosophy of democratic politics. Rather, it can be attributed to the attitude of the sculpture itself, a psychological disposition, and not least from a sculptural principle based on dignity and a sense of authority. Schütte intentionally addresses the now-problematic issue of the symbolism of power. In fact, the figure sternly looks over all that is before him. *Vater Staat* is no peaceful sovereign, such as is the case with Hobbes; he is a frightening, unpredictable monument. Yet Schütte by no means fails to break with this impression. He disallows any iconographic ascriptions. The confrontation is decisive; the encounter of the sculptural body with the living, mobile body of the observer. There is a decisive characteristic in this encounter, which demonstrates the relationship between he who has power with his own ego. The vigorous head rests on a bodiless shell. The cloak, knotted at the belly, covers a chimera, a pretence. *Vater Staat* represents a body without a core. I am very proud that I was able to convince Thomas Schütte to lend this exceptional statue to Kunsthalle Mainz and also that the *FAZ* (German newspaper *Frankfurter Allgemeine*) portrayed this impressive piece of art in its review with a stately image measuring more than 40 centimetres.

We reencounter a monumental presence in the last room. However, this is not compact and erect, but set aside, dissipated and divided. Large drifting copper blocks lie on the floor (Ill. p. 72, 73/75 – 79). Others lean against the wall. Others in turn are placed on large wooden pallets. With some, the substructure is revealed. Thin rods and beams keep the shapes together. The reinforcements are paltry. The front sides of the sheets display wave-like forms, broad bulges, and riveted recesses. These are

Betrachter/innen. In dieser Begegnung, die den Machtträger mit dem eigenen Ich in Beziehung bringt, fällt eine entscheidende Eigenschaft auf. Der markige Kopf sitzt auf einem körperlosen Leib. Das Gewand, das um den Bauch geknotet ist, umhüllt eine Chimäre, einen Vorwand. *Vater Staat* repräsentiert einen Körper ohne Mitte. Ich bin sehr stolz, dass ich Thomas Schütte überzeugen konnte, die herausragende Statue für die Kunsthalle Mainz zu leihen und, dass die FAZ das imposante Bildwerk in einer Besprechung in einem stattlichen Ausmaß von mehr als 40 Zentimetern ablichtete.

Monumentale Präsenz begegnet uns im letzten Raum, jedoch nicht kompakt und aufgerichtet, sondern abgelegt, zerstreut und gespalten. Große getriebene Kupferblöcke liegen auf dem Boden (S. 72, 73/75 – 79). Andere sind an die Wand gelehnt. Wieder andere sitzen auf groben Holzpaletten auf. Bei einigen ist die Unterkonstruktion zu sehen. Dünne Stäbe und Streben halten die Formen zusammen. Die Armierungen sind dürftig. Die Vorderseiten der Bleche zeigen wellenförmige Formen, breite Wülste oder genietete Ausnehmungen. Es sind offenkundig Ausschnitte eines größeren, zusammenhängenden Werks. Danh Vo wird in Vietnam geboren und als einer der Boat People von einem dänischen Frachter aufgenommen. Seither ist er europäischer Staatsbürger, der jedoch die westlichen Werte von Freiheit, Selbstbestimmung und Rechtsstaatlichkeit mit kritischem Blick einfordert. Seine aus Kupfer getriebenen Fragmente sind maßstabgetreue Nachbildungen der amerikanischen *Freiheitsstatue*. Die *Freiheitsstatue* ist trotz ihrer antik-römischen Erscheinung eine monumentale *Marianne*. Die Republik Frankreich schenkte die Statue den Vereinigten Staaten. Das Werk, das von Frankreich in Teilen in die USA verschifft wird, ist etwa gleich alt wie die *Germania*. Es geht um den Transfer des republikanischen Gedankens, um die erste Globalisierung der Idee der Menschenrechte. Danh Vo greift dieses Motiv auf und stellt es dennoch infrage. Seine Kupferteile liegen in der Ausstellungshalle wie in einem Frachtraum, bereit abgeschickt zu werden oder kaserniert und in Quarantäne gesteckt, wie Edward Snowden, der die Wochen der Ausstellungsvorbereitung am Flughafen in Moskau festsitzt. Er ist ein Staatenloser. Der Friedensfürst des Hobbes, der die Untertanen in seinem Körper versammelt, fühlt sich für ihn ebensowenig zuständig, wie das Land, das die Freiheitsrechte feiert und in seine Verfassung geschrieben hat. *We the people* heißt das Werk von Danh Vo. Es zitiert damit die ersten Zeilen dieser Verfassung. Die Rechte, die danach aufgezählt werden, scheinen mittlerweile korrumpiert, die heroischen Satzungen der Humanität infrage gestellt. Am Tag der Eröffnung der Ausstellung in der Kunsthalle Mainz wird die *Statue of Liberty* in New York groß gefeiert, nicht nur weil sie nach einem Jahr der Restaurierung wieder zugänglich ist, sondern weil der 4. Juli der amerikanische Nationalfeiertag ist. Man feiert die Unabhängigkeitserklärung und die Menschenrechte. Es bleibt jedoch die Frage berechtigt, ob dieses Land, ja dieser Erdkreis die Werte der Freiheit noch stützt. Der Zerfall ihrer Bilder, die Fragmentierung der Skulptur zeigt es uns an.

obvious extracts from a larger, cohesive piece of work. Born in Vietnam, Danh Vo was one of the "Boat People", rescued at sea by a Danish cargo ship. Since then, he has become a European citizen, who views the occidental values of freedom, self-determination, and state justice from a critical perspective. His drifting fragments made of copper are true-to-scale reproductions of the American Statue of Liberty. Despite its antique-Roman appearance, the Statue of Liberty is in fact a monumental *Marianne*. The statue is a gift from the Republic of France to the United States. The statue, which was shipped from France to the USA in pieces, is just about as old as *Germania*. It represents the transfer of the republican philosophy, the very first globalization of the principle of human rights. Danh Vo takes up this motif and yet questions it. His copper elements lie around the exhibition hall as if they were in a cargo hold, ready for shipment, in barracks, or placed in quarantine. Like Edward Snowden, who was trapped at Moscow Airport during the weeks the exhibition was being prepared, he is stateless. Hobbes's Prince of Peace, whose subjects are contained in his body, feels just as little obligation towards him as the country that celebrates the rights of freedom and has documented them in its constitution. *We the people*, the title of Danh Vo's work, is taken from the first lines of the US constitution. The rights that follow today seem corrupted; the heroic articles of humanity are being questioned. The day the exhibition opened at the Kunsthalle Mainz is the day the Statue of Liberty is celebrated in New York — not because it is once more accessible after a year of restoration, but because the 4th of July is a national holiday in the United States. It is a celebration of independence and of human rights. However the question is still justifiable as to whether this country, actually the entire world, still commits itself to the principles of freedom. The decay of its images, the fragmentation of this sculpture, is an indication.

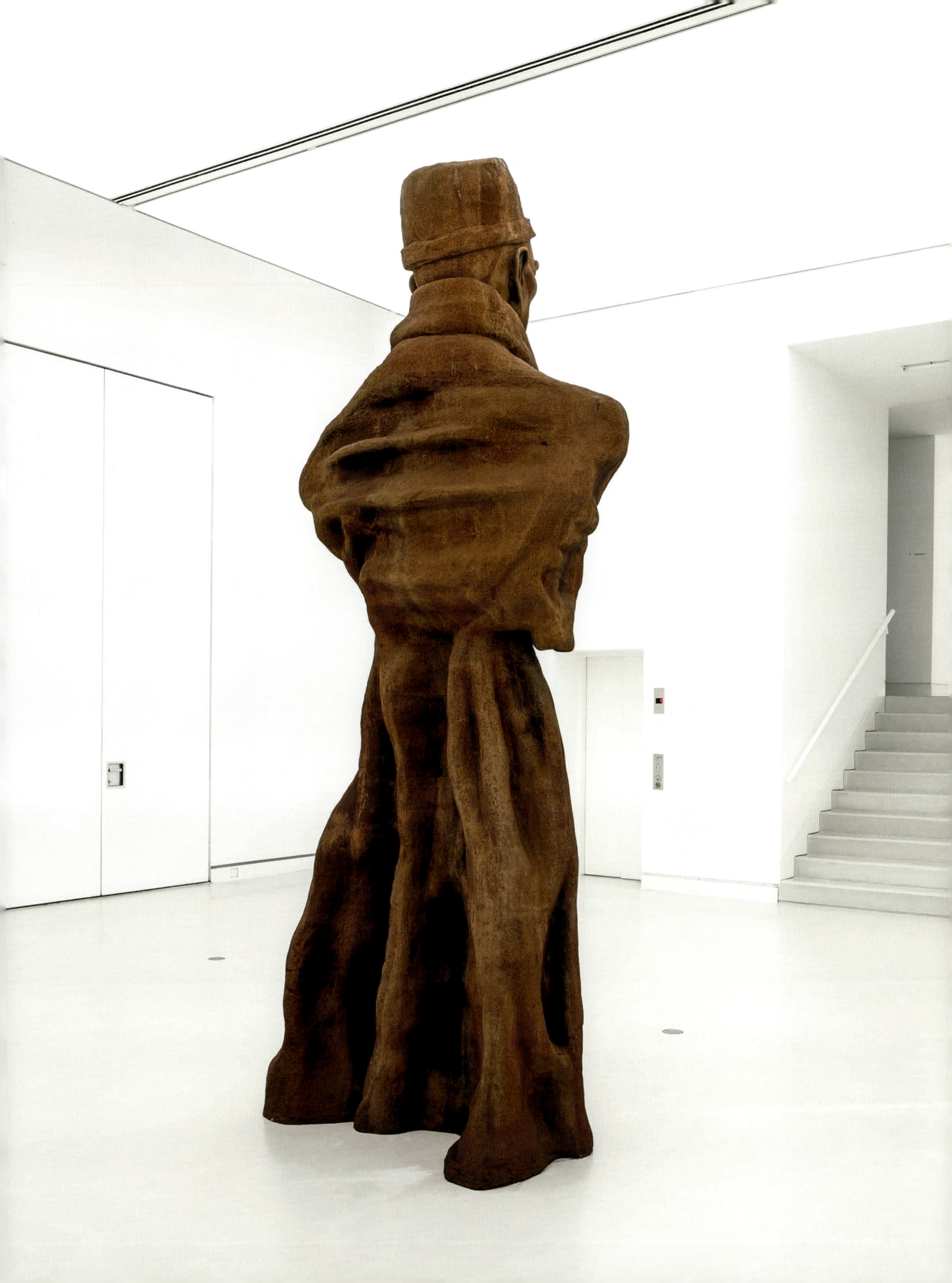

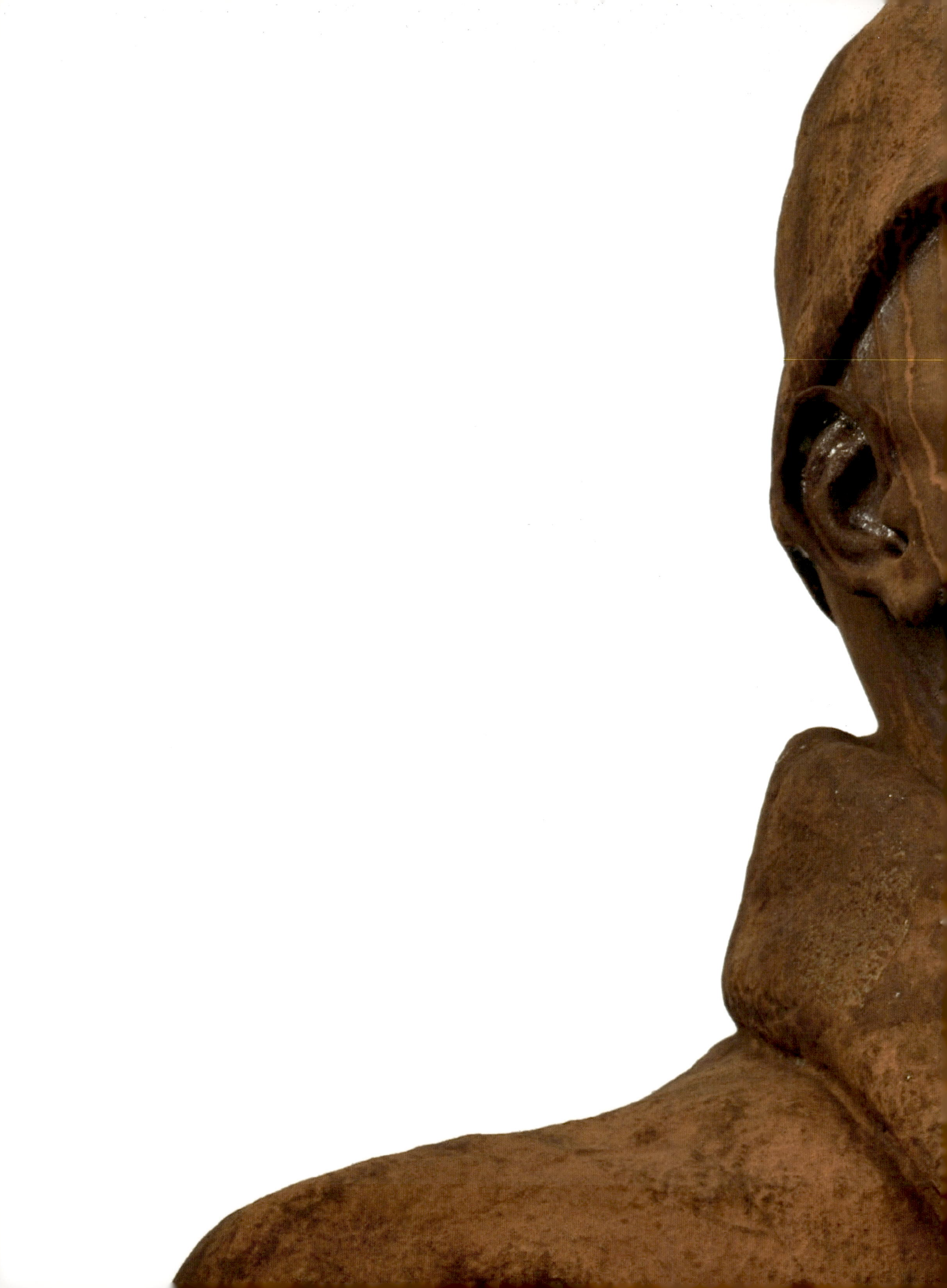

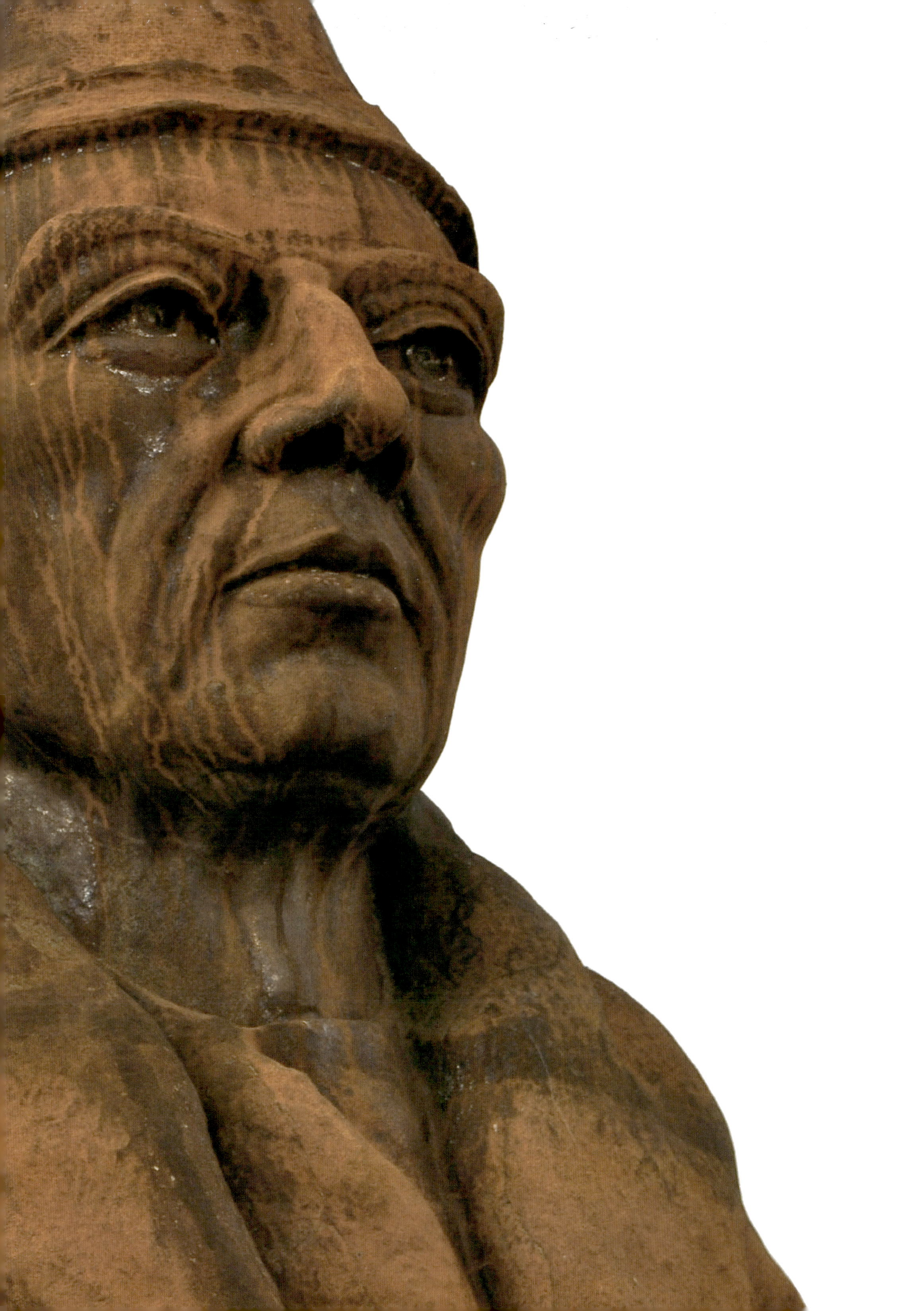

Thomas Schütte
Vater Staat

2012, Stahl/Steel, 373 × 155 × 110 cm
Courtesy: Thomas Schütte, Konrad Fischer
Galerie, Berlin/Düsseldorf

Thomas Schütte begegnet der Frage nach staatlicher Repräsentation mit einem figürlichen Bildnis (Abb. S. 2 – 3, Abb. S. 17 – 21). Sein *Vater Staat* wäre unzureichend verstanden, interpretierte man ihn als spezifisches Porträt oder als gegenwärtige Allegorie heutiger Gemeinwesen. Schütte setzt sich ausdrücklich vom beauftragten, staatlichen Bildwerk ab. Was staatliche Auftraggeber befürworten, nennt er „abstrakten Konformismus" oder „Bekenntnis-Skulptur". Im Gegensatz dazu erinnert seine Figur an vormoderne Figürlichkeit: an Rodins Balzac, an die Bildnisse Bismarcks oder die italienischen Condottieri der Renaissance, an Nathan den Weisen, wegen seiner Mütze an Hamid Karzai vielleicht oder – wie die Assistenten in seinem Studio meinen – an Wolfgang Schäuble. Thomas Schütte, 1954 in Oldenburg geboren und einer der bedeutendsten Künstler Deutschlands, zeigt die monumentale Figur in langem, schwerem Rock. Die männliche Statue, die keinen Sockel besitzt, ist knapp vier Meter hoch und mehr als eine Tonne schwer. In der Kunsthalle beherrscht sie den leeren, klinischen Raum. Der *Vater Staat* thront darin als mächtiger und unbarmherziger Patriarch. Beeindruckend sind sein rostiges Rot, die imposante Größe und seine stumme, unbestechliche Gegenwart. Kopf, Mund, Augen und Teile der Büste sind plastisch ausgearbeitet. Die Glieder sind wie bei einem Flaschengeist unter dem Gewand gefangen, die Arme damit handlungsunfähig. Es fehlen die für monumentale Statuen typischen deutungsvollen Gesten. Auch andere Attribute, wie sie die *Germania*, eigentlich eine „Mutter Staat", reichlich besitzt, fehlen. Nur der Mantel wird eigentümlich robust vor dem Bauch geknotet. Er betont die fehlende, körperlose Mitte.

Thomas Schütte approaches the question of state representation with a figurative image (Ill. pp. 2 – 3, Ill. pp. 17 – 21). His *Vater Staat* would not be sufficiently understood if he were interpreted as a specific portrait or as a contemporary allegory of current community. Schütte explicitly breaks away from the commissioned state sculpture. What state commissioners endorse, he calls "abstract conformism" or "confession sculpture". In contrast, his figure is reminiscent of pre-modern figurative work: of Rodin's *Balzac*, the portrait of Bismarck or the Italian Renaissance condottiere, Nathan the Wise, perhaps Hamid Karzai because of his hat or — as the assistants in his studio think — like Wolfgang Schäuble. Thomas Schütte, born 1954 in Oldenburg and one of Germany's most prominent artists, dresses the monumental figure in a long, heavy cloak. The male statue has no pedestal, is nearly four metres high, and weighs more than a tonne. At the Kunsthalle, the figure commands an empty, sterile room. There, *Vater Staat* is enthroned as a powerful and merciless patriarch. The rusty red, the stately size, and his silent unerring presence are impressive. Head, mouth, eyes, and parts of the torso have been sculpted. Like a genie, his extremities are caught beneath the cloak, the arms therefore unable to act. The statue does not possess the gestures so typical for monumental statues. Also, other attributes are missing that *Germania*, actually a kind of "Mother State", would have in abundance. Only the cloak is tied at the belly as is customary, underscoring the missing, bodiless centre.

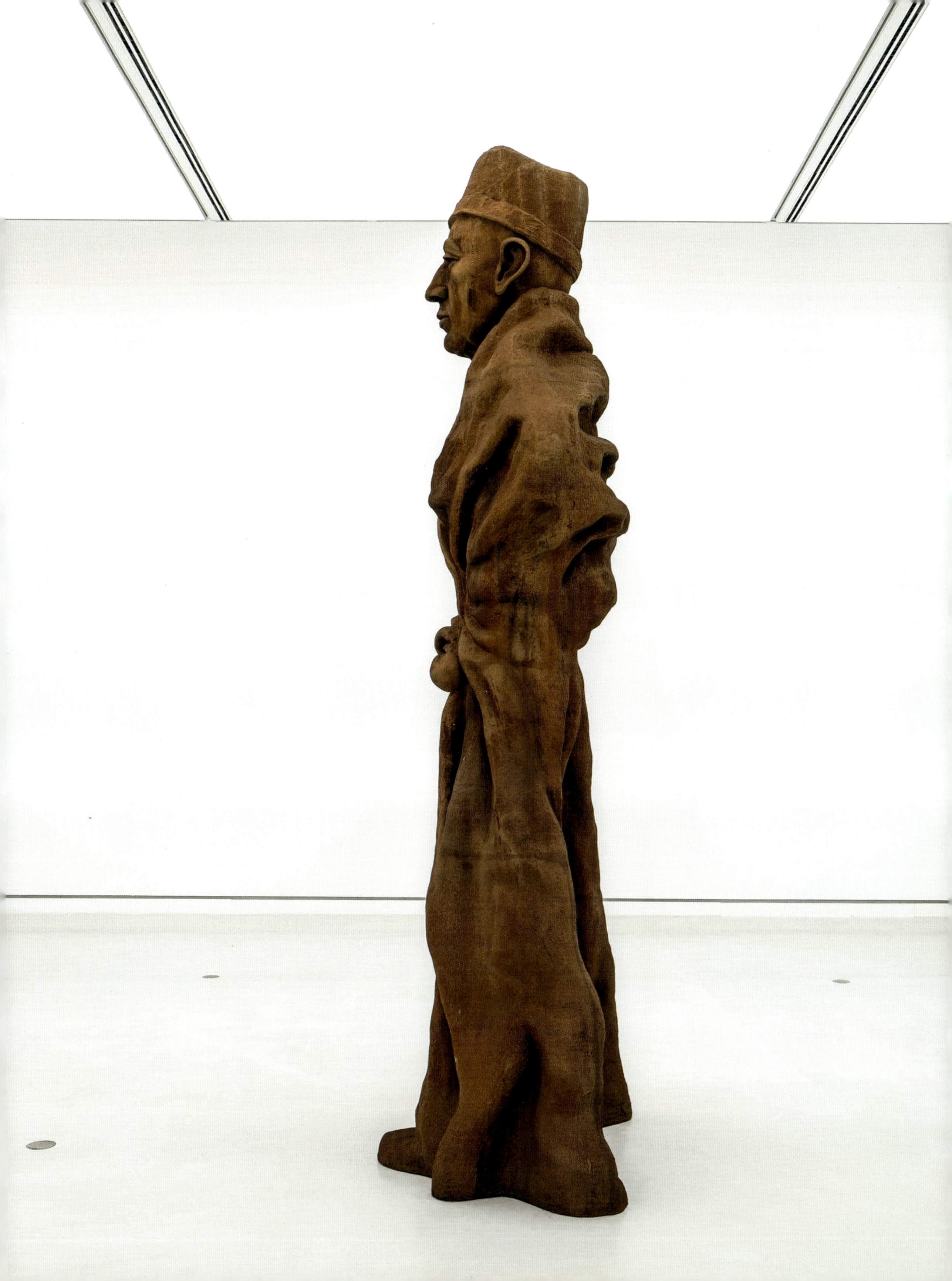

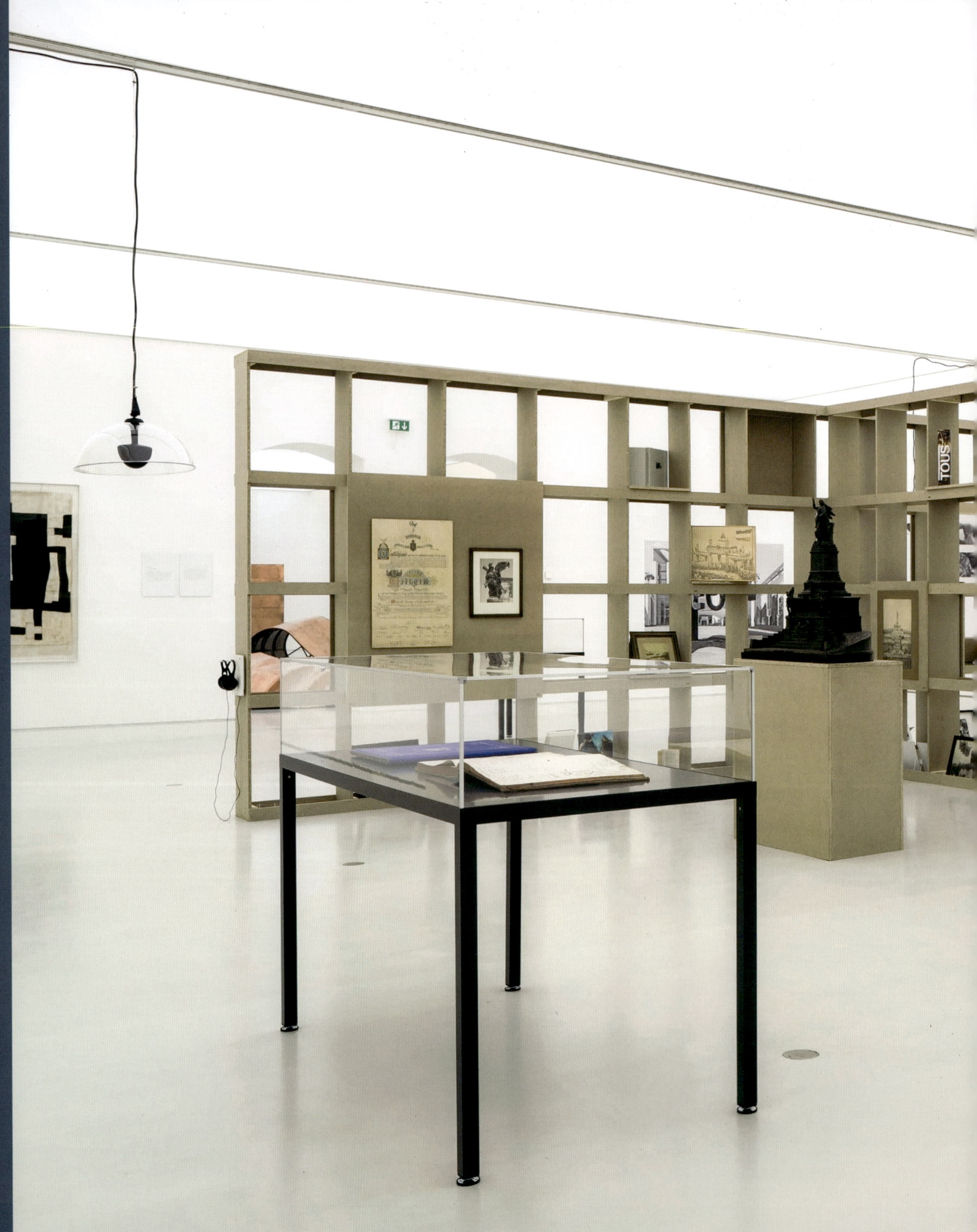

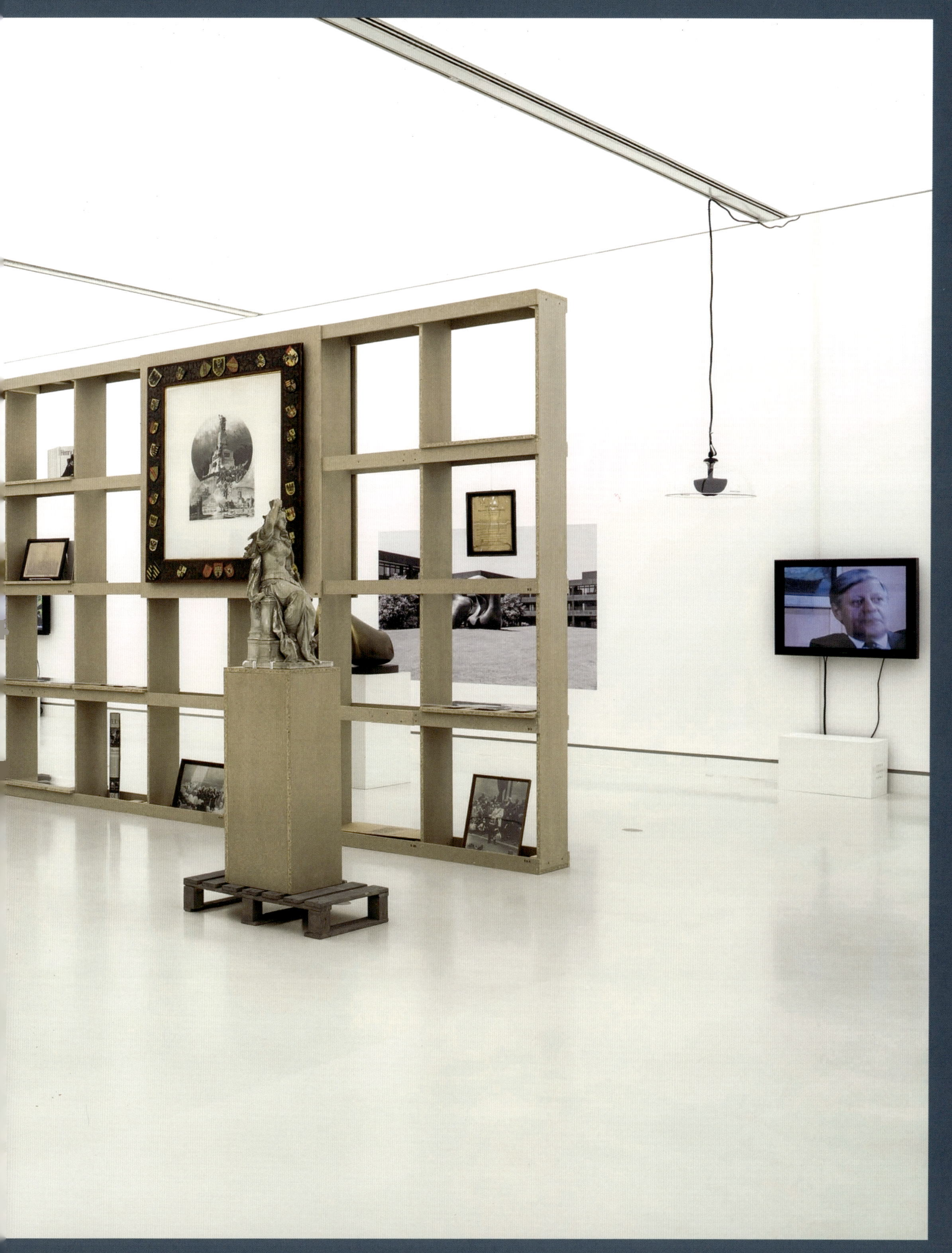

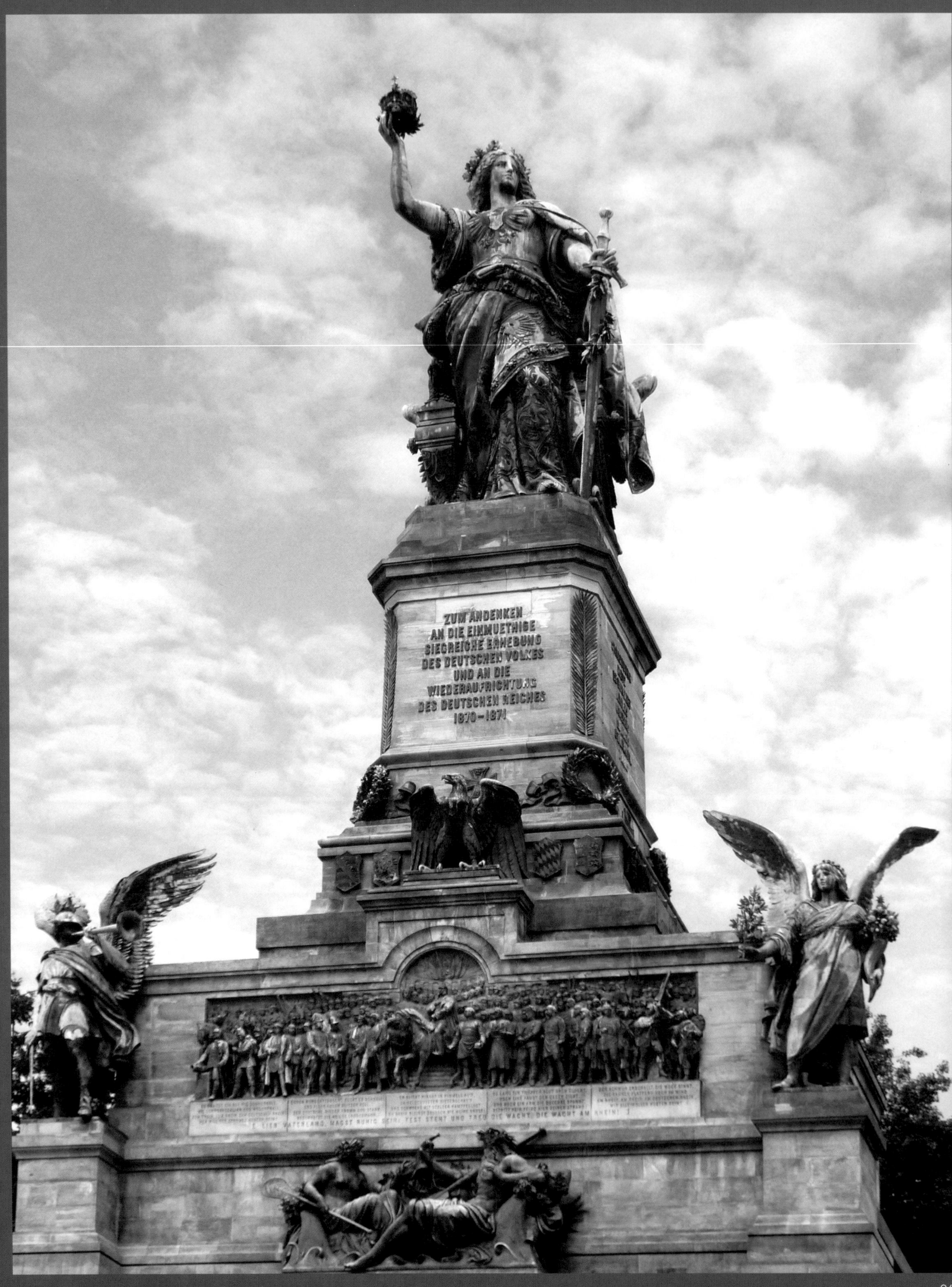

ZUM ANDENKEN
AN DIE EINMUETHIGE
SIEGREICHE ERHEBUNG
DES DEUTSCHEN VOLKES
UND AN DIE
WIEDERAUFRICHTUNG
DES DEUTSCHEN REICHES
1870 – 1871

„Wer will des Stromes Hüter sein?"

"Who wants to be the guardian of the river?"*

Germania von/by Johannes Schilling

04
———

Johannes Schilling, Karl Weißbach
Germania
1883
Bronze
38,18 m (Gesamthöhe/Total height)
Rüdesheim am Rhein
Foto/Photo: Fabienne Rosenbach

Ein Million Besucher zählt das Denkmal jährlich. Eine Seilbahn führt Touristen bis an den Fuß der Skulptur. Über der Stadt Rüdesheim, unweit von Mainz, erhebt sich das Niederwalddenkmal. Von Johannes Schilling stammt die Skulptur, Karl Weißbach entwarf Sockel und architektonische Anlage. Bis heute sorgen Reproduktionen und Souvenirs dafür, dass der Ort an den Weinhängen über dem Rhein Erwartungen stillt und von Neuem anregt. Die überlebensgroße Frauenfigur ist eine Verherrlichung der *Germania*. Die Darstellung mit erhobener Krone und Adlerthron geht auf ein bellizistisches Lied zurück: *Die Wacht am Rhein*. 1871 feiert Deutschland seinen Sieg über Frankreich und die Vereinigung als Kaiserreich. Das Lied wird als inoffizielle Kaiserhymne zur Einweihung angestimmt und bleibt patriotische Erkennungsmusik bis weit in das 20. Jahrhundert. Die Frauenfigur von Johannes Schilling personifiziert die neu erwachte Stärke, obwohl sie eigentlich auf ein Vorbild des „Erbfeindes" und eine republikanische Gesinnung, die französische *Marianne*, zurückgeht. Auffallend verbinden sich wortreiche Kundgebung und skulpturales Vertikalstreben zu nationaler Botschaft. Daneben werden in dem üppigen Ensemble, das vor keiner Theatralik zurückschreckt, verschiedenste Medien und Stile aufgerufen: Text, Bilder, Zeichen und Musik greifen eklektisch ineinander. Zum Beispiel erzählt der Sockel die Entstehungsgeschichte als rechtwinkeliges Flachrelief in Bronze. Der Kaiser ist umgeben von seinen Militärs zu sehen. An der westlichen Seite befindet sich die freistehende Allegorie des *Krieges*, die kraftvoll die Fanfare bläst. Die Gegenspielerin, der *Friede*, steht am gegenüberliegenden Eckpunkt. Dazu kommen heraldische Zeichen und mittelalterlichen Symbole. Am Fuße lagert der *Vater Rhein* im Stile eines römischen Flussgotts und seine *Tochter Mosel.* /

One million people visit the monument every year. A funicular takes tourists up to the base of the sculpture. The Niederwald monument rises high above the town of Rüdesheim, not far from the city of Mainz. The sculpture was made by Johannes Schilling; Karl Weißbach designed the pedestal and architecture. To this day, reproductions and souvenirs ensure that the city, surrounded by vineyards above the Rhine, continues to inspire over and over again. The larger-than-life female figure is a glorification of *Germania*. The depiction with raised sword and eagle's throne is based on a bellicose anthem, "Die Wacht am Rhein" (The Watch on the Rhine). In 1871, Germany celebrated its defeat of France and the unification of the Empire. The song was initially performed as an unofficial Emperor's anthem and remained a patriotic hymn long into the 20th century. Johannes Schilling's female figure personifies the new-found strength, despite the fact that it emanates from an effigy of the "arch enemy" and republican ethos, France's *Marianne*. Eloquent declaration and sculptural vertical aspiration merge into a national statement. In addition, the abundant ensemble, undaunted by any degree of pomposity, makes use of various types of media and styles: text, images, drawings, and music are employed eclectically. For instance, the pedestal tells the story of its creation with a right-angled bas-relief in bronze. The Emperor is depicted surrounded by his soldiers. The western side contains the free-standing allegory of War, which vigorously sounds the trumpet. The antagonist, Peace, stands at the opposite corner. Added to this are heraldic and medieval symbols. The base of the pedestal depicts Father Rhine, in the style of a Roman river god, and his daughter Moselle.

---

* Liedtext: Die Wacht am Rhein. Kat. 30.
  Lyrics: cat. 30.

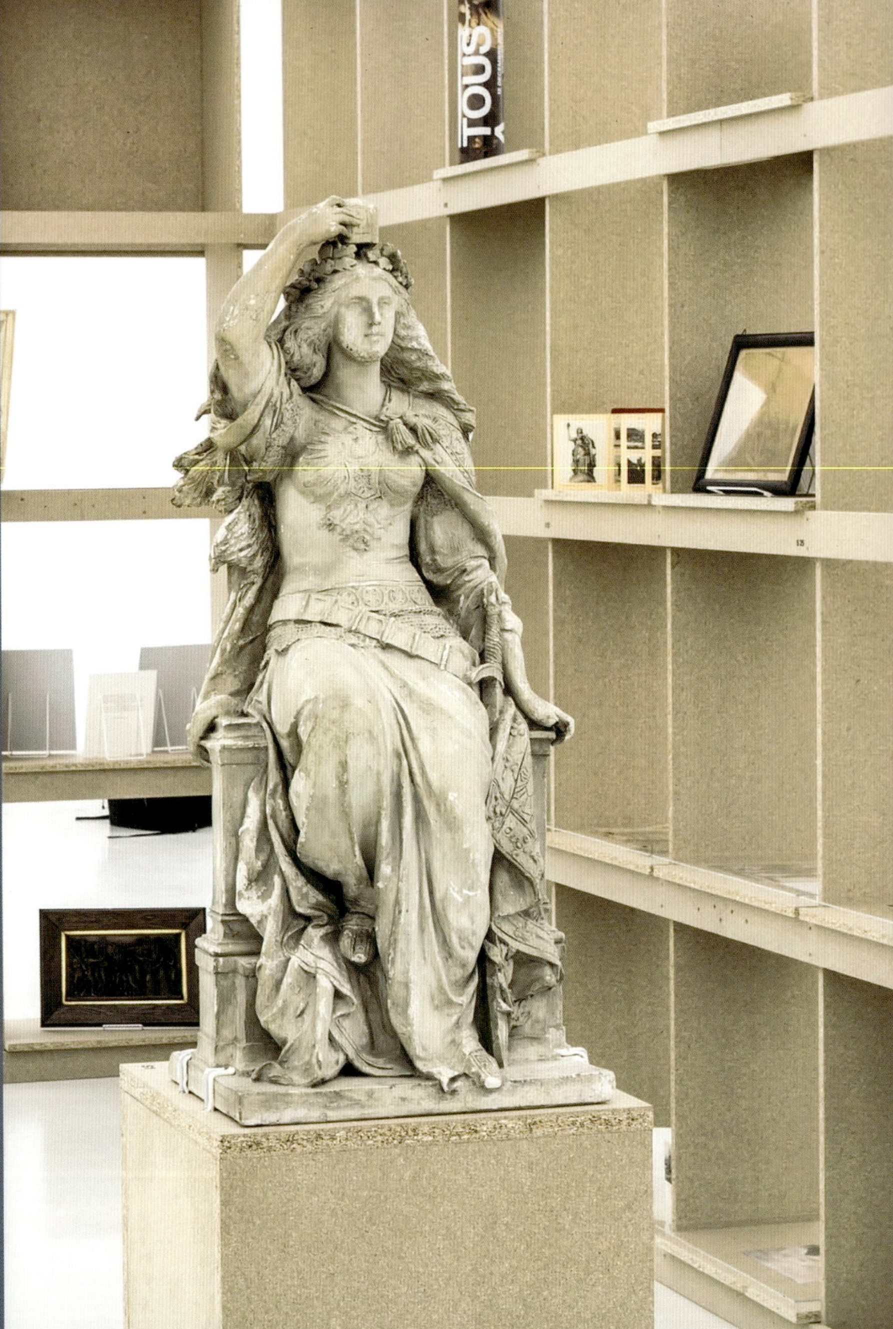

05

Johannes Schilling
Germania (sitzend/seated)
1871/1872
Gips/Plaster
72,5 × 31,5 × 30,5 cm
Johannes-Schilling-Haus, Mittweida/
Johannes Schilling House, Mittweida

In diesem Gipsentwurf hat sich *Germania* noch nicht erhoben. Auch wird sie im späteren Original die Krone weit über dem Kopf halten. Die über dem Rheintal thronende *Germania* ist einer Serie kolossaler Statuen zuordenbar, die nach dem Deutsch-Französischen Krieg 1870/1871 die Vereinigung des Deutschen Reiches verherrlichen und die „Erbfeindschaft" mit dem Nachbarn sinnbildlich versiegeln. Viele der schamlos pathetischen, gigantischen Bauwerke stehen in engem Zusammenhang mit der Glorifizierung Kaiser Wilhelms I., so wie das Barbarossadenkmal auf dem Kyffhäuserberg (1890–1896) oder das mächtige Reiterstandbild des Kaisers am Deutschen Eck in Koblenz (1888–1897). Andere erinnern an historische Schlachten: wie das Hermannsdenkmal bei Detmold im Teutoburger Wald (1838–1875), das Völkerschlachtdenkmal in Leipzig (1895–1913) oder die bereits vor der Reichsgründung vom bayrischen König Ludwig I. in Auftrag gegebene Walhalla bei Donaustauf (1842). /
In this plaster model, *Germania* has not yet revolted. In the later original, she will hold the crown far above her head. To *Germania*, whose throne overlooks the Rhine valley, can be ascribed a series of massive statues that glorify the unification of the German Empire following the Franco-Prussian war (1870–71) and symbolically seal the "enmity" between the two neighbouring countries. Many of the blatantly pathetic, gigantic structures are closely connected to the glorification of Emperor Wilhelm I, as is the Kyffhäuser monument on Kyffhäuserberg (1890–96) or the powerful equestrian statue of the Emperor at Deutsche Eck in Koblenz (1888–97). Others are reminiscent of historical battles, such as Hermannsdenkmal near Detmold in Teutoburger Forest (1838–75), the Monument to the Battle of the Nations (Völkerschlachtdenkmal) in Leipzig (1895–13), or the Walhalla (1842) near Donaustauff, commissioned by the Bavarian King Ludwig I.

——

*Festordnung, Einweihung des National-
denkmals auf dem Niederwald
am 28. September 1883*
*Order of ceremony, inauguration of the
national monument on Niederwald on
September 28, 1883*
Papier/Paper
33,2 × 26,6 cm (mit Rahmen/Framed)
Stadt Rüdesheim am Rhein/
The city of Rüdesheim am Rhein

Das Flugblatt, das sowohl recto (Kat. 06.1)
als auch verso (Kat. 06.2) zu lesen ist, gibt
Auskunft über das Protokoll der feierlichen
Enthüllung des Denkmals im Jahr 1883. Auffällig ist der besondere Stellenwert der Musik.
Unter anderem ist auf der Rückseite „Nun
danket alle Gott" mit Text und Notation abgedruckt. Das Lied wird 1630 anlässlich der
Hundertjahrfeier der „Augsburger Konfessi-
on" von dem Geistlichen Martin Rinckart
verfasst und ist seither fester Bestand des
deutschen Kirchenliedguts. Seine weltliche
Bedeutung gewinnt das protestantische Kir-
chenlied durch die Schlacht bei Leuthen im
Jahr 1757, als die Preußische Armee unter

Friedrich II. die Österreicher im Siebenjähri-
gen Krieg besiegt. Am Abend nach der
Schlacht sollen einer Legende zufolge 25 000
Soldaten das Lied spontan angestimmt haben.
1955 wird es im Lager Friedland bei Göttingen
im Zuge der Heimkehr des offiziell letzten
deutschen Kriegsgefangenen aus der Sowjet-
union, die Konrad Adenauer erwirkt hatte,
angestimmt./
The flyer, printed on both sides (cat. 06.1, 06.2),
provides information on the ceremonial unveiling of the monument in 1883. The significance of the music warrants particular merit.
The reverse contains the text and annotation
"Nun danket alle Gott" (All thank God). The
song was written on the occasion of the 100th
anniversary of the Augsburg Confession by
clergyman Martin Rinckart and has since
become an inherent part of Germany's legacy
of hymns. The protestant hymn obtains its
secular significance from the Battle of Leuthen
in the year 1757, when the Prussian Army,
under the command of Frederick the Great,
defeated the Austrians during the Seven
Years' War. According to legend, 25,000 are
said to have spontaneously joined in to sing
the hymn on the evening after the battle.
In 1955, the same piece was sung at the Fried-

land Camp during the official welcome for
the last German prisoners of war, who returned from the Soviet Union as a result of
efforts by Konrad Adenauer.

——

07.1

Gruss vom Niederwald
Greetings from Niederwald
Postkarte/Postcard
gestempelt 22. Juni 1897/
Postmarked 6/22/1897
15,2 × 8,9 cm
Sammlung/Collection
Günter Höhmann, Wiesbaden

07.2

Enthüllungsfeier des Nationaldenkmals
*Unveiling ceremony of the national mon-
ument*
Postkarte/Postcard
1883
13,8 × 8,4 cm
Sammlung/Collection
Günter Höhmann, Wiesbaden

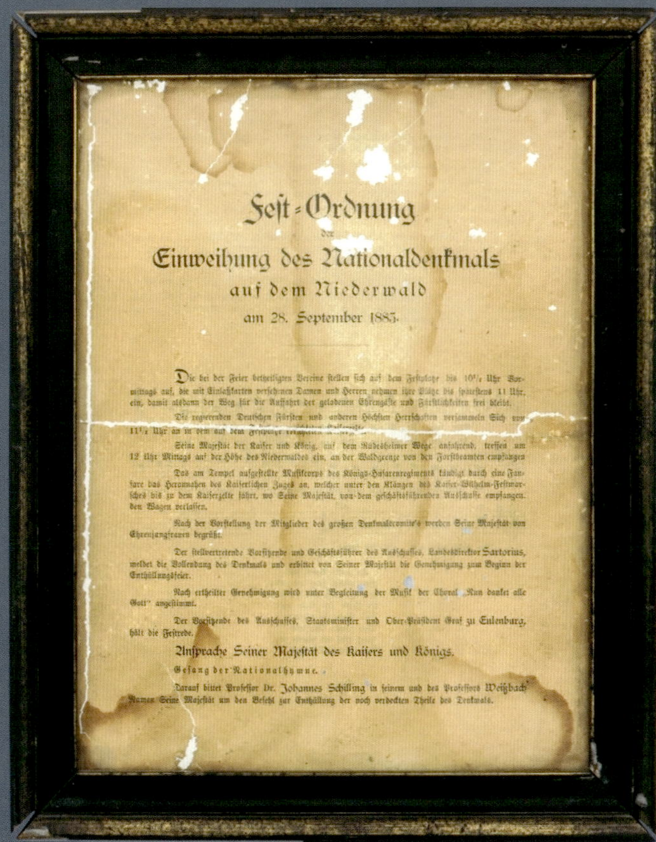

06.1

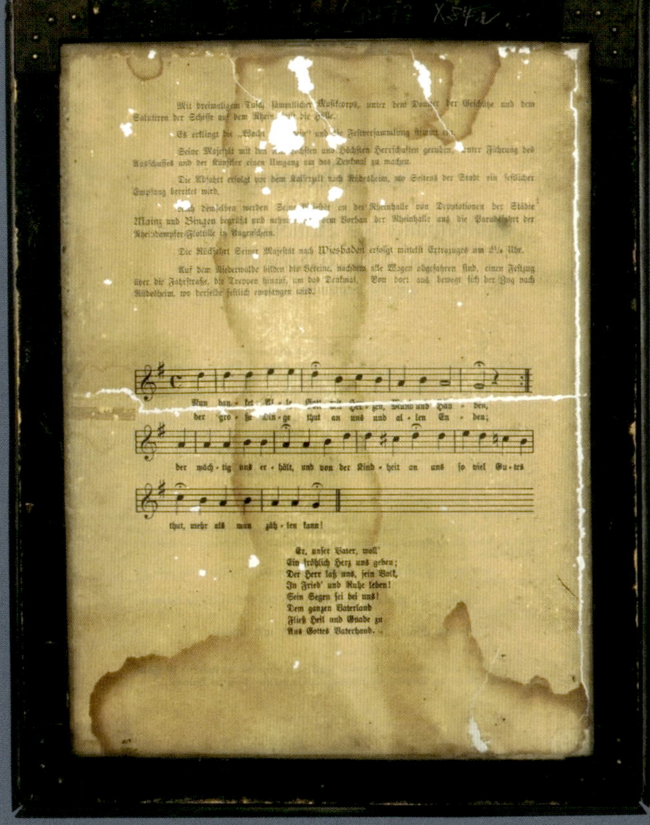

06.2

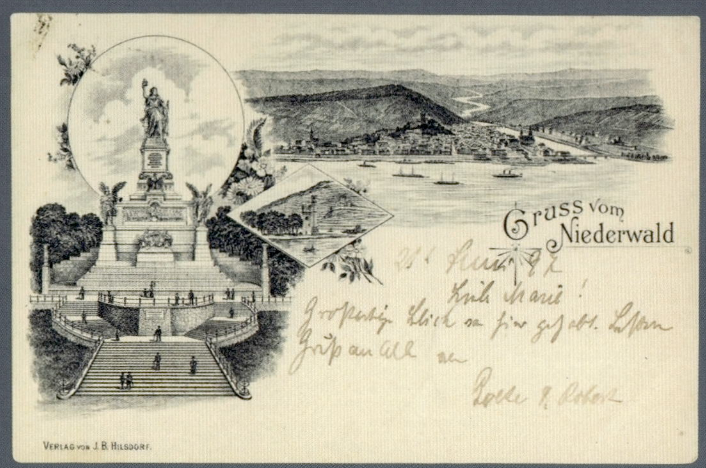

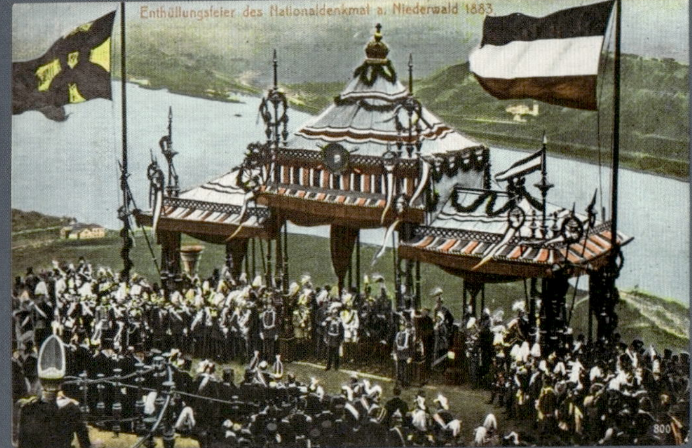

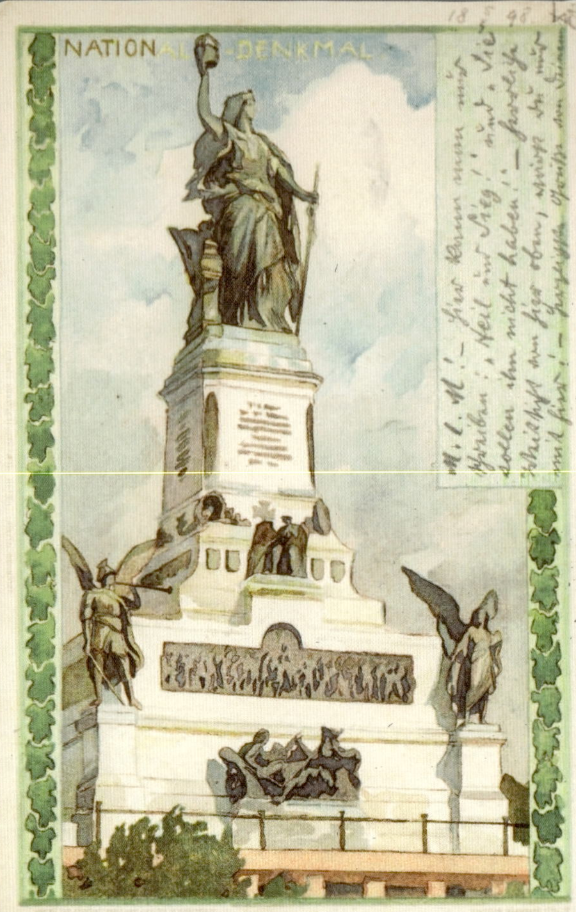

07.1, 07.2

07.3

07.3
National-Denkmal
National monument
Postkarte/Postcard
gestempelt 5. September 1898/
Postmarked 9/5/1898
9,2 × 13,2 cm
Sammlung/Collection
Günter Höhmann, Wiesbaden

Die Popularität der *Germania* als Bildsujet
ist nicht einzig auf ihre weithin sichtbare
topografische Position zurückzuführen,
sondern ebenso auf neue Kommunikations-
formen und Medien. In Deutschland wird
die „Correspondenzkarte" mit ihrem stan-
dardisierten Format 1870, ein Jahr nach
Österreich-Ungarn, eingeführt. Der Vorläufer
der Ansichtskarte entwickelt sich rasch zum
Verkaufsschlager. Anfangs ist die Rückseite
ausschließlich für die Adresse reserviert.
So muss die Vorderseite Bild und Text auf-
nehmen. Viele Motive zeigen daher Leerstellen, die für den Text reserviert sind. Während
des Deutsch-Französischen Kriegs 1870/1871

kommt es erstmals zur Verwendung in grö-
ßerem Umfang. Für mobile Truppen gilt ab
Juli 1870 Portofreiheit, noch bis Dezember
1870 werden rund zehn Millionen „Feldpost-
Correspondenzkarten" in die Heimat verschickt. /
The popularity of *Germania* as a subject cannot be solely attributed to her topographical
position, but also to new forms of communi-
cation and media. The "correspondenzkarte"
(correspondence card) with its standardized
format was first introduced in Germany in
1870, one year after its introduction in
Austria-Hungary. This predecessor of the
postcard quickly became a bestseller. At first,
the reverse of the postcard was reserved just
for the address. Image and text had to be put
on the front, which is why many designs have
spaces left empty for the writer to add their
text. The correspondence card was first put to
large-scale use during the Franco-Prussian
War in 1870 – 71. From July 1870, mobile
troops had free postal services, and by 1870
some 10 million correspondence cards had
been sent home by army postal services.

08

08.1
Ottomar Anschütz
Niederwald-Denkmal Militär
bei der Einweihung
Niederwald monument. Military troops
at the inauguration
1883
SW-Fotografie/Black and
white photograph
32,4 × 44,2 cm
Stadt Rüdesheim am Rhein

08.2
Ottomar Anschütz
Nahaufnahme des Kaisers
A close-up of the Emperor
Einweihungsfeier am 28. September 1883/
Inauguration on 9/28/1883
1883
SW-Fotografie/Black and
white photograph
41,6 × 30,5 cm
Stadt Rüdesheim am Rhein

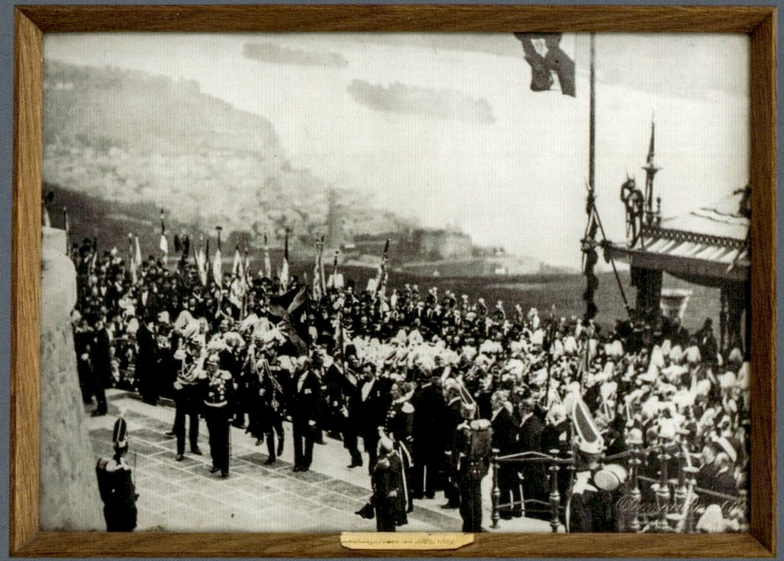

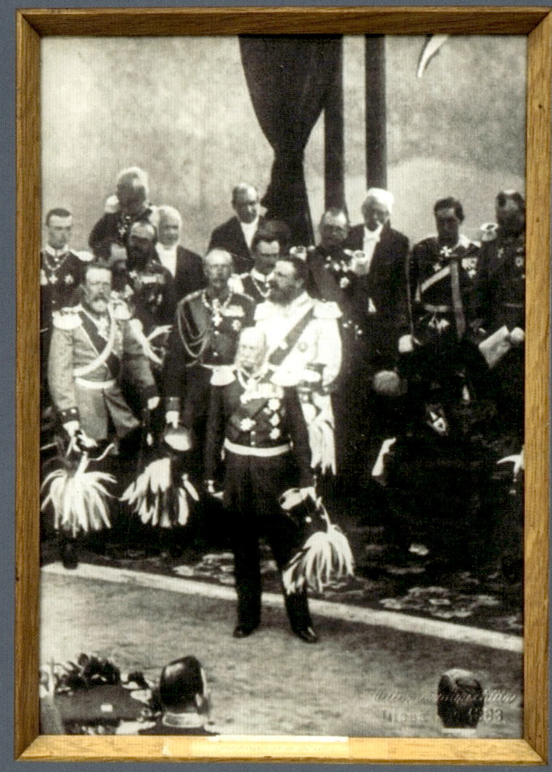

08.1

08.2

Die feierliche Einweihung des Niederwalddenkmals findet am 28. September 1883 in Anwesenheit des Kaisers statt. Der Fotograf Ottomar Anschütz fotografiert die Gäste. Die geladenen Ehrengäste ziehen zur Mittagszeit zu dem über dem Rhein gelegenen Festplatz hinauf. Auch auf dem Rhein ist das Spektakel von Schiffen aus zu beobachten. Wie schon bei der Grundsteinlegung wird *Die Wacht am Rhein* angestimmt und Kaiser Wilhelm I. hält eine Rede, auf die Salutschüsse der Offiziere neben dem kaiserlichen Festzelt und auf den Rheinschiffen folgen. Als feierlicher Höhepunkt enthüllt Johannes Schilling das Hauptrelief des Niederwalddenkmals. /
The festive inauguration of the Niederwald monument took place on 28 September 1883 in the presence of the Emperor. The photographer Ottomar Anschütz took pictures of the guests. During lunchtime, the guests of honour went to the fairgrounds situated high above the river Rhine. A spectacular array of ships was observed on the Rhine. During the laying of the foundation stone, "Die Wacht am Rhein" was performed and Emperor Wilhelm I delivered a speech, followed by gun salutes fired by the officers next to the Emperor's pavilion and from the ships below. The festive climax of the celebration was the unveiling of the main relief of the Niederwald monument by Johannes Schilling.

09

Bernhard Mannfeld
Radierung in farbig gefasstem Holzrahmen mit Wappen/Etching in coloured wooden frame with emblem
Beschriftung links unten/Inscription at the bottom left
„Original Radierung v. B. Mannfeld, Frkft. M.", rechts: „Gedruckt i. Städel'schen Kunstinst. z. Frankfurt/M."
65 × 50 cm (ohne Rahmen/unframed)
132 × 113,3 cm (mit Rahmen/framed)
Stadt Rüdesheim am Rhein

Der altdeutsche Rahmen veredelt. Der Adler des Deutschen Reiches krönt in der Mitte das Geschehen. Zu seiner Linken zeigt sich das Königreich Preußen, zu seiner Rechten das Königreich Bayern. Links unten wird Sachsen und rechts unten Württemberg gezeigt. Die Darstellung selbst wird als Rundbild wie in einer Zauberkugel dargebracht. Schwarze Wolken verdunkeln den Himmel. Es gewittert während der Eröffnung. Die Menschen schützen sich mit Schirmen. Einige verlassen das Geschehen, dringen herab in den abgetrennten Raum des Unterbildes, das eine Landschaftscollage von Rüdesheim und Bingen zeigt. Der stürmische Regen hat unter anderem zur Folge, dass die Zündschnur zweier Anarchisten wegen der Feuchtigkeit versagt. Sie hatten beabsichtigt, die Statue auf den Kaiser stürzen zu lassen. Wenig später werden sie in Halle hingerichtet. /
The old German polished frame. The German Imperial Eagle crowns the events in the centre of the scene. To his left is the Kingdom of Prussia, the Kingdom of Bavaria to his right. Saxony is shown at the bottom left and Württemberg at the bottom right. The scene itself is depicted as a cyclorama, similar to that of a crystal ball. Black clouds darken the sky — there is a thunderstorm during the opening. The people protect themselves from the storm with umbrellas. Some leave the scene, moving down into the separate room of the sub-panel, which depicts a landscape collage of Rüdesheim and Bingen. A consequence of the rainstorm is that the fuse that two anarchists attempt to light fails as it is drenched. Their intention was to make the statue fall on top of the Emperor. A little later, they are executed in Halle.

10.1
Genius des Krieges Postamentfigur am Nationaldenkmal auf dem Niederwald von Prof. Johannes Schilling
The Genius of War Figure on pedestal at the national monument on Niederwald by Prof. Johannes Schilling
1883
Fotografie/Photograph
16 × 10,7 cm
Sammlung/Collection
Günter Höhmann, Wiesbaden

10.2
Genius des Friedens Postamentfigur am Nationaldenkmal auf dem Niederwald von Prof. Johannes Schilling
The Genius of Peace Figure on pedestal at the national monument on Niederwald by Prof. Johannes Schilling
1883
Fotografie/Photograph
16 × 10,7 cm
Sammlung/Collection
Günter Höhmann, Wiesbaden

Auf dem Sockel des Niederwalddenkmals wird programmatisch die Entstehungsgeschichte des Deutschen Kaiserreichs erzählt. An seiner westlichen Seite befindet sich eine überlebensgroße Allegorie des *Krieges*, die kraftvoll in die Fanfare bläst. Die Gegenspielerin zur Allegorie des *Krieges* ist der *Friede*. Diese trägt auf dem Kopf einen Blütenkranz und hält ein mit Früchten gefülltes Füllhorn im Arm, welches den Wohlstand des Kaiserreiches ausdrückt. /
The historical origin of the German Empire is explained on the pedestal of the Niederwalddenkmal. A larger than life allegory of the war, powerfully blowing a fanfare, is located on its western side. The adversary of the allegory of war is peace. She wears a wreath of flowers on her head and holds a cornucopia stuffed with fruit in her arm, expressing the prosperity of the Empire.

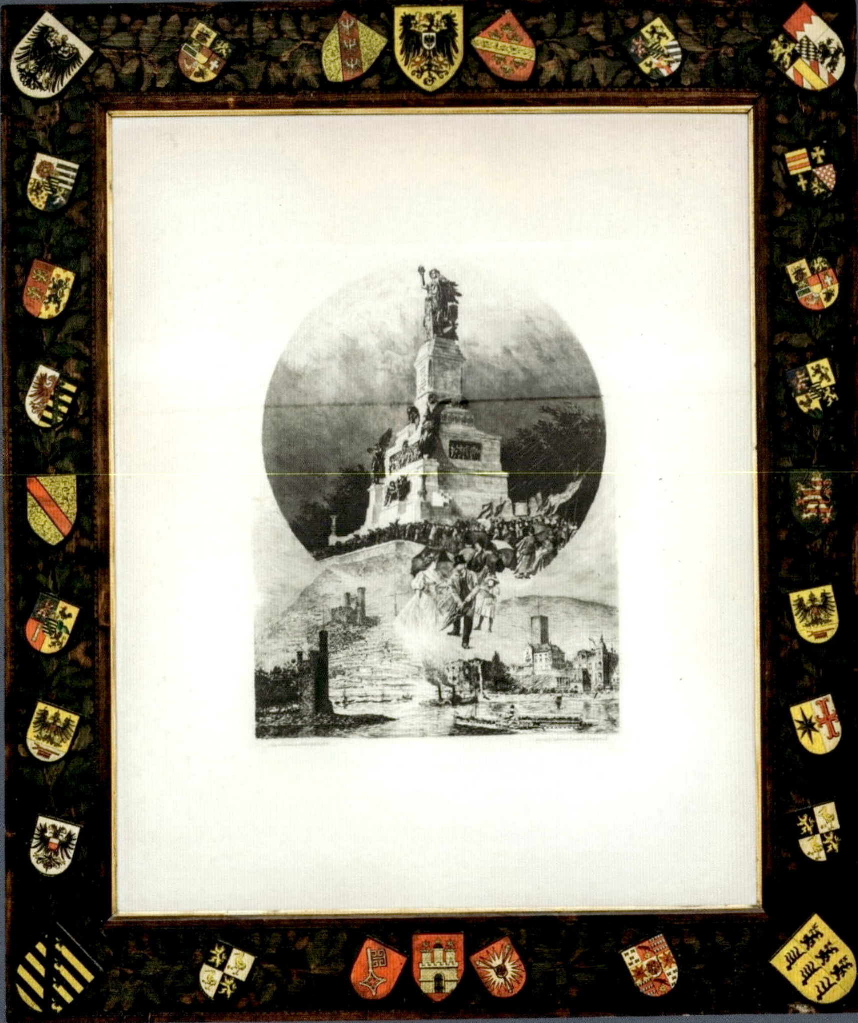

09

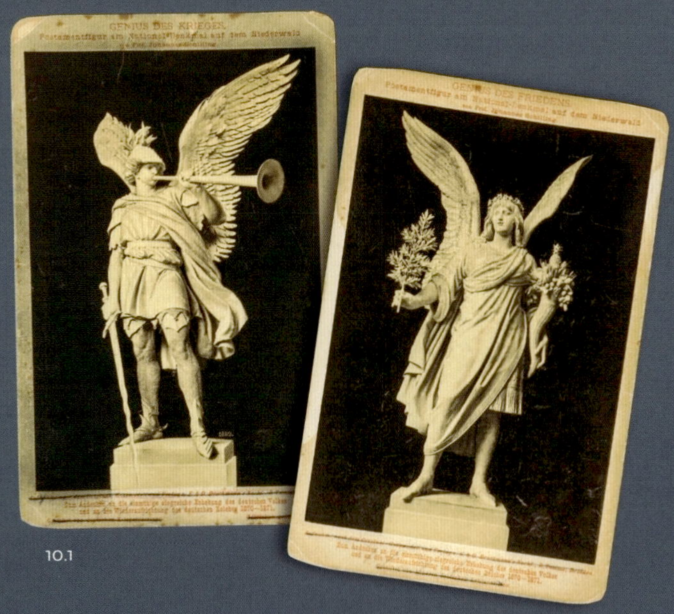

10.1

10.2

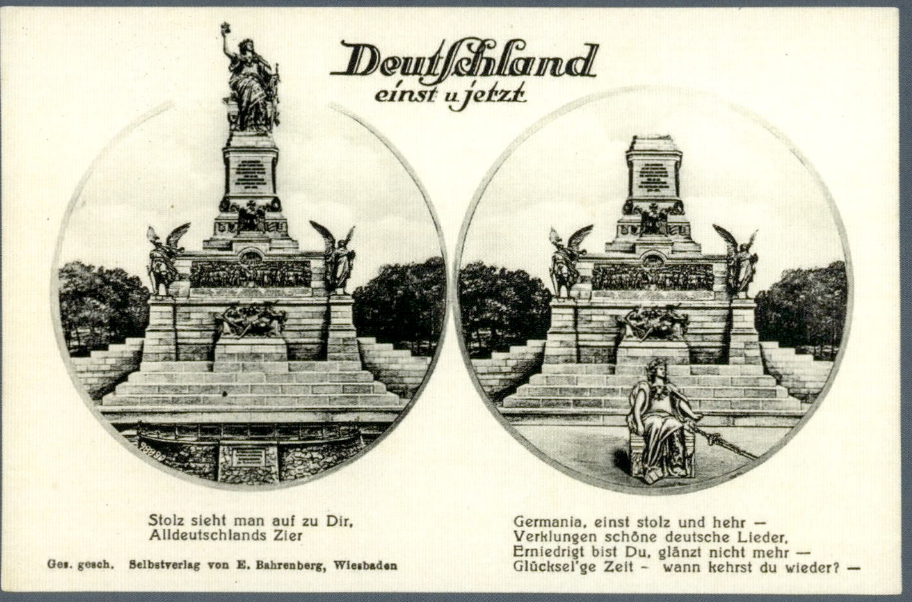

11

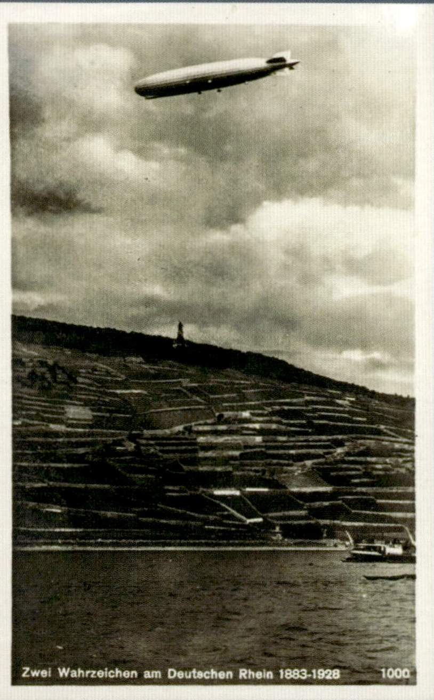

12

11

———

Deutschland einst u. jetzt
Germany, then and now
Postkarte/Postcard
ungestempelt/Unstamped
8,6 × 14 cm
Postkarte Selbstverlag E. Bahrenberg,
Wiesbaden
Sammlung/Collection
Günter Höhmann, Wiesbaden

In dieser Postkarte wird die *Germania* zum
Anlass von nostalgischer Trauer. Der Autor
sieht Deutschlands Ruhm verblasst. Wahr-
scheinlich ist das Sujet nach dem Ersten Weltkrieg entstanden. Wie unter einem Fernglas
wird das Denkmal zweimal in einem Rundbild vorgestellt. Darunter sind jeweils gereimte
Zeilen zu lesen. In dem rechten Sujet ist die
Statue von ihrem Thron herabgestiegen. Sie
sitzt hilflos vor dem Postament. Darunter ist
zu lesen: „Germania, einst stolz und hehr –
Verklungen schöne deutsche Lieder Erniedrigt bist Du, glänzt nicht mehr – Glücksel'ge
Zeit – wann kehrst du wieder?" – /
In this postcard, *Germania* becomes the object of nostalgic grief. The author sees that
Germany's glory has faded. It was most likely
created after the First World War. As if observed through binoculars, the monument is
depicted in two circular images. A rhyme
is written beneath. In the image on the right,
the statue has descended from her throne.

She sits helplessly in front of the pedestal. The
text beneath the image reads: "Germania, einst
stolz und hehr — Verklungen schöne deutsche
Lieder Erniedrigt bist Du, glänzt nicht mehr –
Glücksel'ge Zeit – wann kehrst du wieder?"
(*Germania*, once proud and sublime — fine
German songs have faded, you no longer
shine — blessed times when will you return?)

12

———

Zwei Wahrzeichen am Deutschen Rhein
Two Landmarks on the German River
Rhine
Postkarte/Postcard
1883 – 1928
ungestempelt/Unstamped
12,6 × 9 cm
Sammlung/Collection
Günter Höhmann, Wiesbaden

Die *Germania* ist bis heute ein Tourismus-
magnet mit rund einer Million Besucher pro
Jahr. Die Position der Statue ist topografisch
gewählt, ihr Blick schweift über den Rhein.
Bemerkenswerterweise ist die Statue umgekehrt jedoch am besten von einem fiktiven
Standpunkt aus zu betrachten. Vor Ort zwingt
sie zur krassen Untersicht, von Bingen aus
gesehen ist sie zu klein. Dies vermittelt diese
Fotografie wohl ungewollt. Ideal ist die Vogel-
perspektive, wie hier aus der Kabine eines
Zeppelins im Jahr 1928. /

To this day, *Germania* has great appeal among
tourists, attracting some one million visitors
per year. The position of the statue was chosen
for topographical reasons; her gaze looks over
the Rhine. Remarkably, on the reverse side it
should be observed from a fictitious perspective. Here, the perspective is observed from
directly below, from the town of Bingen, and
the statue appears to be much too small. This
is most likely not the intention of the photograph. A bird's-eye view, as taken here from
the cabin of a zeppelin in 1928, offers the ideal
perspective.

13

———

Deutscher Gruss! Lieb' Vaterland,
magst ruhig sein: Fest steht und treu
die Wacht am Rhein!
Dear fatherland, no fear be thine:
Firm and True stands the Watch,
the Watch at the Rhine
Postkarte/Postcard
gestempelt 13. Mai 1916/
Postmarked 5/13/1916
13,4 × 9,1 cm
Sammlung/Collection
Günter Höhmann, Wiesbaden

Zwei Flaggen der Marine säumen das Bildnis
der Statue. Links ist das so genannte *Kriegs-*
schiffgösch zu sehen, welche von 1871 bis 1903
in Gebrauch war, rechts die Lotsenflagge, die

auch noch während des Ersten Weltkriegs
benutzt wurde./
Two naval banners adorn the image of the
statue. To the left, we see the so-called
"Kriegsschiffgösch" (jack), which was used
from 1871 to 1903, and to the right, the
"Lotsenflagge" (pilot jack), which was still
in use during the First World War.

14

Erinnerung an das National-Denkmal
Commemoration of the
National Monument
Leporello/Leporello

21 SW-Aufnahmen des Niederwalddenkmals, Details der Statue, des Sockels
und der Umgebung mit deutschen,
französischen sowie englischen Bild-
unterschriften o. J.
21 monochrome photographs of the Niederwald monument, details of the statue,
the pedestal and the surroundings, with
German, French and English captions,
undated.

Druck und Verlag/
Printing and publishing
v. G. Blümlein & Co., Frankfurt/M.
Sammlung/Collection
Günther Höhmann, Wiesbaden

Einerseits ist es die Industrialisierung, die
Verkehrswege beschleunigt und dem Touris-
mus Auftrieb verleiht, andererseits sind es
Bilder und poetische Texte, welche die Vor-
aussetzung für die Rheinromantik und den
Fremdenverkehr liefern. Die Landschaft mit
ihren Ruinen, Felsen und Flusswindungen
entsteht durch eine ästhetisch gefärbte Sicht.
Das Leporello zeigt verschiedene Ansichten
von Rüdesheim, Bingen und Umgebung.
Es ist eines der vielen bis heute publizierten
Souvenirs./
On the one hand, it is industrialisation that
facilitates the development of infrastructures,
which in turn give impetus to the tourism industry; on the other hand, it is the imagery
and poetic texts that give life to the romanti-
cism of the Rhine region and tourism. The
landscape with its ruins, cliffs, and river
bends, is founded on an aesthetically tainted
perspective. The leporello depicts various
views of Rüdesheim, Bingen, and the surroun-
ding area. It is one of the many souvenirs
still published to this day.

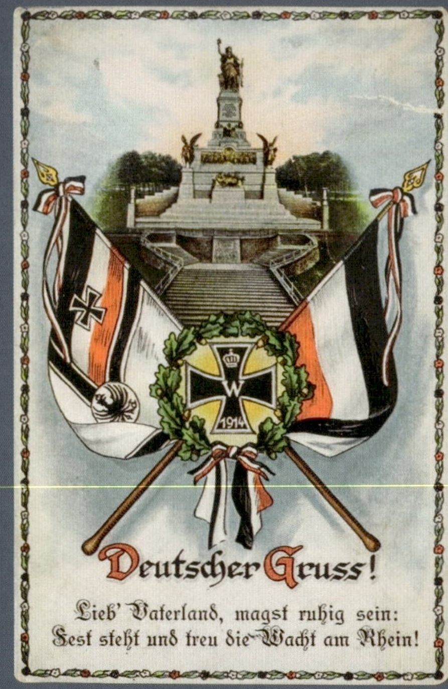

13

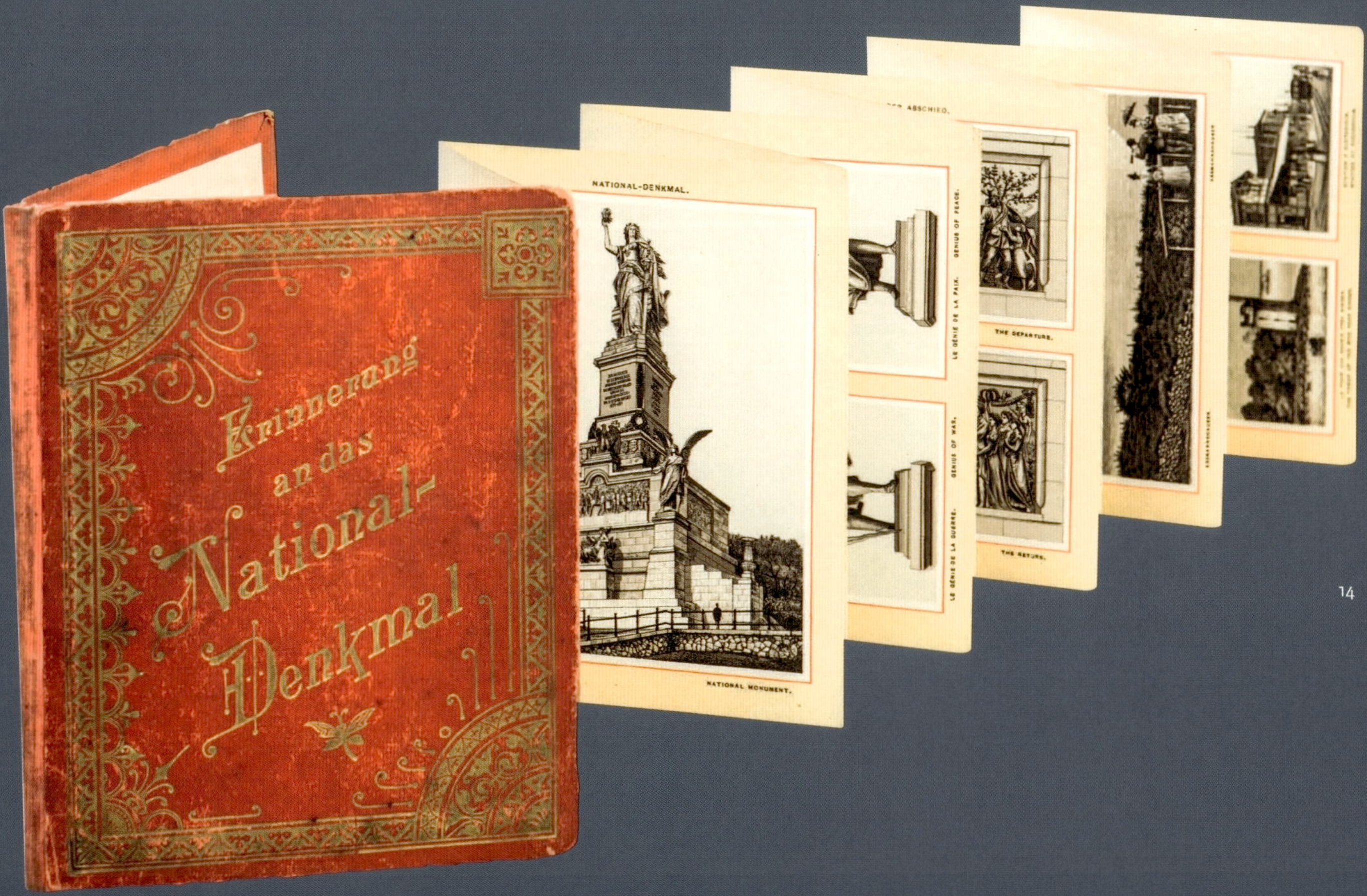

14

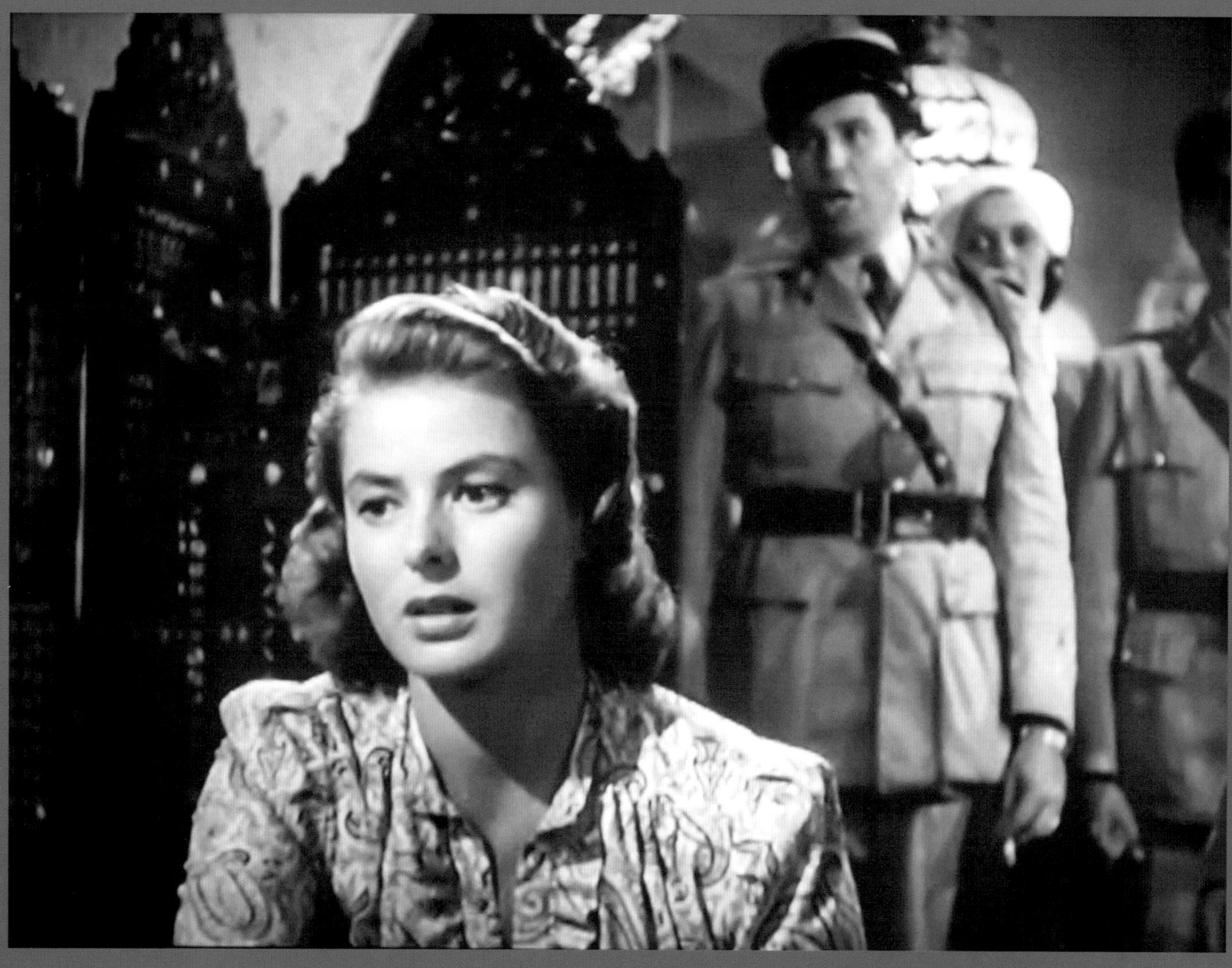

15

Casablanca (Film still)
USA 1942, Länge/Duration 102 min,
Regie/Director: Michael Curtiz

Besetzung/Cast:
Richard (Rick) Blaine: Humphrey Bogart
Ilsa Lund: Ingrid Bergmann
Victor László: Paul Henreid
Capt. Renault: Claude Reins
Major Strasser: Conrad Veidt

In der Gestalt der *Germania* erhebt sich eine markige Frauenfigur gegen ihr symbolisches Gegenstück: *Marianne*, die weibliche Allegorie des republikanischen Frankreich. *Die Wacht am Rhein*, die das Niederwalddenkmal ideologisch vorbereitet, bleibt durch die Feindseligkeit der beiden Länder über Jahrzehnte aktuell. Nazideutschland benutzt die ersten Takte des Liedes als Kennmelodie seiner Wehrmachtsberichte im Radio. Der Einsatz zur deutschen Propaganda führt zu einem Zitat in *Casablanca*, dem berühmten Hollywood-Film aus dem Jahr 1942. Die amerikanischen Filmproduzenten reagieren auf den Kriegseintritt der Vereinigten Staaten. Die Dreharbeiten beginnen Ende Mai des Jahres. Noch im selben Jahr wird der Film fertig gestellt. Die Handlung: Die marokkanische Stadt Casablanca – unter der Verwaltung des Vichy-Regimes – wird von einem korrupten französischen Polizeichef kontrolliert. Capitaine Renault handelt mit Transit-Visa für durchziehende Flüchtlinge. Viktor László, ein tschechischer Widerstandskämpfer, der den Nazis bereits mehrmals entkommen ist, will sich mit seiner Frau Ilsa Lund nach Amerika absetzen. Der deutsche Major Strasser verfolgt ihn bis nach Marokko. László bittet den amerikanischen Inhaber des Cafés, Rick Blaine, um Unterstützung. Rick, gespielt von Humphrey Bogart, verweigert ihm die Hilfe. Die beiden werden jedoch im Gespräch unterbrochen. Von unten, aus dem Café dröhnt *Die Wacht am Rhein*. Die deutschen Soldaten rund um Major Strasser haben sich ans Klavier gesetzt. László fordert im Gegenzug die Kapelle auf, die Marseillaise zu spielen. Es kommt zu einem Wettstreit der Lieder, bei dem die Deutschen letztlich übertönt werden. Strasser zwingt Capitaine Renault, das Café umgehend zu räumen.

Viele der Schauspieler sind Emigranten aus Nazi-Deutschland: Conrad Veidt (Major Strasser), Peter Lorre (der Schwarzmarkt-

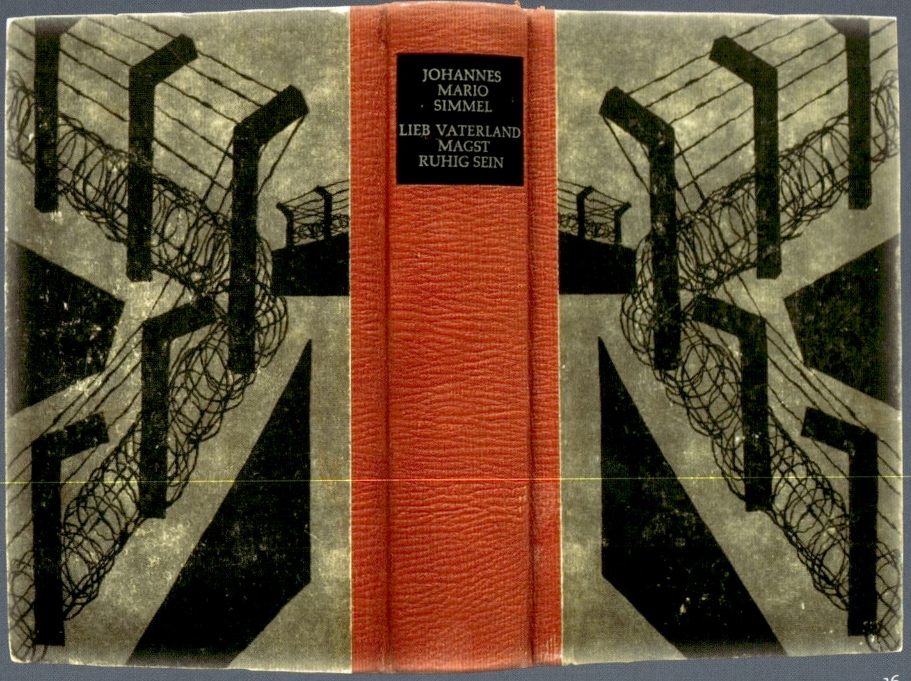

16

händler Bugate) sowie Paul Henreid (Viktor László). Henreid bleibt 1940 selbst auf der Flucht in die USA in London stecken. In der Bundesrepublik wird der Film erstmals 1952 gezeigt. Alle Szenen mit Major Strasser – so auch der in der Kunsthalle Mainz gezeigte Ausschnitt – werden herausgeschnitten. Die um 25 Minuten gekürzte Version ist eine leicht verträgliche Romanze ohne politische Brisanz. Erst 1975 strahlt die ARD die originale Fassung erstmals für das deutsche Publikum aus. /
In the form of *Germania*, a pithy female figure arises to face her counterpart: *Marianne*, the female allegory of France. "Die Wacht am Rhein" [The Watch on the Rhine], which ideologically made way for the Niederwald monument, remained a topical issue for several decades as a result of the animosity between the two nations. Nazi Germany made use of the first bar of the anthem as an introductory tune for its Wehrmacht broadcasts on the radio. Its use as German propaganda led to a quote in the famous Hollywood feature film, *Casablanca*, in the year 1942. American filmmakers responded to the US's entry into the war; filming started late May of that year. The film was completed that very same year. The plot: The Moroccan city of Casablanca — under the administration of the Vichy Regime — is controlled by a corrupt French police commissioner, Captain Renault, who deals in transit visas for refugees. Viktor László, a Czech resistance fighter, who has

managed to evade the Nazis several times, wants to settle down in America with his wife Ilsa Lund. German Major Strasser follows him all the way to Morocco. László asks the American owner of a café, Rick Blaine, for help. Rick, played by Humphrey Bogart, refuses to help him. The two, however, are interrupted during their conversation. From downstairs, we hear the song "Die Wacht am Rhein" being played. The German soldiers are seated around Major Strasser at the piano. László responds by telling the band to play *La Marseillaise.* This results in duelling songs, during which the Germans are ultimately drowned out. Strasser forces Captain Renault to close the café.

Many of the actors in the film were German emigrants from Nazi Germany: Conrad Veidt (Major Strasser), Peter Lorre (the black market dealer Bugate), and Paul Henreid (Viktor László). Henreid, himself a refugee since 1940, spent time in the USA and London. The film was shown in Germany for the first time in 1952. All scenes with Major Strasser — including the scene shown at the Kunsthalle Mainz — were cut out of the movie. The 25-minute shorter version is a light romance without any politically explosive elements. It wasn't until 1975 that German broadcaster ARD aired the original version for a German audience.

16

Johannes Mario Simmel
Lieb Vaterland magst ruhig sein
Dear fatherland, no fear be thine
Verlag/Publisher
Reinhard Mohn OHG, Gütersloh
Ersterscheinung/Initial release:
Knaur, München 1965
Privatbesitz/Private collection,
Mainz

Der Refrain der *Wacht am Rhein* wird im 20. Jahrhundert zur Vorlage verschiedenster Bearbeitungen. Ab den 1960er-Jahren schreibt Johannes Mario Simmel (1924 – 2009) Bestseller im Unterhaltungsgenre. *Lieb Vaterland magst ruhig sein* spielt zwischen West- und Ostberlin im Jahr 1964. Bruno, ein kleiner Ganove aus Ostberlin, gerät zwischen die Fronten des Kalten Krieges, als er im Auftrag der DDR in den Westteil der Stadt geschleust wird. /
The refrain of "Die Wacht am Rhein" has been used for various purposes in the 20th century. Johannes Mario Simmel (1924 – 2009) wrote light fiction from the 1960s. *Lieb Vaterland magst ruhig sein* (Dear fatherland, no fear be thine) takes place between West and East Berlin in the year 1964. Bruno, a small-time crook from East Berlin, ends up on the Cold War front when ordered by East German authorities to enter West Berlin.

Tous à Lens
Plakat zur Eröffnung des Louvre Lens
Tous à Lens
*Poster on the occasion of the opening of
the Louvre-Lens*
Detailausschnitt aus „La liberté guidant
le peuple" von Eugène Delacroix, 1830
Detail from *La liberté guidant le peuple*
by Eugène Delacroix, 1830

12. Dezember 2012
60 × 40 cm
Privatbesitz/Private collection,
Mainz

La Liberté guidant le peuple ist ein großformatiges Ölgemälde, das Eugène Delacroix (1798 – 1863) im Jahr der Julirevolution 1830 malt. Pressezensur und die Abschaffung der Abgeordnetenkammer führen zu blutigen Protesten der Pariser Bevölkerung gegen die Obrigkeit. Flankiert von zwei Kämpfern stürmt *Marianne* mit Bajonette und Fahne über die Gefallenen hinweg. Dahinter raucht Pulverdampf. Das hier gezeigte Plakat bewirbt die Eröffnung der Dependance des Louvre in der französischen Provinzstadt Lens im Dezember 2012. Weniger als zwei Monate nach der Überstellung des Gemäldes von Paris, am 7. Februar 2013, kommt es zu einem Anschlag auf das berühmte Gemälde. Eine 28-jährige Frau schreibt auf den rechten unteren Rand mit einem schwarzen Marker den Schriftzug AE911. AE911 steht für *Architects and Engineers for 9/11 Truth*. Diese Gruppe vertritt die Überzeugung, dass das World Trade Center in New York durch Sprengstoff und nicht durch Flugzeuge zerstört worden sei. Der Schriftzug auf Delacroix' Gemälde konnte entfernt werden, ohne es zu beschädigen. /
La Liberté guidant le peuple is a large-scale oil painting, which Eugène Delacroix (1798 – 1863) painted in the year of the July Revolution, 1830. Censorship of the press and the abolishment of the Chamber of Deputies led to bloody protests against the authorities by the Parisian population. Flanked by two combatants, *Marianne* bears a bayonet and flag over the fallen. Behind her is the smoke of gunpowder. The poster exhibited here is an advertisement for the opening of the Louvre branch in the French provincial town of Lens in December 2012. The famous painting was vandalised less than two months after it was moved there from Paris, on 7 February 2013, when a 28-year old woman wrote the inscription AE911 with a black marker on the lower left edge. AE911 stands for *Architects and Engineers for 9/11 Truth*. This group believes that the World Trade Center in New York was destroyed by explosives and not by airplanes. The writing on the Delacroix painting was able to be removed without damaging the painting.

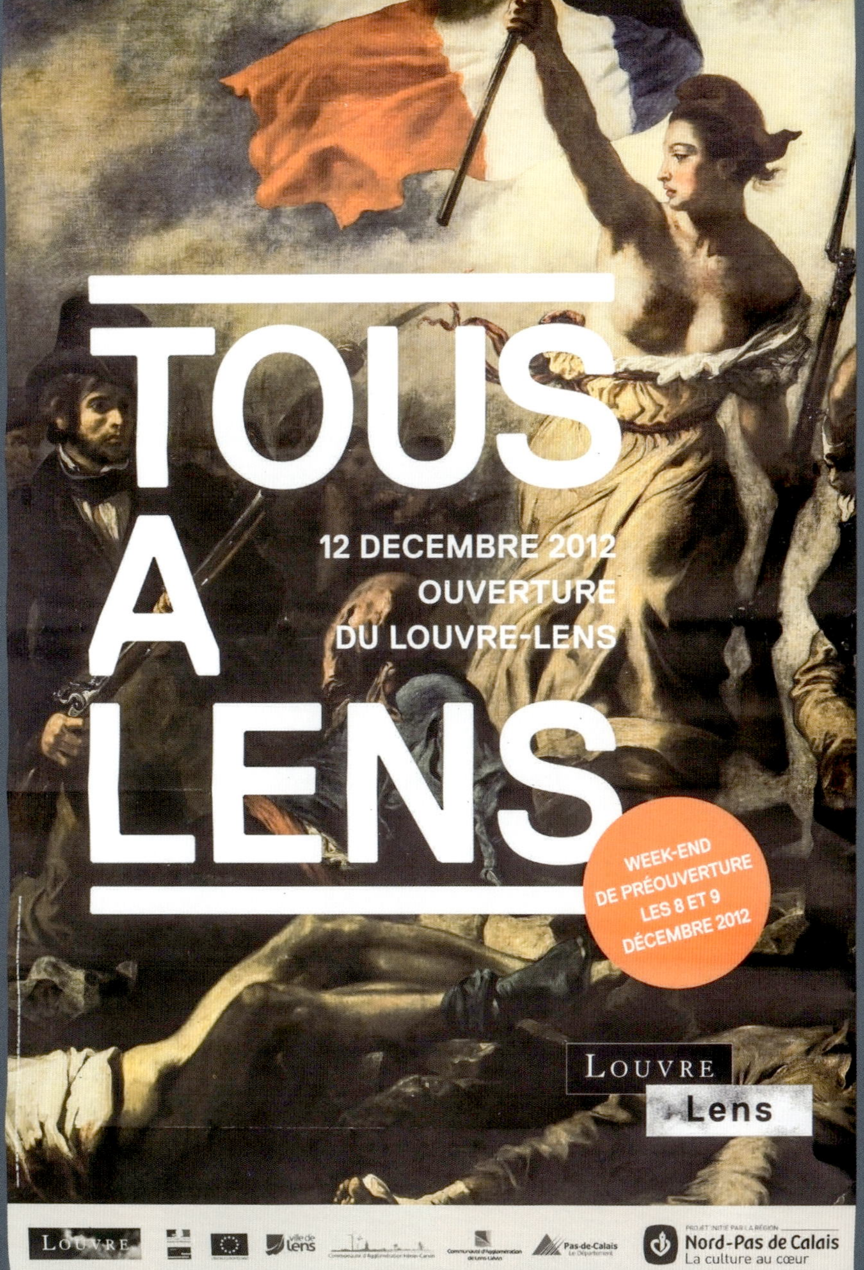

17

—

Heinrich Hanemann
50 Jahre Nationaldenkmal auf dem Niederwald, Erinnerungen an die Errichtung des Nationaldenkmals auf dem Niederwald
50th anniversary on Niederwald, commemoration of the construction of the national monument on Niederwald
1933
Verlag / Publisher:
Filcher und Metz
(Inh.: Fritz Mohr) Rüdesheim a. Rh.
Sammlung / Collection
Günter Höhmann, Wiesbaden

Diese Broschüre entsteht anlässlich des 50. Jubiläums der Aufstellung des Niederwalddenkmals im Jahr der sogenannten Machtergreifung der Nationalsozialisten. Sie beschreibt Wettbewerb, Aufbau und Ikonografie des Denkmals.

Gegen Ende des Zweiten Weltkrieges wird das einst bei der Einweihung des Denkmals gesungene Lied Die *Wacht am Rhein* zum Decknamen der *Ardennen-Offensive*. Es ist die letzte großangelegte militärische Initiative Nazideutschlands. Sie soll von den Alliierten an der Westfront erobertes Gebiet wieder zurückgewinnen. Das Unternehmen beginnt am 16. Dezember 1944. Betroffen sind Gebiete im Osten und Nordosten Belgiens sowie Teile Luxemburgs. /

This brochure was created on the occasion of the 50th anniversary of the erection of the Niederwald monument, in the year that the National Socialists seized power. It describes the competition, erection, and iconography of the monument.

Towards the end of the Second World War, the anthem, "Die Wacht am Rhein", which was performed during the inauguration of the monument, was used as a code name for the Battle of the Bulge, the final major military offensive by Nazi Germany. The plan was to regain the Western Front from the Allied forces. The offensive began on 16 December, 1944. It affected areas throughout eastern and north-eastern parts of Belgium, as well as parts of Luxembourg.

—

50 Jahre National-Denkmal auf dem Niederwald bei Rüdesheim am Rhein
50th anniversary of the national monument, Niederwald near Rüdesheim am Rhein
Postkarte / Postcard
unleserlich gestempelt /
illegible postmarked
8,7 × 14,1 cm
Sammlung / Collection
Günter Höhmann, Wiesbaden

Diese Karte zeigt die 50-Jahr-Feier des Niederwalddenkmals. Vor dem Denkmal sind Hakenkreuzfahnen zu sehen. In Nazdeutschland diente *Die Wacht am Rhein* als heimliche Hymne. Zu Beginn des Zweiten Weltkrieges werden die ersten acht Töne der Melodie als Erkennungsmusik für die täglichen Sondermeldungen der Wehrmacht verwendet. 1941 werden sie durch einen Ausschnitt aus Franz Liszts „Les Préludes" ersetzt. /
This card depicts the 50th anniversary celebration of the Niederwald monument. In front of the monument we see swastika flags. "Die Wacht am Rhein" was a secret hymn in Nazi Germany. At the beginning of the Second World War, the first eight notes of the melody were used as the theme music for the daily special news broadcasts by the Wehrmacht. In 1941, the tune was replaced by a section of Franz Liszt's "Les Préludes".

—

Grosse Saarkundgebung vor dem Führer am National-Denkmal, August 1933
Saar Manifestation before the Führer at the National Monument, August 1933
Postkarte / Postcard
ungestempelt / unstamped
10,3 × 14,9 cm
Sammlung / Collection
Günter Höhmann, Wiesbaden

Am 27. August 1933 findet beim Niederwalddenkmal eine *Saarkundgebung* in Anwesenheit von Adolf Hitler statt. Der Treppenaufsatz ist mit Hakenkreuzfahnen beflaggt. Direkt unter den Figuren von Rhein und Mosel stehen SA Männer Spalier. Wenig später kommt es zu einer ähnlichen Kundgebung der NSDAP am Leipziger Völkerschlachtdenkmal. Schließlich erfolgt die große Saarkundgebung in Zweibrücken am 6. Mai 1934, in der Goebbels ausruft: „Deutsch die Saar immerdar, zurück zum Reich!" Die Propaganda wirkt. Am 13. Januar 1935 stimmen 90,73 % der Wähler und Wählerinnen für die Rückkehr des Saarlandes zum Deutschen Reich. /
The Saar manifestation took place in the presence of Adolf Hitler at the Niederwald monument on 27 August 1933. The stairs are adorned with swastika flags. SA men stand guard directly beneath the figures of the Rhine and Moselle. Shortly thereafter, a similar rally took place at the Monument to the Battle of the Nations in Leipzig, held by the NSDAP. This was followed by the Saar manifestation in Zweibrücken on 6 May 1934, at which Goebbels proclaimed: "Deutsch die Saar im-

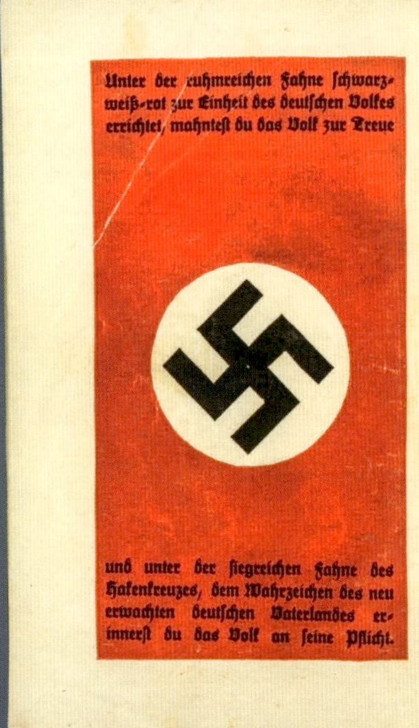

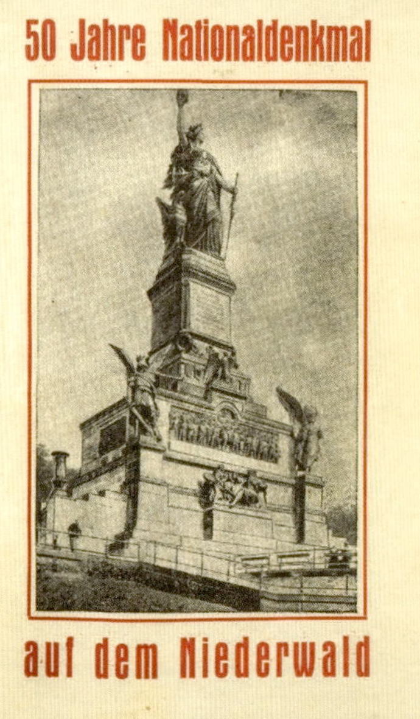

18

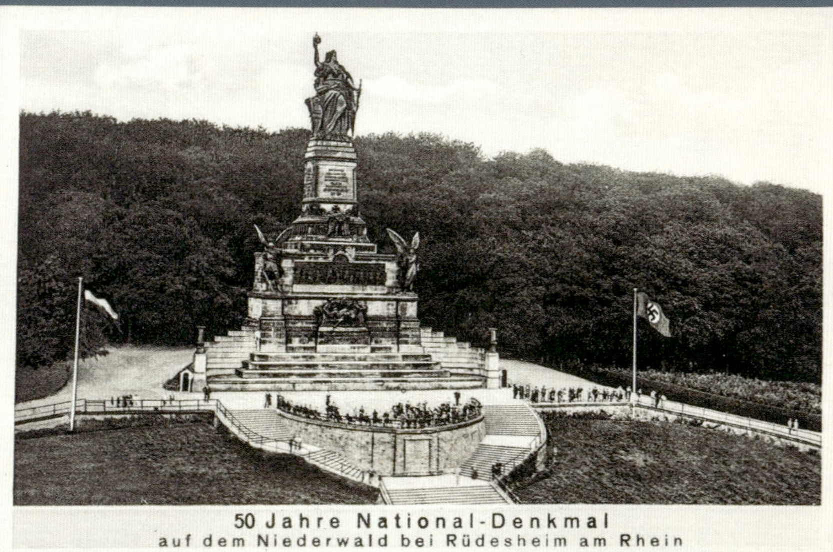

50 Jahre National-Denkmal
auf dem Niederwald bei Rüdesheim am Rhein

19

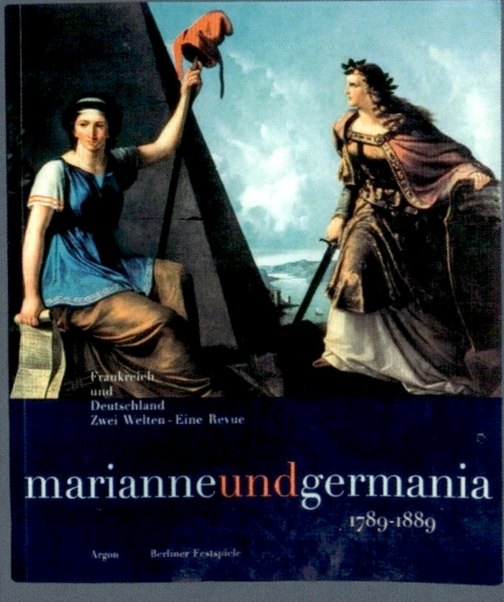

21

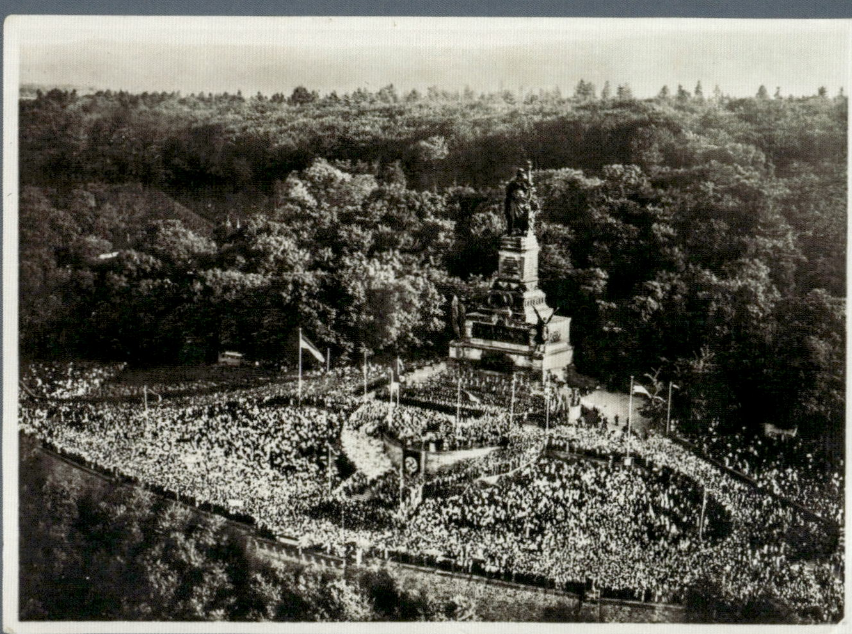

20

merdar, zurück zum Reich!" (Saar is German evermore, return to the Reich!) The propaganda was working. On 13 January 1935, 90.73 % of the voting population voted for the return of Saarland to the German Reich.

21

———

Marianne und Germania 1789 – 1889.
Frankreich und Deutschland.
Zwei Welten – eine Revue,
zur 46. Berliner Festwoche 1996
Hrsg. Marie-Louise von Plessen
Berliner Festspiele GmbH (Hg./Ed.)

Marianne and Germania 1789 – 1889
France and Germany.
Two Worlds – One Look Back
for the 46th Berliner Festwoche 1996
Umschlag/Cover
Nicolaus Ott und Bernard Stein, Berlin
28 × 24 cm
Verlag Argon Verlag GmbH, Berlin

Personifiziert *Germania* das vereinte Deutschland, so steht *Marianne* mit der roten phrygischen Mütze für das republikanische Frankreich. Am bekanntesten ist die Darstellung der *Marianne* auf dem Gemälde *La liberté guidant le peuple* von Eugène Delacroix. Im

Deutsch-Französischen Krieg wurden *Germania* und *Marianne* zu Gegenspielerinnen und Repräsentantinnen ihrer Länder. Das Cover eines Katalogbuches aus Berlin von 1996 vereinigt die beiden Allegorien. Links ein Ausschnitt eines Gemäldes von Nanine Vallain von 1793/1794, das *Marianne* vor einer Pyramide zeigt. Rechts die *Germania auf der Wacht am Rhein*, ein Gemälde von Lorenz Clasen aus dem Jahr 1860. *Marianne* trägt eine antike Tunika und sitzt auf einem Steinblock. In ihrer Linken hält sie eine Lanze mit der Freiheitsmütze. Eine Urne erinnert an die Toten. Im Gegensatz zu ihrer Grazie gibt sich die Germania als unbarmherzige Rächerin. Mit Schwert und Schild mit Doppeladler steht sie auf einem Felsen über dem Rheinufer. Clasen nimmt Schillings Idee vorweg, zeigt sie jedoch entschlossener und aggressiver in ihrer Haltung. /
Whereas *Germania* personifies Germany, *Marianne* with her red Phrygian cap stands for republican France. The most famous depiction of Marianne can be seen on the painting *La liberté guidant le peuple* by Eugène Delacroix. During the Franco-Prussian War, *Germania* and *Marianne* became adversaries and representatives of their nations. The cover of a catalogue from Berlin (1996) combines these two allegories. To the left, a section of a painting by Nanine Vallain, made in 1793 – 94, depicts *Marianne* seated in front of a pyramid. To the right, we see *Germania* depicted in *Die Wacht am Rhein*, an 1860 painting by Lorenz Clasen. *Marianne* is wearing a tunic and sits on a boulder. In her left hand she holds a lance with the Phrygian cap. An urn reminds us of those who have died. In contrast to her poise, *Germania* is

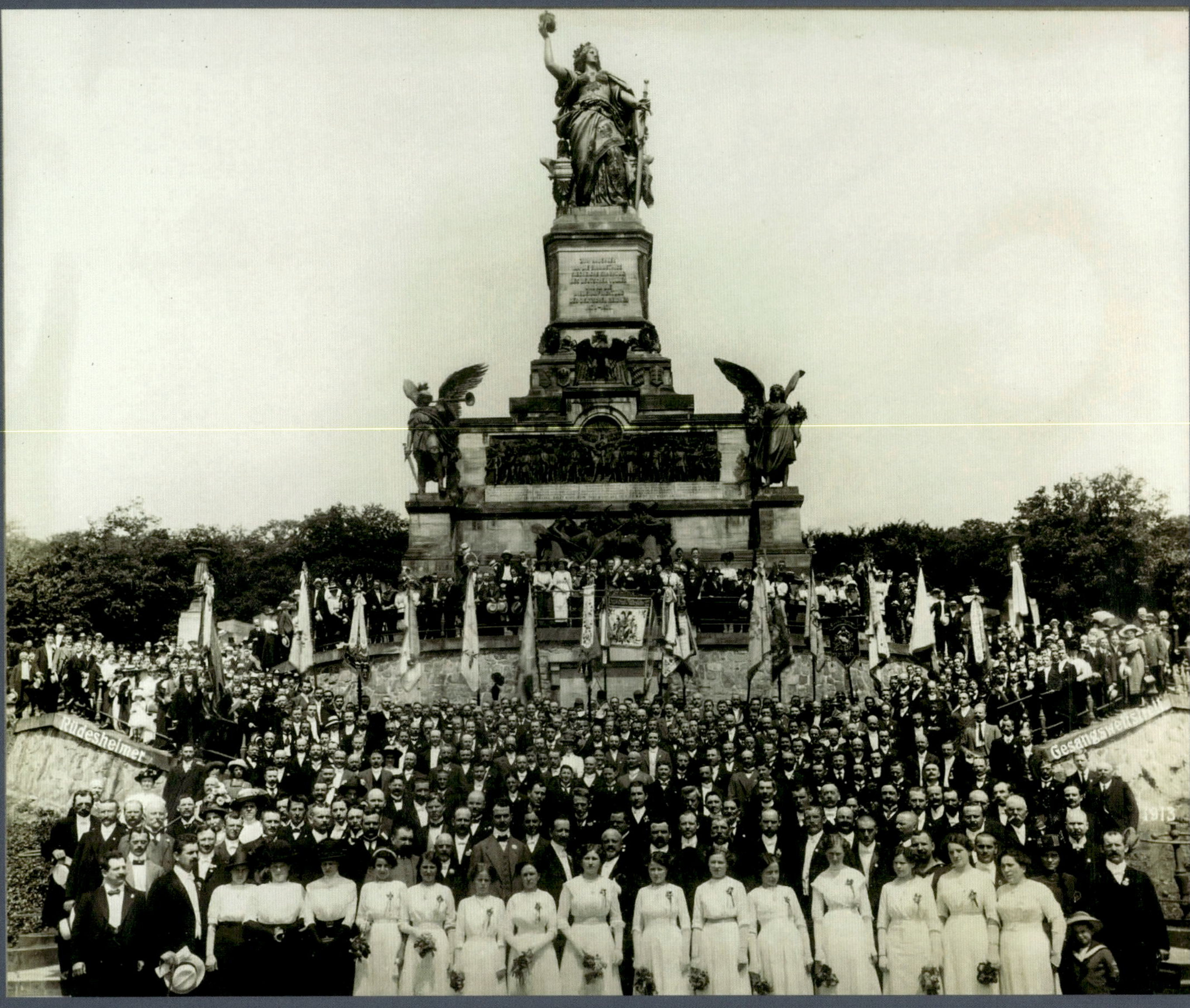

22

depicted as a merciless avenger. With a sword and shield bearing the double-headed eagle, she stands on a cliff above the Rhine embankment. Clasen takes Schilling's idea, depicting it in a more resolute and aggressive manner.

22
—

Gesangswettstreit 1913
Song Contest 1913
SW-Fotografie unten
Beschriftung rechts unten/
Black and white photograph below
Inscription lower right
„Osw. Heiderich Rüdesheim"
22 × 26,7 cm
Stadt Rüdesheim am Rhein

Das Lied machte ursprünglich bei Sängerwettbewerben Karriere. Die Bedeutung der Musik in Verbindung mit dem Niederwalddenkmal besteht auch 1913 noch. Regelmäßig finden am Fuße der *Germania* Gesangstreffen- und Wettbewerbe oder Fahnenweihen mit musikalischer Untermalung statt. /
The song originally was used in singing competitions. The significance of music in connection with the Niederwald monument is still important in 1913. Song festivals, contests, and flag consecration ceremonies with music were held regularly at the base of *Germania*.

23
—

Relief nach/Relief by
Johannes Schilling
Der Abschied (Fehlerhaft benannt, eigentlich „Die Heimkehr")
The Farewell (faulty title, actually "The Homecoming")
29,8 × 43,4 × 3,2 cm
Johannes-Schilling-Haus, Mittweida

Hier ist ein getriebenes Metallrelief als kleinformatiges Souvenir zu sehen. An der Ostseite des Denkmals befindet sich die *Heimkehr der Sieger*. Die linke Hälfte der Darstellung wird von Soldaten verschiedener Waffengattungen und deren Uniformen und Gesten bestimmt. Die rechte Seite ist von Frauen in leichten,

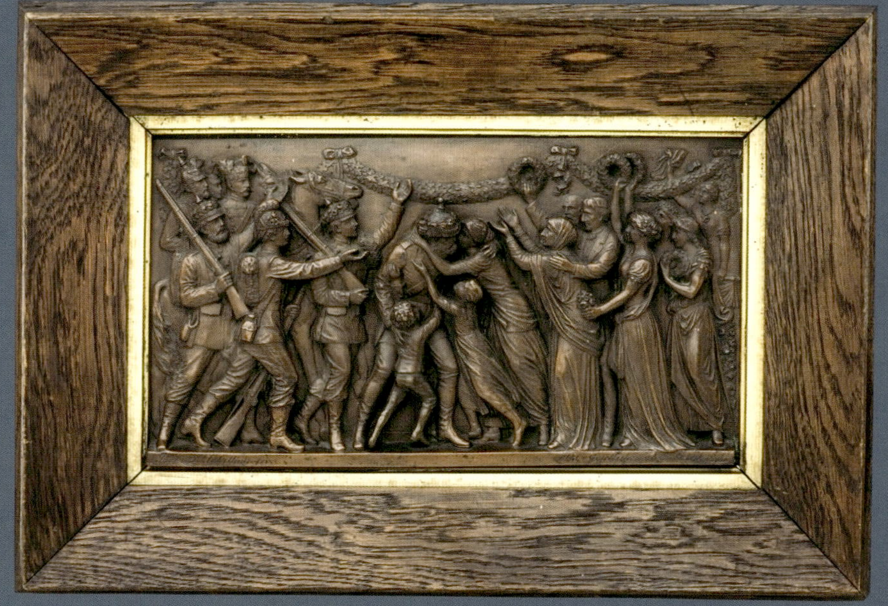

23

tered. The completed monument also lists the names of the battlefields on the sides. One detail of the text merits special attention: "What was hoped for in song and text, fought for by friends of the fatherland — was accomplished by the hour of shared peril …" From the beginning, *Germania* is addressed as a realisation of a linguistic figure, as a symbol of a musical verse. As a sculpture, she is a materialised song.

25

———

SW-Fotografie, gerahmt
Beschriftung rückseitig/
Inscription verso
Denkmalsfeier 1883/
Monument celebration 1883
Black and white photograph, framed
17,3 × 37,5 cm
Stadt Rüdesheim am Rhein

Im Hotel Jung in Rüdesheim findet ein Festbankett statt. Der Bürgermeister ruft einen Toast auf den Kaiser aus, danach wird abermals die *Wacht am Rhein* intoniert. Der Dichter Friedrich Emil Rittershaus trägt ein Gedicht als Apologie auf die anwesenden Künstler vor: "Stoßt an und trinkt die Gläser leer, zu Schilling's und zu Weißbach's Ehr!" /
A festive banquet takes place at Hotel Jung in Rüdesheim. The mayor calls a toast to the Emperor, after which "Die Wacht am Rhein" is sung. The poet Friedrich Emil Rittershaus recites a poem as an apologia to the artists present: "Toast and drink to Schilling's and to Weißbach's honour!"

langen Gewändern und älteren Personen geprägt. In der Mitte des Bildes beugt sich der verwundete Landwehrmann. Er wird von Frau und Kindern begrüßt. Seine Pickelhaube tritt am stärksten in den Reliefraum hervor. Darüber befindet sich als verbindendes Element der Lindenkranz, ein Zeichen der Freude. /
Here, the model is to be regarded as a smallscale souvenir. On the eastern side, the homecoming of the victors is depicted. The left-hand half of the relief shows soldiers of various branches of the service, with their uniforms and salutes. The right side depicts women in light, long robes as well as older persons. In the centre of the image, a wounded Landwehr soldier bows. He is greeted by his wife and children. His spiked helmet is most pronounced in the relief. On top we see the linden wreath, a symbol of joy, as a connecting element.

24

———

*Urkunde zum Grundstein des National
Denkmals auf dem Niederwald*
Foundation stone certificate of the
Niederwald national monument
Beschriftung rückseitig links/
Inscription verso, left
"Text von Otto Satorius, Landesdirektor in Wiesbaden."
Beschriftung rückseitig rechts/
Inscription verso, right

"Entw. U. kalligr. Von G. A. Hohle, R. Sekr. in Wiesbaden."
Beschriftung rückseitig mittig/
Inscription verso, centre
"Carl Jügel's Verlag in Frankfurt/M. (Moritz Abendroth)
Lithographie & Druck von August Usterrieth in Frankfurt/M."
81,6 × 53,8 cm
Stadt Rüdesheim am Rhein

Die Urkunde zur Grundsteinlegung vereint mannigfaltige grafische Elemente und farbliche Töne. In der Mitte ist der Name des Kaisers Wilhelm, reichhaltig dekoriert, zu erkennen. Am untersten Rand sind zwischen Ranken und floralen Verzierungen die Schlachten eingetragen. Auch das vollendete Monument listet auf den Seitenwangen die Schlachtfelder auf. Ein Detail des Textes verdient Aufmerksamkeit: "Was in Lied und Wort erhofft, wonach von den Vaterlandsfreunden jahrelang gerungen – vollendet hat es die Stunde der gemeinsamen Gefahr …" Die *Germania* wird von Beginn an als Verwirklichung eines sprachlichen Bildes angesprochen, nicht zuletzt als Sinnbild einer musikalischen Strophe betrachtet. Als Skulptur ist sie materialisiertes Lied. /
This document combines the ground-breaking ceremony with diverse graphic elements and colours. One can see the name of Emperor Wilhelm, extensively decorated, in the centre. At the very bottom, between the vines and floral decoration, the names of battles are en-

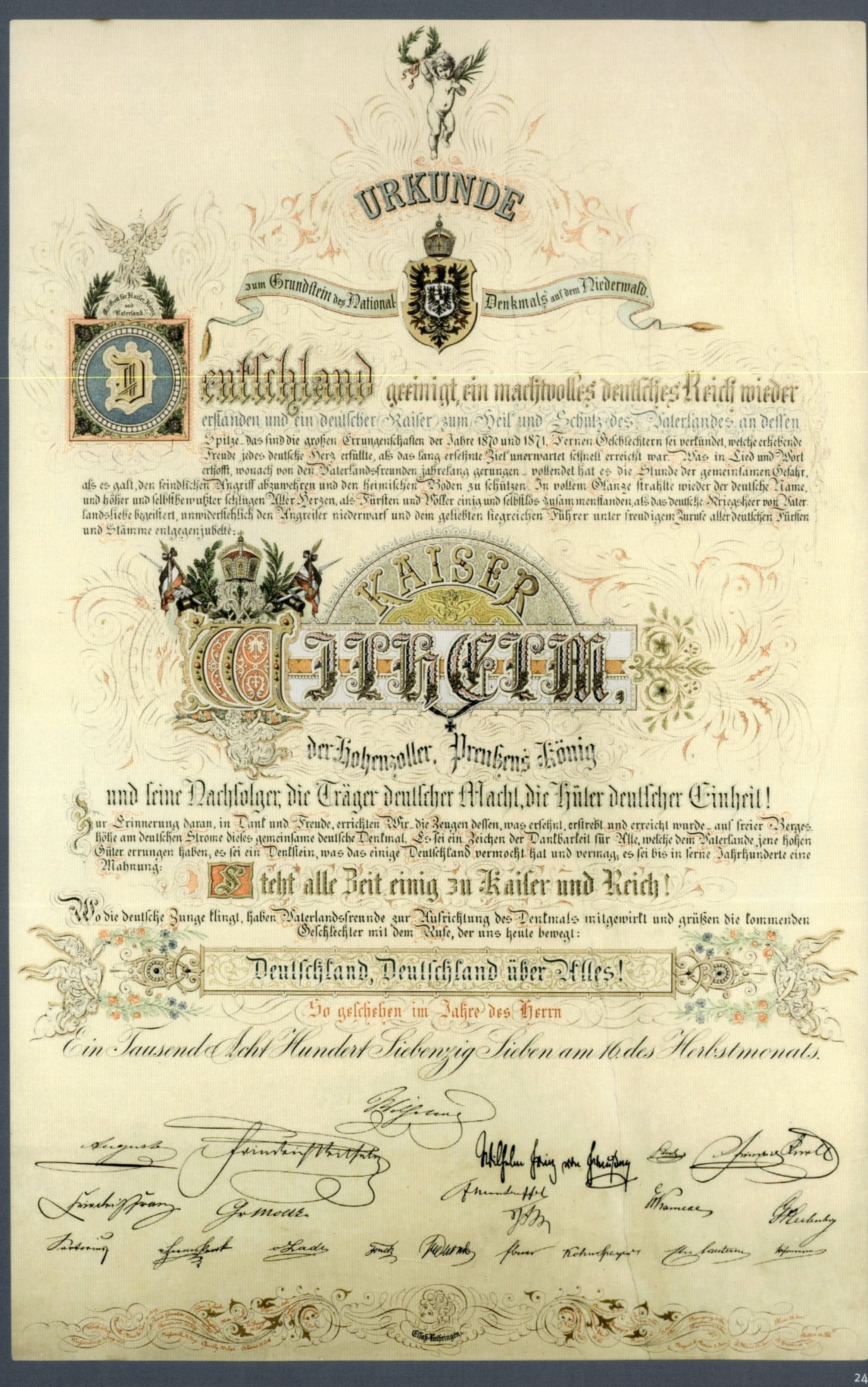

URKUNDE

zum Grundstein des National Denkmals auf dem Niederwald.

Deutschland gereinigt, ein machtvolles deutsches Reich wieder erstanden und ein deutscher Kaiser zum Heil und Schutz des Vaterlandes an dessen Spitze, das sind die großen Errungenschaften der Jahre 1870 und 1871. Fernen Geschlechtern sei verkündet, welche erhebende Freude jedes deutsche Herz erfüllte, als das lang ersehnte Ziel unerwartet schnell erreicht war. Was in Lied und Wort erhofft, wonach von den Vaterlandsfreunden jahrelang gerungen – vollendet hat es die Stunde der gemeinsamen Gefahr, als es galt, den feindlichen Angriff abzuwehren und den heimischen Boden zu schützen. In vollem Glanze strahlte wieder der deutsche Name, und höher und selbstbewußter schlugen Aller Herzen, als Fürsten und Völker einig und selbstlos zusammenstanden, als das deutsche Kriegsheer von Vaterlandsliebe begeistert, unwiderstehlich den Angreifer niederwarf und dem geliebten siegreichen Führer unter freudigem Zurufe aller deutschen Fürsten und Stämme entgegenjubelte:

KAISER WILHELM,

der Hohenzoller, Preußens König

und seine Nachfolger, die Träger deutscher Macht, die Hüter deutscher Einheit!

Zur Erinnerung daran, in Dank und Freude, errichten Wir die Zeugen dessen, was ersehnt, erstrebt und erreicht wurde – auf freier Berges Höhe am deutschen Strome dieses gemeinsame deutsche Denkmal. Es sei ein Zeichen der Dankbarkeit für Alle, welche dem Vaterlande jene hohen Güter errungen haben, es sei ein Denkstein, was das einige Deutschland vermocht hat und vermag, es sei bis in ferne Jahrhunderte eine Mahnung:

Steht alle Zeit einig zu Kaiser und Reich!

Wo die deutsche Zunge klingt, haben Vaterlandsfreunde zur Aufrichtung des Denkmals mitgewirkt und grüßen die kommenden Geschlechter mit dem Rufe, der uns heute bewegt:

Deutschland, Deutschland über Alles!

So geschehen im Jahre des Herrn

Ein Tausend Acht Hundert Siebenzig Sieben am 16. des Herbstmonats.

Elsaß-Lothringen.

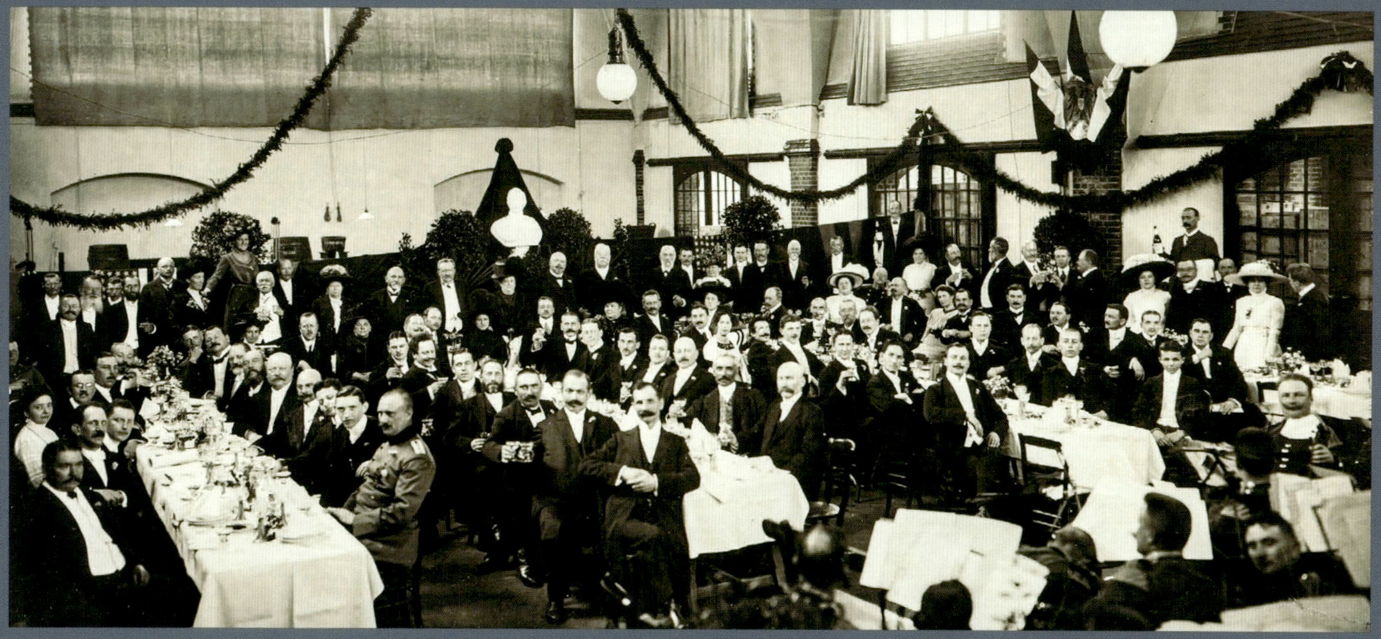

25

26

Unterschriften der Spender
Signatures of the donors
gebundenes Buch/hardcover book
Titel auf Einband: „National-Denkmal"
Beschriftung erste Seite: „Willkommen
am Deutschen Friedens-Denkmal!"
Title on cover: "National-Denkmal"
(National Monument)
Inscription on the first page:
"Willkommen am Deutschen
Friedens-Denkmal!" (Welcome to
the German monument of peace!)
bevor/before 1883

34,2 × 41 cm
Stadt Rüdesheim am Rhein

Das Niederwalddenkmal wurde zum Groß-
teil aus Spendengeldern aus der Bevölkerung
finanziert. Bis 1880 kommen in etwa 800 000
Mark zusammen, der Reichstag zahlte das
letzte Drittel der rund 1,2 Millionen Mark
teuren *Germania*. /
The Niederwald monument was predominantly funded by donations from the public.
By 1880, a total of some 800,000 marks had
been collected and the Reichstag paid the
remaining third of the 1.2 million marks that
Germania cost.

27

Kopf der Germania
The Head of Germania
1883
SW-Fotografie, gerahmt/
Black and white photograph, framed
Prägung mittig unterhalb des Motivs/
Stamp at the centre bottom of the motif
„Fotographische Anstalt J. B. Hilsdorf
B …(?)"
22,4 × 26 cm
Stadt Rüdesheim am Rhein

Der Kopf der *Germania* wird von der Geisenheimer Straße aus auf den Niederwald gebracht. Das Foto ist nicht ohne zeitgebundenen
Charme. Einige Damen und Herren der
Gesellschaft lassen sich mit dem von einem
Laubkranz geschmückten Porträt ablichten,
bevor es mit einem Seilzug nach oben gehoben
wird. Die Gesichtszüge sind von klassischen
Vorbildern inspiriert. Ähnlich bezieht sich
der französische Bildhauer Frédéric Auguste
Bartholdi mit der Freiheitsstatue auf die An-
tike. Bartholdi zitiert das Porträt der *Venus
Ludovisi*, die eine römische Kaisergattin wie-
dergibt. Es wird unter anderem in Schillers
Werk *Briefe zur ästhetischen Erziehung des
Menschen* erwähnt und in jüngster Zeit von
Philosophen wie Jacques Rancière zu neuen
Überlegungen über Kunst, Macht und Wider-
stand herangezogen. /
The head of *Germania* was transported to
Niederwald via the Geisenheimer Straße. The
photo has a certain period-inspired charm.

26

41

Some ladies and gentlemen in the group have their picture taken with the wreath-decorated portrait before it is lifted to its final destination. The facial expressions are inspired by classical likenesses. In a similar manner, the French sculptor Frédéric Auguste Bartholdi makes a reference to antiquity with the Statue of Liberty, quoting the portrait of the Ludovisi Venus, which depicts a Roman emperor's wife. Schiller's work *Briefe zur ästhetischen Erziehung des Menschen* (On the Aesthetic Education of Man), and most recent philosophers such as Jacques Rancière, reflected on new ideas concerning art, power, and resistance.

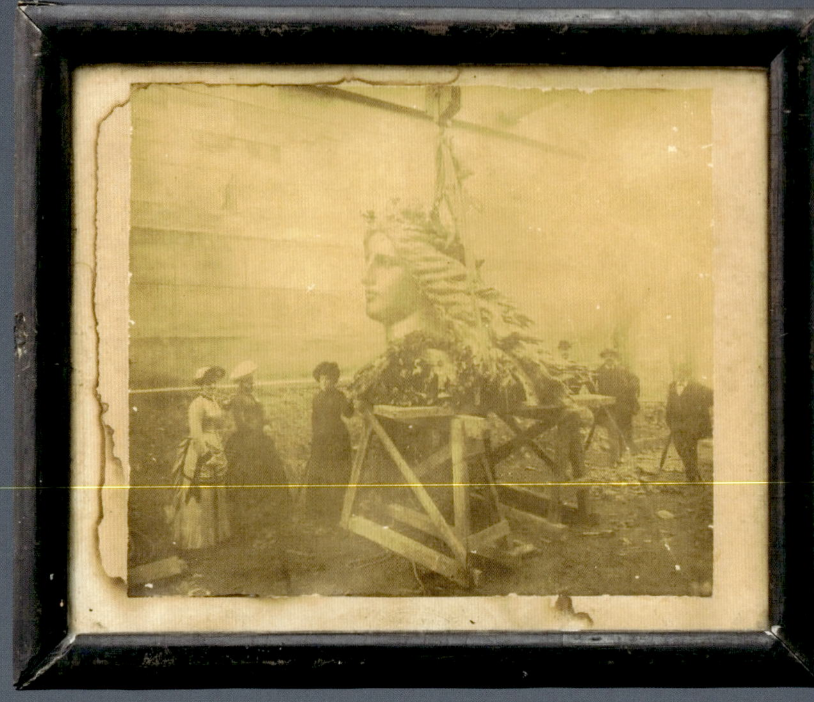

27

28
———
Udo Jürgens
Lieb Vaterland/*Lieb Vaterland
(Dear Fatherland)*
1970
Vinyl Platte/Vinyl gramophone record
18 × 18 cm
Text: Eckart Hachfeld
Edition Montana, 1970
Privatbesitz/Private collection,
Mainz

1970 verfasst der österreichische Schlager-sänger Udo Jürgens (1934 – 2014) ein Lied mit dem Titel *Lieb Vaterland*. Melodisch unab-hängig nimmt es mit Titel und Marschtrom-mel Bezug zur *Wacht am Rhein*. Das Lied versteht sich jedoch als Anklage gegen den Staat im Namen der aufbegehrenden Jugend und des Widerstands der 68er-Generation gegen das Establishment. So lautet etwa die vierte Strophe: „Lieb Vaterland, wofür soll ich dir danken? Für die Versicherungspaläste oder Banken? Und für Kasernen, für die teure Wehr? Wo tausend Schulen fehlen, tausend Lehrer und noch mehr."/

In 1970, the Austrian folk musician Udo Jür-gens (1934 – 2014) composed a song entitled "Lieb Vaterland". Using a different melody, it makes a reference to "Die Wacht am Rhein", with its title and marching drums. The ratio-nale behind the song, however, is a denounce-ment of the state by the youth involved in the protests of 1968 and their resistance against the establishment. This is the fourth verse: "Dear fatherland, what should I thank you for? For the palaces housing the insurance com-panies or for the banks? And for the barracks and expensive defence? While thousands of schools are missing, thousands of teachers, and much more."

29
———
Johannes Schilling
*Modell Niederwalddenkmal, Auschnitt
Model of the Niederwald monument,
detail*
1875
Zinkguss/Cast zinc
Gießerei Hermann Gladenbeck, Berlin
88 × 82 × 46 cm
Otto-von-Bismarck-Stiftung,
Friedrichsruh

Das Niederwalddenkmal zieht viele ästheti-sche Register, um als Mahnmal erinnerung-strächtig und widerspruchsfrei zu wirken. An diesem Modell fehlen einige Details. Den-

noch gibt es Auskunft über die letzte Fassung der *Germania* und ihre überreiche ikonogra-fische Ausstattung. Eine vollständige Abbil-dung ist auf Seite 6 dieses Bandes zu sehen An der Front ist das monumentale Relief des Kaisers zu sehen, der von seinen Generälen und Soldaten umgeben ist. Ein Halbkreis hebt seine Gestalt wie unter einer Apsis her-vor. Die übrigen Dargestellten – allesamt benennbare Militärs – zeigen die typische Gleichschaltung, Reihung und Hierarchie. Darunter – wohl aus Gründen der Lesbarkeit – sind die Tafeln, die am Originalstandort die Strophen der *Wacht am Rhein* enthalten, in der Modellversion durch den Refrain ersetzt./
The Niederwald monument has many forms of aesthetic expression and is a consistent and evocative memorial. Although some details are missing in this model, it still provides in-formation about the last version of *Germania* and her abundant iconographical make-up. A complete illustration can be seen on page 6 of this booklet. At the front, we see the monu-mental relief of the Emperor surrounded by his officers and soldiers. A semi-circle accen-tuates the figure as if from an apse. All the other individuals – each one an identifiable military figure – depict the typical conformity and hierarchy. Beneath this on the model, the panels that at the original location contain the verses of "Die Wacht am Rhein" only depict the refrain, most likely for reasons of legibility.

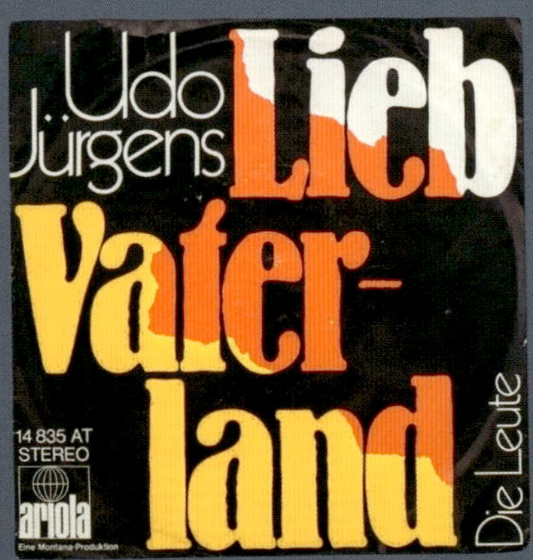

28

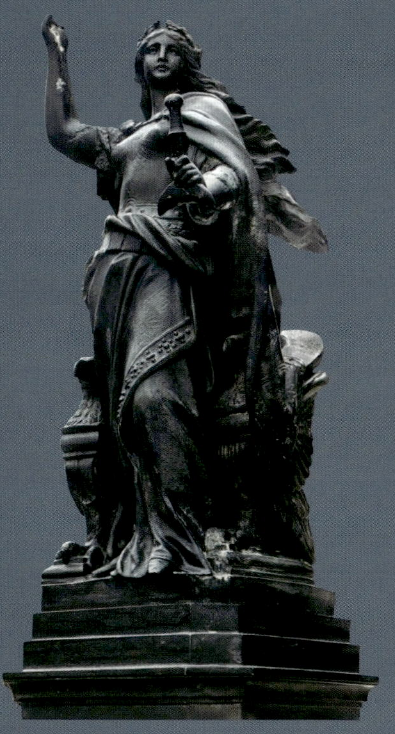

The French government, under Adolph Thiers, called for the Rhine as an eastern border. After a choirmaster from the city of Krefeld write the music to this text in 1854, the song quickly gained popularity, becoming one of the most popular marching songs during the Wilhelmine Imperial era. The troublesome relationship with "arch enemy" France is manifested in "Die Wacht am Rhein". The belligerent text is blood-thirsty and full of pathos. Yet the nationalistic message it conveys still has more of a defensive nature. The Rhine river must be protected against the attempts of the French to conquer it.

31

Sigmar Polke
Leuchtkasten Germania/
Germania Lightbox
aus der Installation „Vor-Ort-Sein"
im Westeingang des Reichstagsgebäudes/
from the "Vor-Ort-Sein" installation in the western entrance hall of the Reichstag building
1998/1999

Sigmar Polke (1941 – 2010) geht mit ironischen *Rasterbildern* und der Idee eines *Kapitalistischen Realismus* während der 1960er Jahre gegen die konservative Gesellschaft der Wirtschaftswunderzeit vor. Seine Kunst besteht in der Verwertung anderer Bilder. Es geht um

Original und Fälschung, um die Überbewertung von Authentizität und Autorschaft, nicht zuletzt um die Verkrustung der Lebenswelt durch selbstverschuldete Normen. Auf die Einladung, ein Werk für das Reichstagsgebäude zu entwerfen, reagiert Polke mit einem Zitat der *Germania*. Während sein Künstlerfreund Gerhard Richter die Farben Schwarz Rot Gelb in monumentaler Fassung zitiert, beschränkt sich Polke auf die Reinzeichnung der Skulptur. Sie taucht unter blauem Dunst auf, verwaschen, verwässert. Aus der Tiefe eines Leuchtkasten blickt sie wie leblos treibende Ophelia. /
Sigmar Polke (1941–2010) voices opposition to conservative society during the German economic miracle by means of ironic *halftone images* and the idea of 1960s *capitalist realism*. His art is comprised of appropriating other images. It is about original creations and forgeries, about placing too high a value on authenticity and authorship, not least about the rigidification of the world we live in by self-imposed norms. On being invited to create a work of art for the Reichstag, Polke responded by referencing the iconic figure of *Germania*. While his artist friend Gerhard Richter quoted the black, red and gold colors of the German flag in monumental form, Polke restricted himself to a fair drawing of the sculpture. Germania looms up in blue mist, washed out, watery, peering out from deep inside the lightbox like the lifeless form of Ophelia floating in water.

30

Die Wacht am Rhein
Reproduktion des Liedtextes
"Die Wacht am Rhein"
(The Watch on the Rhine).
Reproduction of the lyrics
G. Blümlein & Co., Frankfurt/M.
ca. 1900
21 × 29,7 cm
Privatbesitz/Private collection, Mainz

Die *Wacht am Rhein* entsteht 1840. Der Berner, Max Schneckenburger, verfasst den Text unter dem Eindruck wachsender Gefahr eines neuen Krieges. Die französische Regierung unter Adolph Thiers, fordert den Rhein als Ostgrenze. Nachdem der Text 1854 von einem Krefelder Chorleiter mit neuer Musik versehen wird, erlangt das Lied bei Sängerfesten zügig Beliebtheit. In der wilhelminischen Kaiserzeit wird es zum populärsten Marschlied. In der *Wacht am Rhein* manifestiert sich das problematische Verhältnis zum „Erbfeind" Frankreich. Der kämpferische Text ist blutdürstig und pathetisch. Dennoch ist die nationalistische Botschaft eher von defensivem Charakter: Der Rhein soll gegen die Eroberungsversuche der Franzosen verteidigt werden. /
Die Wacht am Rhein was written in 1840. Max Schneckenburger, from Bern, wrote the lyrics in reaction to an imminent new war.

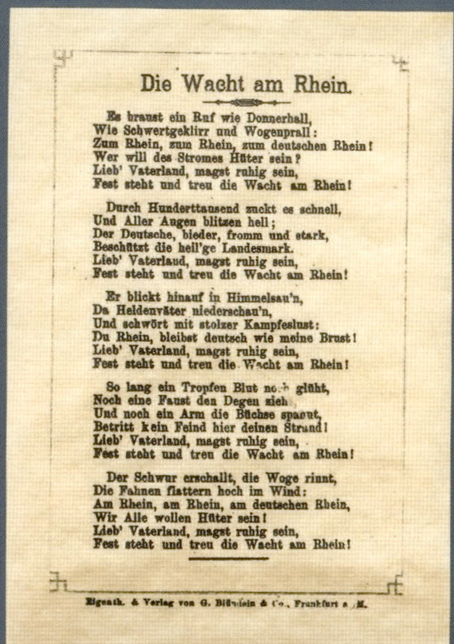

Die Wacht am Rhein.

Es braust ein Ruf wie Donnerhall,
Wie Schwertgeklirr und Wogenprall:
Zum Rhein, zum Rhein, zum deutschen Rhein!
Wer will des Stromes Hüter sein?
Lieb' Vaterland, magst ruhig sein,
Fest steht und treu die Wacht am Rhein!

Durch Hunderttausend zuckt es schnell,
Und Aller Augen blitzen hell;
Der Deutsche, bieder, fromm und stark,
Beschützt die heil'ge Landesmark.
Lieb' Vaterland, magst ruhig sein,
Fest steht und treu die Wacht am Rhein!

Er blickt hinauf in Himmelsau'n,
Da Heldenväter niederschau'n,
Und schwört mit stolzer Kampfeslust:
Du Rhein, bleibst deutsch wie meine Brust!
Lieb' Vaterland, magst ruhig sein,
Fest steht und treu die Wacht am Rhein!

So lang ein Tropfen Blut noch glüht,
Noch eine Faust den Degen zieh,
Und noch ein Arm die Büchse spannt,
Betritt kein Feind hier deinen Strand!
Lieb' Vaterland, magst ruhig sein,
Fest steht und treu die Wacht am Rhein!

Der Schwur erschallt, die Woge rinnt,
Die Fahnen flattern hoch im Wind:
Am Rhein, am Rhein, am deutschen Rhein,
Wir Alle wollen Hüter sein!
Lieb' Vaterland, magst ruhig sein,
Fest steht und treu die Wacht am Rhein!

Eigenth. & Verlag von G. Blümlein & Co., Frankfurt a. M.

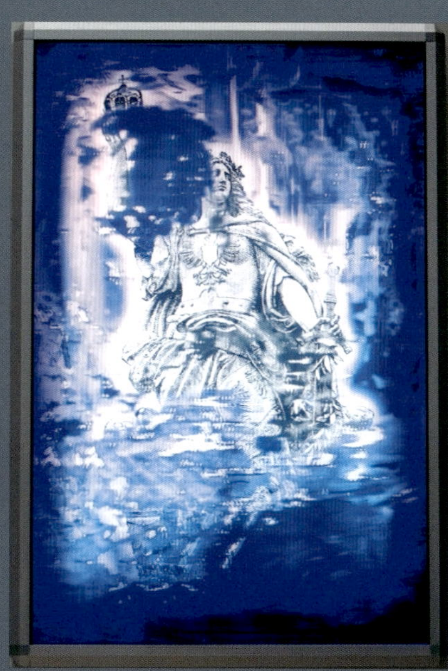

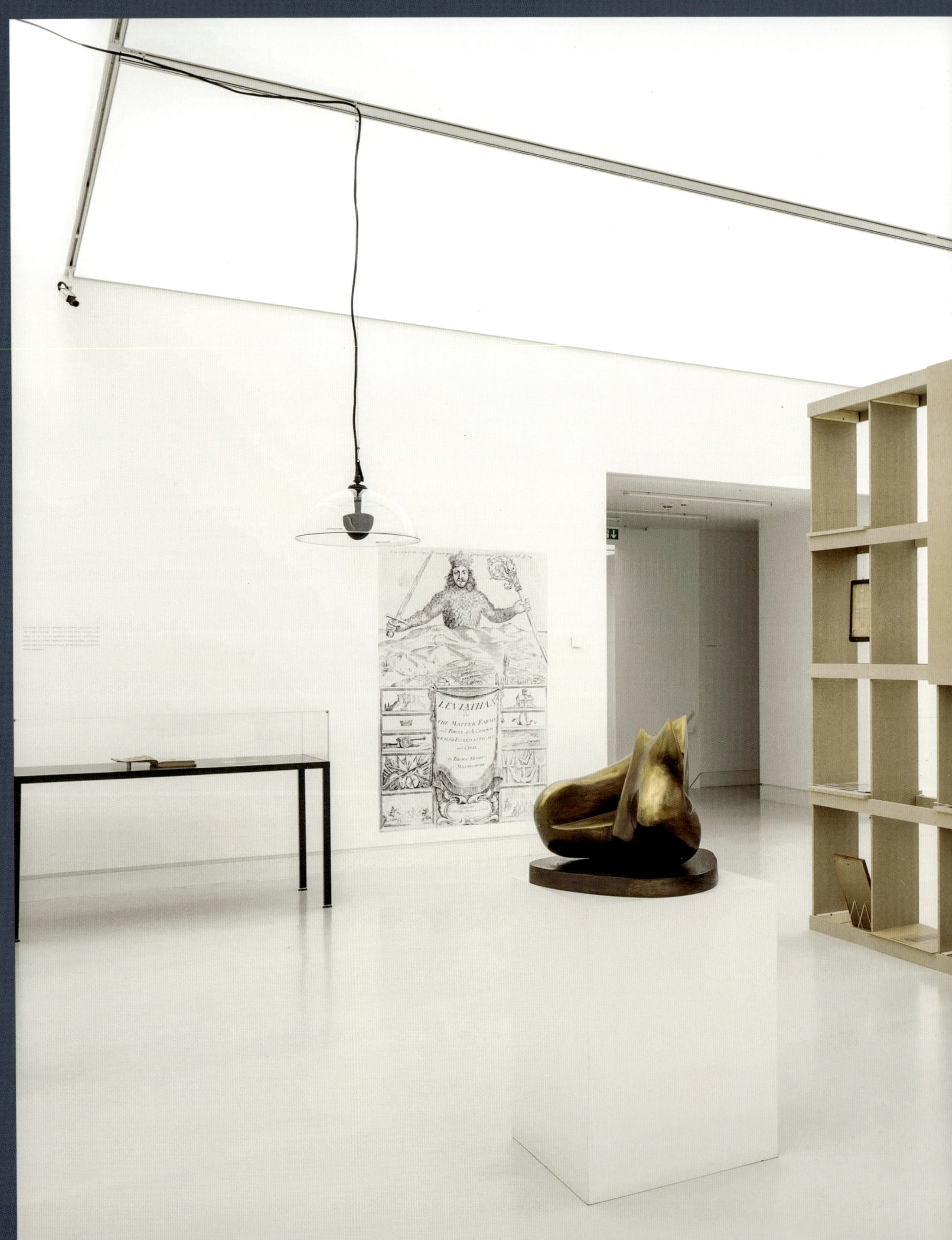

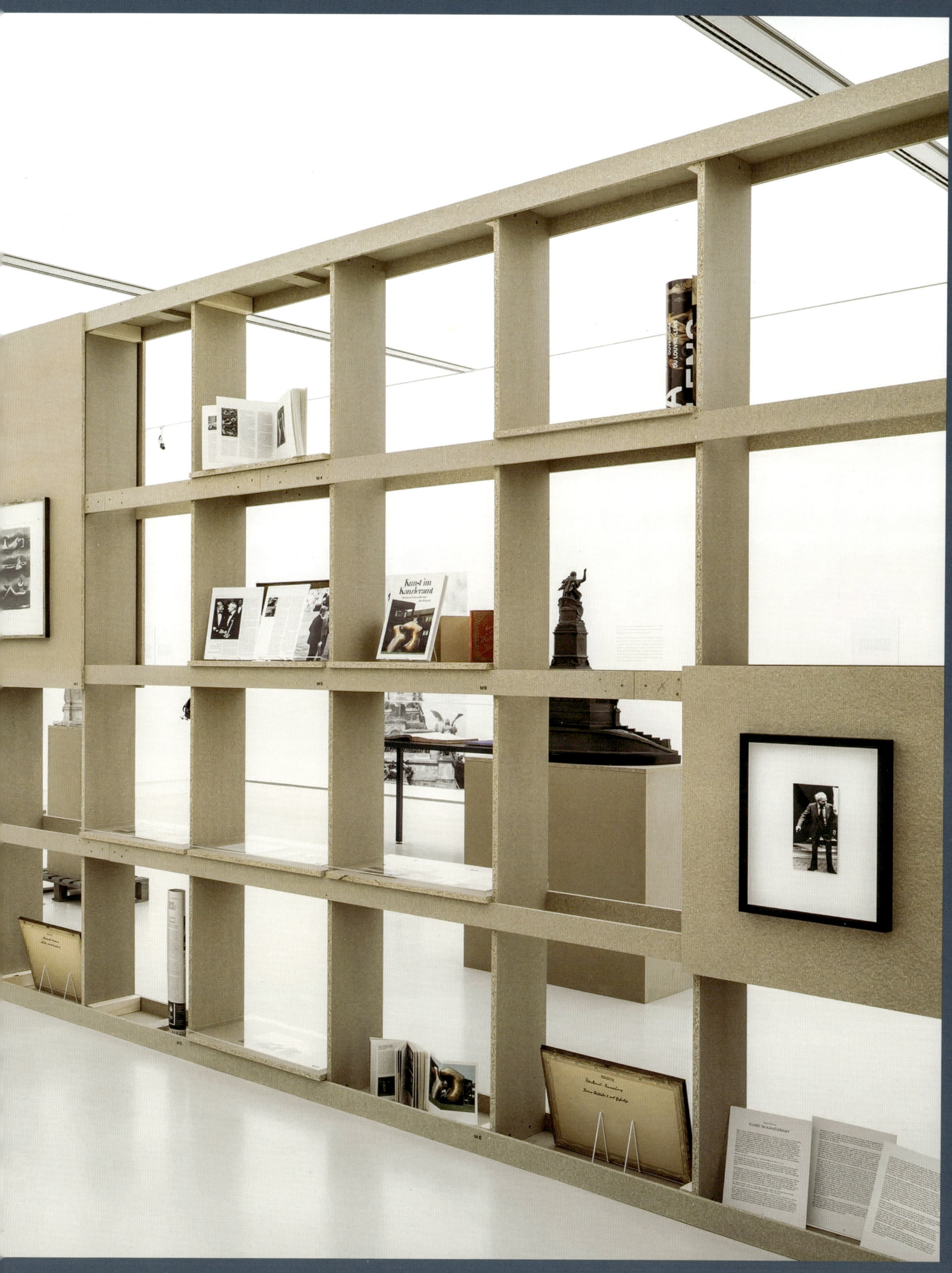

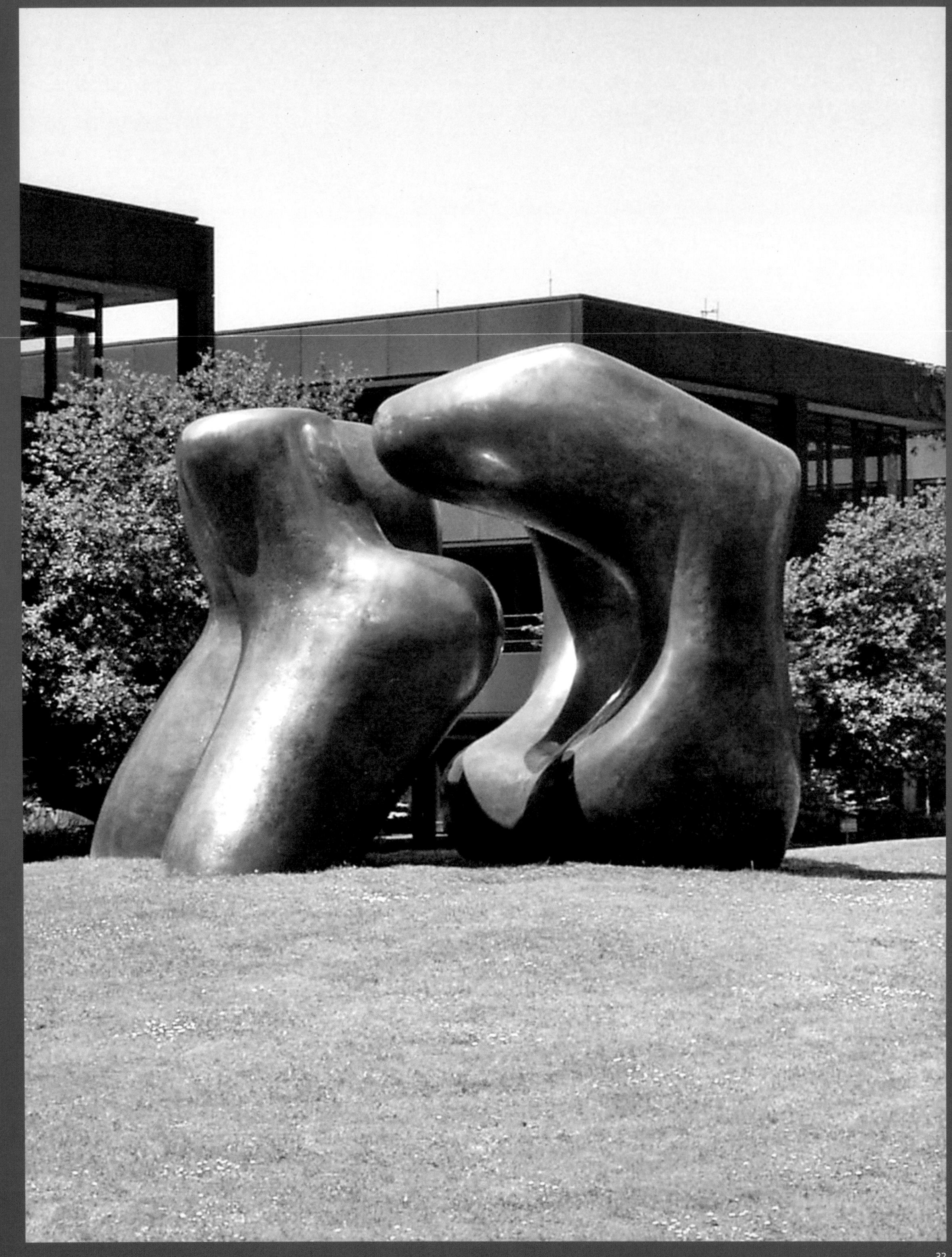

„Soweit ich mich erinnere, habe ich kurz Luft geholt."

"As far as I can remember, I took a quick breath."*

Large Two Forms von/by Henry Moore

32

———

Henry Moore
Large Two Forms
1966/1977
Bronze
610 cm (Länge)
Ehem./Former Bundeskanzleramt Bonn
Heute/Now Bundesministerium für
wirtschaftliche Zusammenarbeit
und Entwicklung
Foto: Michael Sondermann

Henry Moore zeigt zwei ineinandergreifende Formen in Bronze. Das Vertikalstreben der *Germania* ist nach hundert Jahren durch eine Begegnung in der Waagrechte ersetzt. Der Titel *Large Two Forms* verweigert Metaphorik. Er beschränkt sich auf sachliche Darstellung. Tatsächlich besteht das Skulpturenpaar aus zwei mächtigen, körperhaft gerundeten Volumen, die als Komplementärstücke einander begegnen. Es sind weich polierte Gelenke oder Glieder, Kontinente, die zueinander triften oder Geschlechter. Der Engländer Henry Moore wird als Bildhauer weiblicher Form und eleganter Durchbrüche bekannt. Sein Werk, das vor allem ab den 1950er Jahren Berühmtheit erlangt hat, gilt dabei lange Zeit als Inbegriff moderner, abstrakter Plastik. Moore entwickelt seine Formen dennoch aus dem Gesehenen: aus den Schwellungen des menschlichen Körpers und dem plastischem Formenwerk der Natur, wie Kieseln, Knochen oder Muscheln. Abstraktion ist vereinfachte Nachbildung, Politik bleibt darin fern. Auf Ersuchen von Bundeskanzler Helmut Schmidt, eine Skulptur für den Standort Bonn zu fertigen, entschließt sich Moore für einen Abguss eines bereits zehn Jahre davor ausgefertigten Figurenpaars. Das Ensemble wird schließlich im Innenhof des Kanzleramtgebäudes errichtet. Auf einen Sockel wird ebenso verzichtet wie auf ein weithin sichtbares Höhenzeichen. Der demokratische Staat vermeidet markige Botschaften und theatralisch laute Inszenierung. Anstelle dessen setzt er auf ein Kunstwerk von intimem Charakter, rätselhafte Stille in begrüntem Innenhof und die Verweigerung eindeutig lesbarer Botschaft./

Henry Moore depicts two forms in bronze reaching into one another. After one hundred years, the vertical reach of *Germania* has been substituted by a horizontal encounter. The title *Large Two Forms* rejects any metaphors. It is limited to the objective expression. In fact, the pair of sculptures consist of two powerful, body-like rounded forms that confront one another as complementaries. They are soft, polished joints or limbs, continents that drift towards one another, or sexes. The Englishman Henry Moore is known as a sculptor of female forms and elegant apertures. His work, for which he became known from the 1950s, had been the epitome of modern, abstract sculpture for quite some time. Moore, however, developed his forms based on what he saw: from the curves of the human body and the sculptural shapes of nature, such as gravel, bones, or shells. Abstraction is simplified reproduction, politics has no place here. Having been requested by Chancellor Helmut Schmidt to make a sculpture for Bonn, Moore decided to make a cast of a pair of figures he had created ten years earlier. The ensemble was ultimately installed in the inner courtyard of the Chancellery building. There is no base or pedestal nor any visible symbols of exaltation. The democratic state avoids any pithy statements or orchestrations. Instead, it opts for a work of art of an intimate nature, an enigmatic silence in a leafy inner courtyard, and denies any clearly readable statement.

* Bundeskanzler Helmut Schmidt Kat. 42
  German Chancellor Helmut Schmidt, cat. 42

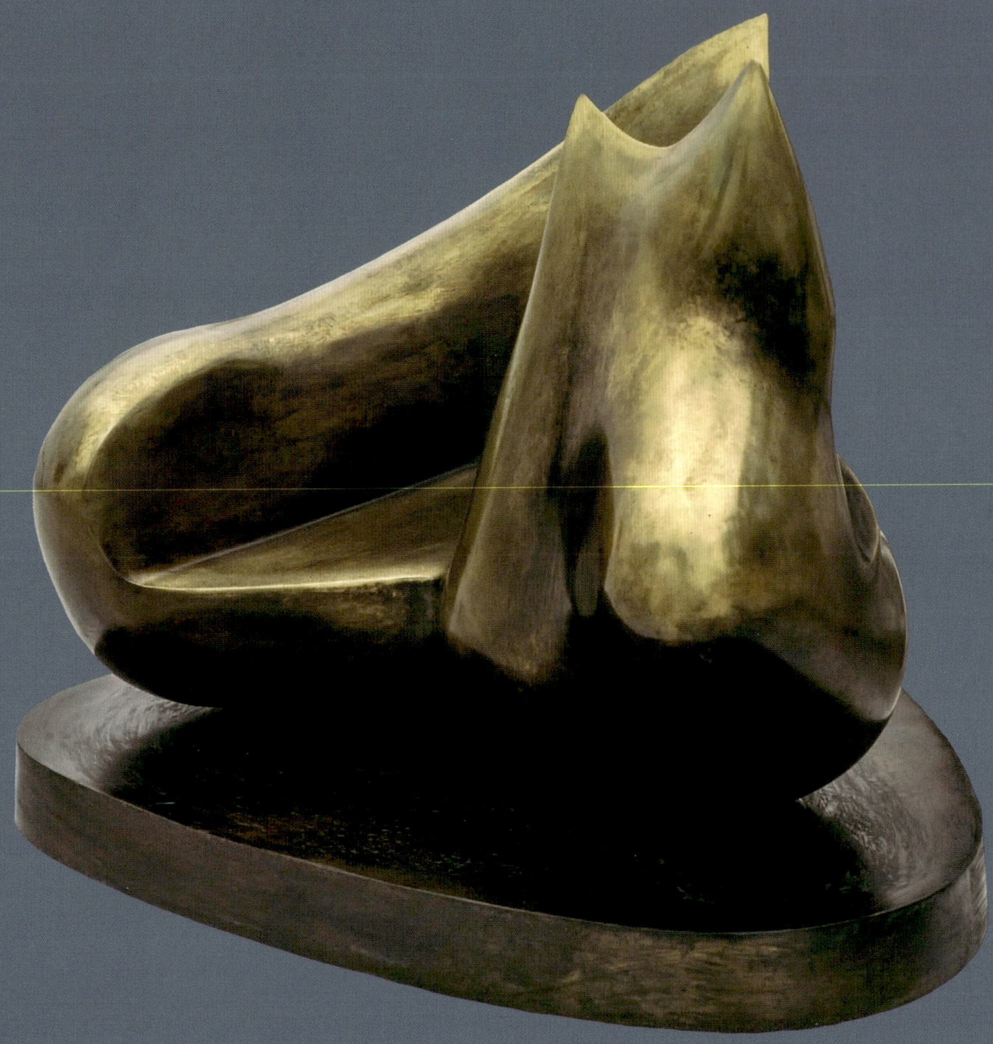

33

33

———

Henry Moore
Architectural Project
1969
Bronze
51 × 61 × 73 cm (Höhe Bronzesockel /
Height bronze pedestal: 5,2 cm)
Privatsammlung / Private collection
Berlin

Die Figur ist in sich kompakt und ohne die
für Moore so charakteristischen Öffnungen.
Ihre unregelmäßig polierten und metallisch
malerischen Oberflächen sind sichtbar bewegt.
Von Energieströmen aufgewühlt, entstehen
Kerben, Schatteninseln und gletscherartige
Flächen. Neben Raum kommt Zeit ins Spiel.
Die Plinthe zeigt die Maserung und Farbig-
keit von Tropenholz, ist aber aus Bronze.
In den oberen Partien greifen die Volumen
dramatischer ineinander. Es entsteht eine

gebirgsartige Masse, deren Umrisse wie
Flammen flackern. *Architectural Project* entsteht kurz nach der ersten Ausführung von
Large Two Forms. /
The figure itself is compact and lacks Moore's
characteristic openings. Its irregular and metallic artful surfaces appear to move. Stirred
by energy fluxes, notches, areas of shadow
and glacier-like surfaces are formed. Besides
space, time comes into play. The plinth portrays the texture and colouration of tropical
wood, yet it is made of bronze. In the upper
parts, the volumes dramatically reach into
one another. A mountainous mass arises,
with contours that flicker like flames. *Architectural Project* was made shortly after the
first presentation of *Large Two Forms.*

34

———

Jörg Albrecht
*Kanzlers Krempel. Henry Moore bleibt
in Bonn, Berlin erhält einen Ehrenhof*
in: *Die Zeit*, 15. Juli 1999
*The Chancellor's Rubbish Henry Moore
stays in Bonn, Berlin gets a Court of
Honour*
Die Zeit, 15 July 1999

Mit dem Umzug des Bundeskanzleramtes
von Bonn nach Berlin und unter dem neuen
Kanzler Schröder stellt sich die Frage, ob
auch *Large Two Forms* von Henry Moore als
Wahrzeichen des ehemaligen Regierungs-
sitzes mitgenommen werden sollten. „Moore
hat seine Schuldigkeit getan und bleibt in
Bonn und basta", fasst der Autor zusammen.
Heute sieht man vor dem Bundeskanzleramt
in Berlin die Plastik *Berlin* von Eduardo
Chillida. /

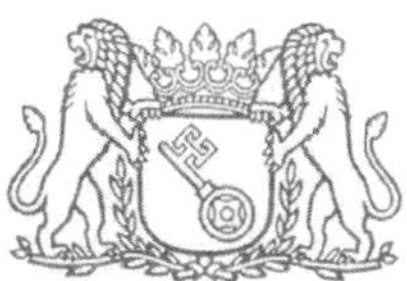

Kanzlers Krempel

Henry Moore bleibt in Bonn, Berlin erhält einen Ehrenhof

Vor langer, langer Zeit, als der deutsche Kanzler noch Willy Brandt hieß und in einem ehemaligen Palais des Prinzen von Schaumburg-Lippe residierte, machte sich eine Kommission daran, den wichtigsten, bedeutendsten, oder sagen wir wenigstens: mit Abstand am häufigsten gefilmten Platz der Republik zu verschönern. Nämlich den sogenannten Vorfahrtsbereich des neuen Kanzleramtes, wo die Mächtigen und Wichtigen dieser Welt künftig aus ihren dunklen Limousinen steigen sollten. Es gab auch einen Wettbewerb, am Ende viel Pflaster, garniert mit Granitblöcken und streng geschnittenen Taxushecken. Aber bald schon einen neuen Kanzler, dem dies gar nicht gefiel. Und weil am Taxus sowieso der Rüsselkäfer nagte und das Pflaster die Verkehrssicherheit im gesamten Vorfahrtsbereich gefährdete, schaffte sich der neue Kanzler (Schmidt hieß er übrigens) einen echten Henry Moore an. *Large Two Forms,* zwei große Formen sahen wir fortan, wenn wieder mal große Politik gemacht wurde. Die kam uns, Moore sei Dank, immer etwas rundlich ins Wohnzimmer.

Zwei Kanzler später stehen wir heute vor neuerlichen Wettbewerbsergebnissen, betreffend den künftigen wichtigsten Platz der nunmehr berlinischen Republik. Der Neue (Schröder heißt er übrigens) hat schon deutlich werden lassen, dass er Bonn nicht vermissen wird und gut auf den alten Krempel vor seiner Haustür verzichten kann; man schleppt ja auch Tantchens Plumeau nicht ewig mit. Der Moore hat seine Schuldigkeit getan und bleibt in Bonn und basta. Entschlossen das Neue wagen, heißt das vermutlich im neuen Kanzlerdeutsch. Oder so.

Die Frage ist nur, ob die Kameraleute in Berlin mit dem neuen, amtlicherseits bereits abgenickten Schwenkmaterial glücklich sein werden. Es handelt sich um zirka 30 sogenannte Stelen aus Beton, die das Architektenpaar Schultes und Frank gleich als Kunst am Kanzlerbau mitgeliefert hat. Die Hälfte davon soll im Ehrenhof stehen, also da, wo in Zukunft die Mächtigen und Wichtigen dieser Welt aus ihren dunklen Limousinen steigen. Man muss sich wohl noch ein paar Fahnen hinzudenken, eventuell eine Grüßkompanie sowie je einen winkenden Regierungschef.

Werden wir den Beton lieben lernen? So wie Moores Bonner Bronze? Mal sehen. Mit des Altkanzlers (übrigens schon damals erstaunlich richtungsweisenden) Worten: „Ein Kunstwerk trifft uns häufig im Zustand der Fassungslosigkeit."

JÖRG ALBRECHT

With the relocation of the Chancellery from Bonn to Berlin under then new Chancellor Schröder, the question was asked as to whether *Large Two Forms* by Henry Moore should be taken along as a memorial of the former Chancellery. "Moore has done his part and will remain in Bonn, and that's that", the author concludes. Today, the Chancellery in Berlin is adorned by a sculpture made by Eduardo Chillida.

35

Henry Moore
Figures with Smoke Background
1976
Farblithographie/Colour lithograph
38 × 28 cm
Dr. Dorothea van der Koelen, Mainz

Im Zweiten Weltkrieg zeichnet Henry Moore Menschen in den Luftschutzkellern. Die Studien einer Liegenden vermitteln eine ähnliche Stimmung. Ihre dunklen Gründe sind vom Existenzialismus und dem Versuch eines künstlerischen Humanismus geprägt. In der obersten Variante wird der Kopf aus zwei knopfartigen Augen gebildet, der sich auf einen rechtwinkligen Arm stützt. Der Körper wird wie ein Spannleintuch über angewinkelte Beine und Rumpf gezogen. Das Vorbild Picasso ist zu erkennen. Besonders an der untersten Liegenden, deren Mundsichel und Augenperle auf einem konischen Hals aufsitzt. /

During the Second World War, Henry Moore drew people in air-raid shelters. The studies of a reclining figure convey a similar atmosphere. Their dark rationales are characterised by existentialism and an attempt at artistic humanism. In the upper version, the head is comprised of two button-like eyes, which rest on a right-angled arm. The body is pulled like a fitted sheet over the half-bent legs and back. The influence of Picasso is apparent. Particularly with regard to the lower reclined figure, whose crescent lips and eye-beads rest on a conically shaped neck.

36

Bundeskanzleramt (Hrsg.)
Gerhard Bott
Henry Moore. Marquette, Bronze, Handzeichnungen
Grafische Gestaltung: Fritz Fischer
Buchcover, erschienen anlässlich der Übergabe von *Large Two Forms* im

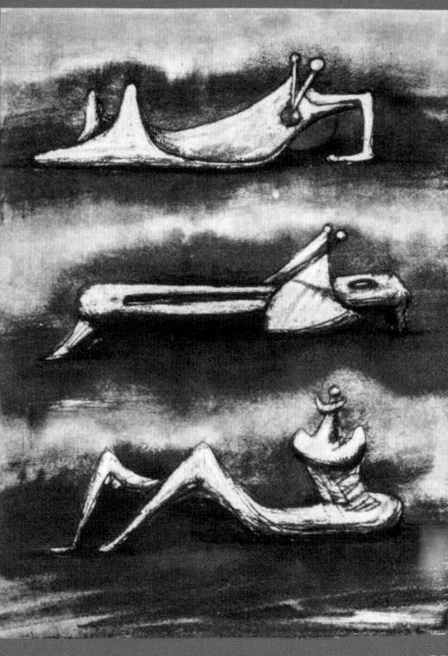

35

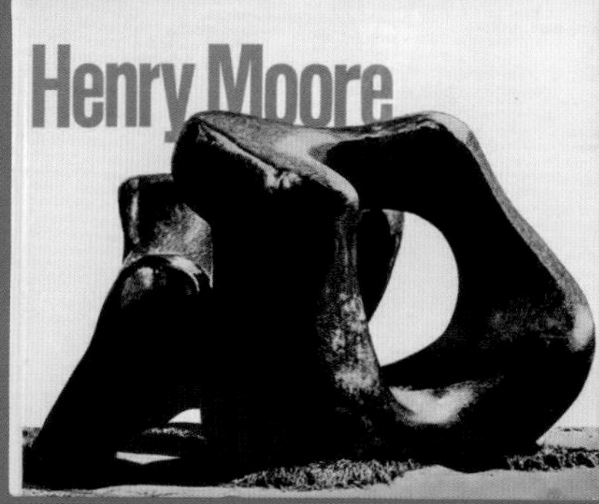

36

Bundeskanzleramt in Bonn 1979
Henry Moore. Marquette, Bronze, Sketches
Book cover, published on the occasion of the presentation of *Large Two Forms* at the Chancellery in Bonn, 1979
Eduard Roether Verlag Darmstadt

37

SW-Fotografie/Black and white photograph
1979
Henry Moore Foundation, Much Hadham

Auf dieser Fotografie spaziert der Bundeskanzler mit dem Künstler über den Rasen vor dem Bildwerk. Das Werk ist eine Ausnahme. Die künstlerische Ausstattung des Bundeskanzleramtes in Bonn beinhaltet mehrheitlich Werke von deutschen Künstlerinnen und

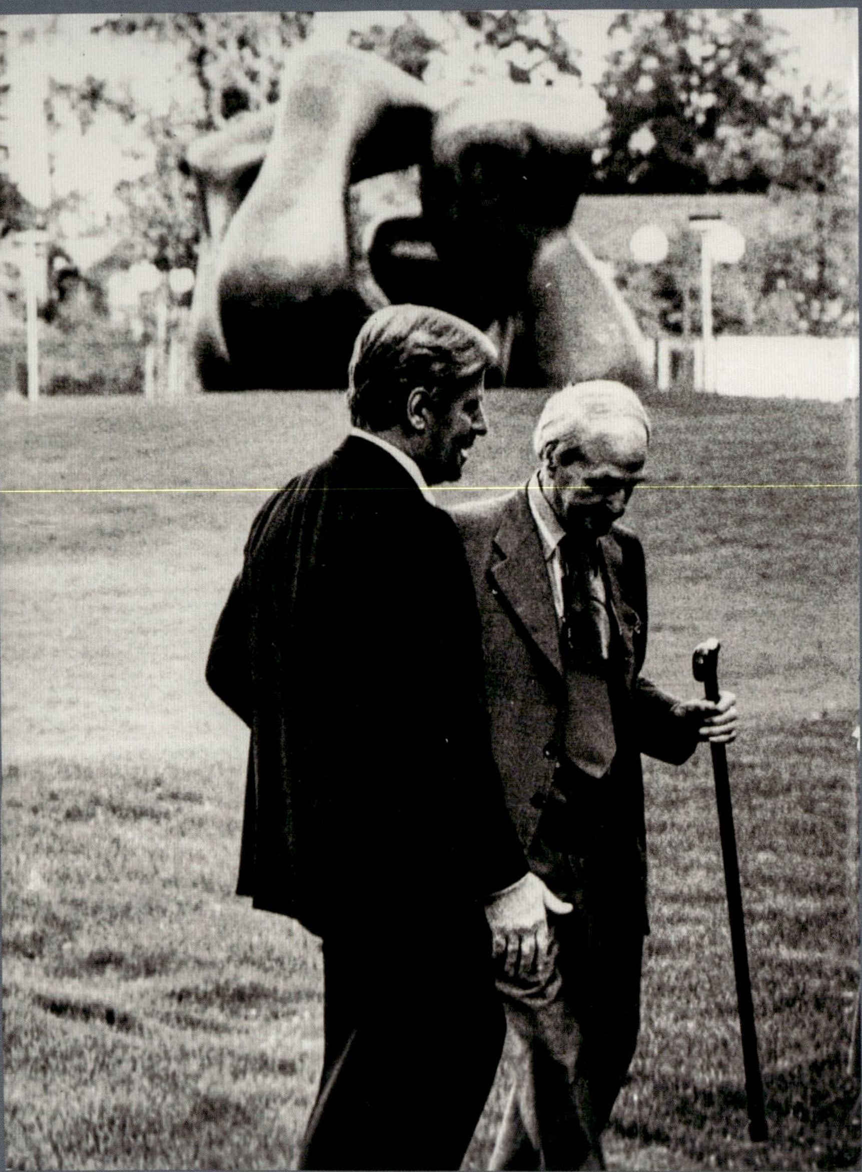

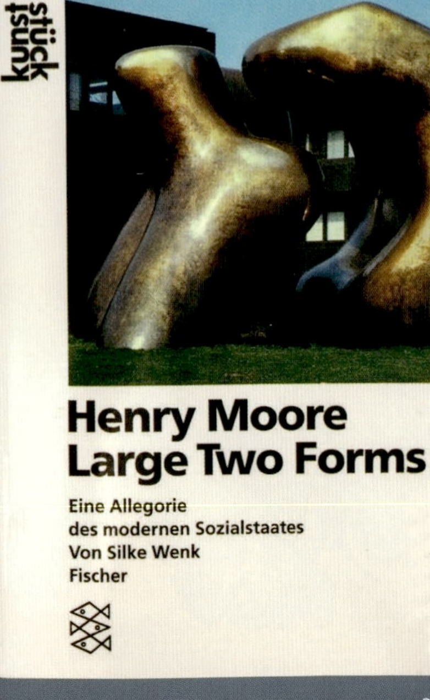

38

37

38

Silke Wenk
Henry Moore. Large Two Forms. Eine Allegorie des modernen Sozialstaates
Fischer Taschenbuch Verlag: Frankfurt, 1997
Grafische Konzeption/Graphical concept
Max Bartholl und Christoph Krämer

Die *Large Two Forms* von Henry Moore wurden zu einem der Wahrzeichen der Bonner Republik. Politische Absichten waren dem Werk ursprünglich nicht eigen. Henry Moore orientiert sich bei seinen Plastiken vielmehr an natürlichen und vor allem weiblichen Formen, in denen Silke Wenk einen Ersatz für die früheren Herrschermonumente sieht. /
Large Two Forms by Henry Moore became a monument to the Bonn republic. The work originally had no political intentions. Rather, Henry Moore's sculptures are based on natural and especially female forms, in which Silke Wenk sees a substitute for the ruler-inspired monuments of bygone days.

39

Brief von Henry Moore an Kanzler Helmut Schmidt
Reproduktion in: „Henry Moore", Gerhard Bott, anlässlich der Übergabe von *Large Two Forms*

Künstlern, die während der nationalsozialistischen Diktatur verfemt wurden. Henry Moore war einer der ersten ausländischen Künstler, dessen Werk für das Bundeskanzleramt gewählt wurde. Seine Bedeutung war zu diesem Zeitpunkt jedoch unbestritten. Moore war ein Klassiker der Moderne geworden, dennoch sieht sich der Kanzler zur Rechtfertigung aufgerufen. Schmidt betont die Aufgabe der Kunst, Völker und Kulturen über Grenzen hinweg zu verbinden. Das Werk Henry Moores kann „von allen Menschen verstanden werden, gleich, welche Sprache sie sprechen". /
In this photo, the Chancellor is walking across the lawn with the artist in front of the sculpture. The work is an exception. The art collection of the Chancellery in Bonn predominantly consists of works by German artists who were ostracised during the National Socialist dictatorship. Henry Moore was one of the first foreign artists whose work was chosen for the Chancellery. Its significance at the time, however, was undisputed. Moore was an icon of modernity, yet the Chancellor was called upon to justify his decision. Schmidt pointed out that it was the task of art to connect people and cultures beyond borders. The work of Henry Moore can "be understood by all people, whatever language they may speak."

HENRY MOORE. O.M.C.H.

TELEPHONE MUCH HADHAM 2566

(STD 027984)

HOGLANDS.
PERRY GREEN.
MUCH HADHAM.
HERTS.

Dear Chancellor Schmidt,

I want to tell you how pleased I am that you are having my bronze sculpture "LARGE TWO FORMS" for long-loan at the new Chancellery building in Bonn.

I'm happy that we worked out the placing + setting for the sculpture, so that people can see it from all round.

At the same time, to have a small exhibition of my drawings + maquettes, is a good idea — and I have tried to make the selection to complement some of the ideas connected with the 'LARGE TWO FORMS'

With warmest regards.

Yours sincerely

Henry Moore

Zusage zu *Large Two Forms*
am 18. Oktober 1978
*Letter from Henry Moore to
Chancellor Helmut Schmidt*
Reproduction in: "Henry Moore",
Gerhard Bott, on the occasion of the
presentation of *Large Two Forms*
Letter of acceptance of *Large Two Forms*
on 18 October 1978

Helmut Schmidt engagierte sich erkennbar
für Kunst im Kanzleramt. Um das seiner
Meinung nach problematische Architektur-
ensemble des Bundeskanzleramtes in Bonn
aufzuwerten, denkt er an die Aufstellung
einer Statue am Vorplatz. Bis zur Übergabe
der Skulptur am 19. September 1979 stehen
Henry Moore und Kanzler Helmut Schmidt
in engem Kontakt. /
Helmut Schmidt was clearly committed to art
in the Chancellery. To enhance the problematic architectural ensemble of the Federal
Chancellery in Bonn, he thought about in-
stalling a statue in front of it. Henry Moore
and Chancellor Schmidt were in close contact

up until the presentation of the sculpture on
19 September 1979.

40
———

SW-Fotografie/Black and
white photograph
1979
Persönliche Widmung „With best
wishes to Henry Moore, 20 July 77,
Helmut Schmidt"
Henry Moore Foundation,
Much Hadham

Parlamentarischer Widerstand ist in Sachen
Moore zu erwarten. Um seinen Auftrag dennoch möglich zu machen, nimmt Helmut
Schmidt den Habitus eines Privatgelehrten
oder Mäzenaten an. Er stellt sich als Sammler
und Kenner dar, der die guten Beziehungen
zum Künstler nutzt, um für die Gemeinschaft –
zum Teil gegen ihren Mehrheitswillen – Wert
zu stiften. / Parliamentary resistance with
regard to Moore was to be expected. To make

this commission possible, Helmut Schmidt
acted as a scholar or patron. He assumed
the position of a collector and expert who
makes use of his good connections to artists
to generate value for the community – in
part against the wish to the majority.

41
———

*Kunst im Kanzleramt. Helmut Schmidt
und die Künste*
*Art in the Chancellery. Helmut Schmidt
and the Arts*
*Gemeinschaftsproduktion der
Verlage Burda, Offenburg, und
Goldmann, München*
Wilhelm Goldmann Verlag/Publisher,
1982
Umschlaggestaltung: Atelier Adolf
und Angelika Bachmann, München
Verlage Burda, Offenburg
Goldmann, München

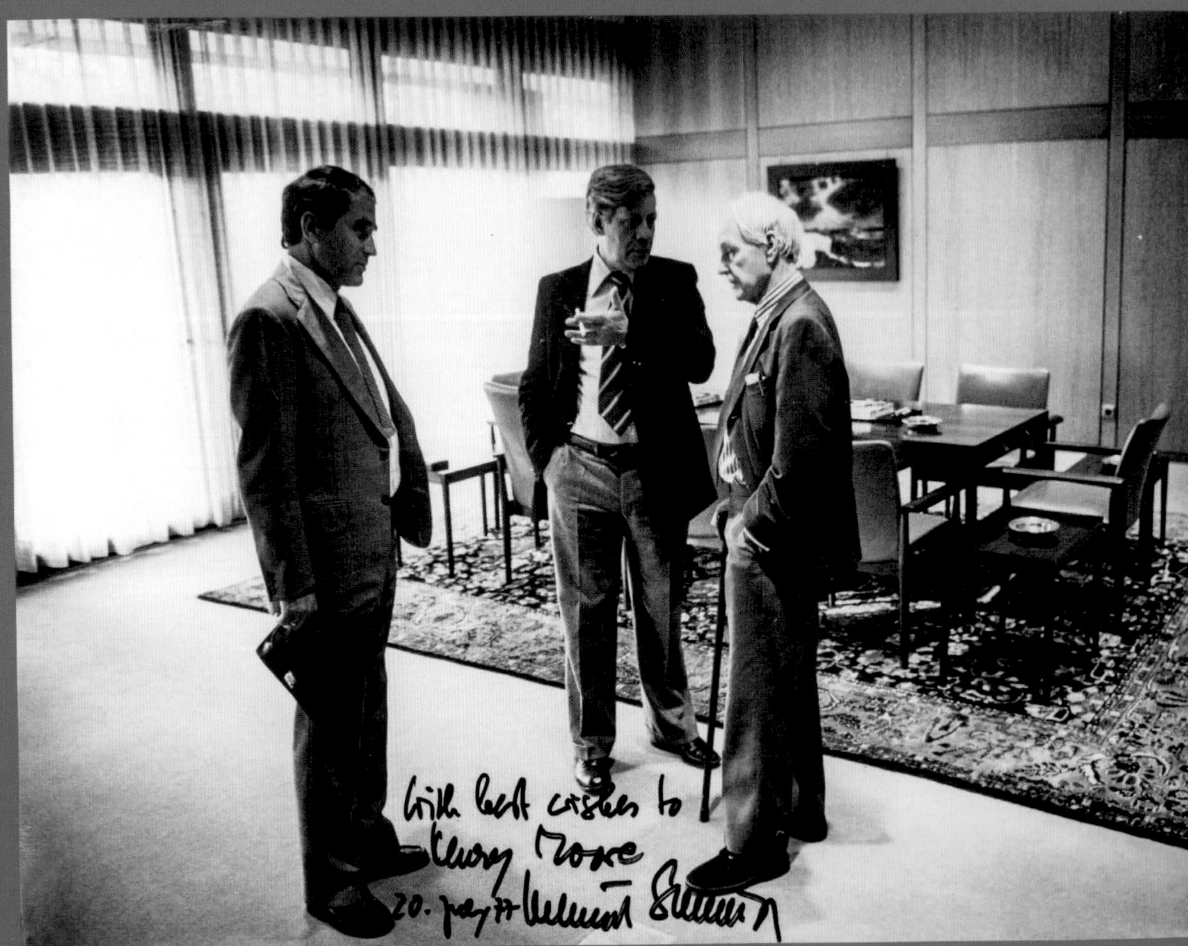

40

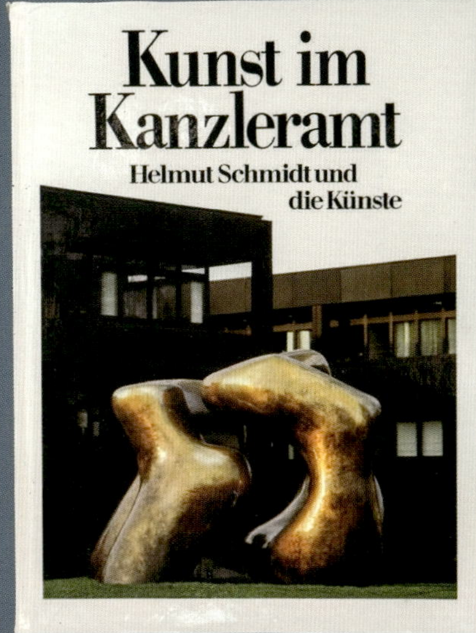

41

42

---

*Henry Moore vor seiner Skulptur
„Large Two Forms"*
*Henry Moore in front of his sculpture
"Large Two Forms"*
29. August 1979
SW-Fotografie/Black and
white photograph
20,5 × 10 cm (ohne Rahmen/unframed)
Quelle/Source:
General-Anzeiger/Heinz Engels

Die Plastiken von Henry Moore gehen vom
Bild des Menschen aus. Ähnlich einer Anwei-
sung zum abstrakten Sehen entwickelt der
englische Bildhauer aus der Körperform seine
künstlerische Sprache. Dabei sind Durchbrüche, Rundungen und Positiv-Negativ-
Formen charakteristisch. „Obwohl mich die
menschliche Gestalt am meisten interessiert,
habe ich Naturformen wie Knochen, Muscheln
und Kieselsteine aufmerksam beobachtet",
schreibt Moore. Die Großskulptur umfasst
zwei getrennte Teilstücke, die sich einander
zuwenden, jedoch nicht berühren. /
Henry Moore's sculptures are based on people.
The English sculptor developed his artistic
language from an abstract vision of the shape
of the body. Breakthroughs, roundings and
positive-negative forms are characteristic of his
work. "Although I am most interested in the
human form, I have also closely observed
natural shapes such as bones, shells and
gravels," Moore writes. The large sculpture
encompasses two separate parts, turned towards each other, but not touching.

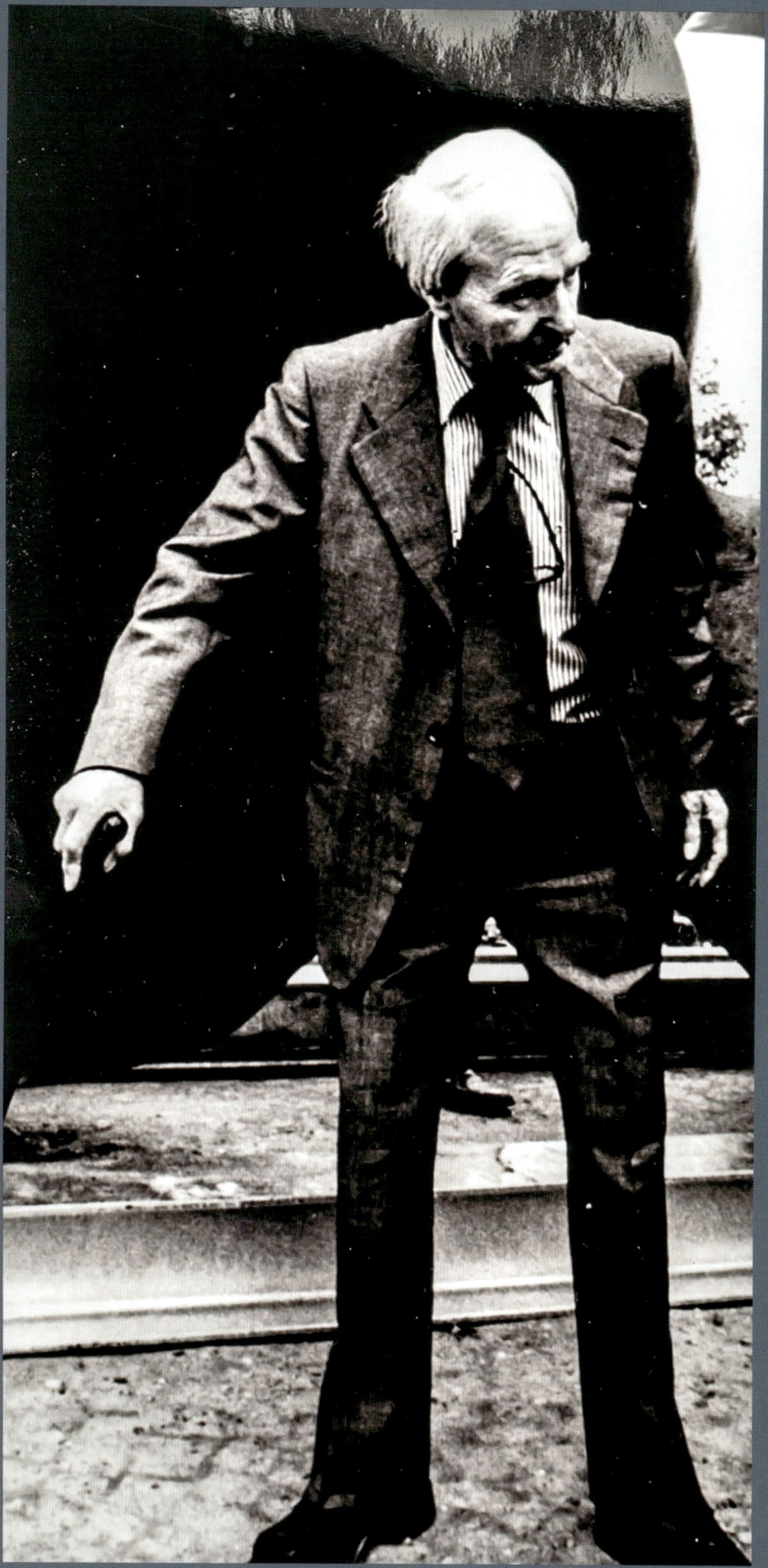

42

Helmut Schmidt
Kunst im Kanzleramt
Rede anlässlich der Eröffnung, in:
„Festschrift für Gerhard Bott zum
60. Geburtstag. 14. Oktober 1987",
Ulrich Schneider (Hg.), 1987

Es ist die Zeit der sozialliberalen Regierung und der Ostverträge. Die Existenz zweier deutscher Staaten wird als historisch und auf lange Zeit unveränderlich gesehen. Durch die Entscheidung Schmidts, Henry Moores Skulptur vor den Amtssitz zu setzen, wird ein kulturpolitisches Bekenntnis abgegeben. Schmidt, der Kunstwerke des deutschen Expressionismus in Büroräume und Flurbereiche hängen lässt, möchte Deutschland als ein der Moderne aufgeschlossenes und international ausgerichtetes Land darstellen. Die Entscheidung fällt auf ein Skulpturenpaar, das eigentlich für Saudi-Arabien bestimmt war. Die Anlehnung an körperliche Form nährt in Moore den Verdacht, es könnte im bilderskeptischen Kulturraum des Islam nicht am richtigen Ort sein. Für Djidda ist es zu wenig abstrakt, für Bonn und den Geschmack vieler Zeitgenossen zu sehr.

[...] Die Geschichte von Large Two Forms für Bonn ist, soviel ich weiß, noch nirgendwo vollständig niedergeschrieben worden. [...]

Ende 1975 und Anfang 1976 fanden im Kanzlerbungalow zwei größere Besprechungen eines dazu von mir einberufenen Beraterkreises statt. Der Neubau des Bundeskanzleramtes, ein Gebäude, das vor meiner Zeit begonnen worden war und das ich – bei allem ehrlichen Respekt für seine Funktionalität- ästhetisch nie sehr geliebt habe, stand vor seiner Vollendung. Man hatte für Räume und Schreibtische und Maschinen geplant. Kunst war nicht vorgesehen. Dem galt es abzuhelfen. [...]

In den erwähnten Terminen ging es um vieles, um Bilder für die Wände vor allem.

Der riesige, gepflasterte und mit Taxushecken umrahmte Vorplatz war nur ein Punkt [...]. So hat es dann noch bis März 1977 gedauert, bis diesbezüglich etwas konkret in Angriff genommen wurde. Die räumliche wie architektonische Situation war schwierig: ein gewaltiger steinerner Platz vor einer überaus strengen, buchstäblich alles zermalmenden Architektur in prägender schwärzlich- brauner Farbe. Die um Beratung Gebetenen waren sich schnell einig, dass nur ganz wenige es schaffen könnten, diese Vorgegebenheiten zu zähmen, sie zu prägen und nicht in ihnen unterzugehen. [...] Einer der ganz wenigen Vorschläge von Anfang an war Henry Moore, dem man es zutraute, die Raummasse zu bändigen.

Henry Moore, diesen liebenswürdigen, in seinem Lebensalter fast grazilen Menschen, dem man von seinem Erscheinungsbild her den Umfang mit seinen Formkolossen kaum zugetraut hätte, habe ich zu diesem Zeitpunkt persönlich noch gar nicht gekannt. Ich hatte einige Hemmungen, ihm – am 29. April 1977 – aus heiterem Himmel einen Brief zu schreiben [...] und ihn, unter Betonung der Möglichkeit einer Leihgabe, um seine Hilfe zu bitten. [...]

Schon am 29. Mai 1977 hielt ich eine handschriftliche Antwort von Moore in Händen, er wolle sich das alles einmal ansehen kommen. Am 13. Juni 1977 war er da; eine kleine, schlanke Person auf einem großen Exerzierplatz. [...]. Ich führte ihn, Vollständigkeit halber, auch in den auf der anderen Seite des neuen Bundeskanzleramtes gelegenen wunderschönen Park des Palais Schaumburg. Nach einer Stunde erklärte Moore mir spontan, er wolle gern für den Park eine Leihgabe zur Verfügung stellen, für einen Punkt etwa auf halber Wegstrecke zwischen Kanzleramt und dem Kanzlerbungalow. Der Vorplatz aber sei ungeeignet. Soweit ich mich erinnere, habe ich kurz Luft geholt und ihm erwidert, ich sei dankbar gerührt, doch löse das mein Problem nicht ganz. Wir sind freundlich voneinander geschieden. Er versprach zu überlegen und lud meine Frau und mich auf sein Anwesen in Much Hadham ein. [...]

Dort, in dieser prachtvollen englischen Grünlandschaft, angefüllt mit seinen eigenen Schöpfungen, [...] ist mir Moores Bonner Reaktion, auch wenn ich sie schon in Bonn begriffen hatte, noch nachträglich förmlich physisch erlebbar geworden. [...]

Im Juli 1978 feierte Moore seinen 80. Geburtstag und erhielt dazu eine große berühmt gewordene Freiluftausstellung in den Londoner Kensington Gardens; am 17. August empfing er meine »Emissäre«. [...]

Moore hatte sie zunächst nach Kensington Gardens geschickt, damit sie sich umsehen sollten, [...]. Von der Art und vom erforderlichen Volumen her kamen sie im Wesentlichen auf Large Two Forms. Bei Moore zurück, stellte sich heraus, dass von dieser in vier Exemplaren bei der berühmten Berliner Gießerei Noack hergestellten Skulptur keines mehr verfügbar war. Die eher vorsichtige und bedeckte Frage nach der Möglichkeit eines zusätzlichen Gusses beschied Moore, wie nicht anders zu erwarten, abschlägig. [...]

Immerhin erwähnte Moore tröstend, er wolle sich erkundigen, ob nicht das letzte Exemplar von Large Two Forms, das schon für einen Komplex in Djidda vergeben sei, noch zurückgeholt werden könne. [...].

Im September rief Moore unversehens an und ließ zur übergroßen Überraschung wissen, dass das Djidda- Exemplar verfügbar sei. Viel, viel später habe ich den Künstler gefragt, wie er das denn fertiggebracht habe. Er hat erzählt, ihm seien wegen der in der Figur künstlerisch reduziert enthaltenen anatomischen Formen Bedenken gekommen. Der Islam verbiete die Abbildungen. So habe er eine besser geeignete andere Skulptur angeboten. [...]

[...] As far as I know, the story of Large Two Forms for Bonn has never been recorded. [...]

Late 1975 and early 1976 two larger meetings took place at the Chancellor's Bungalow, one of which with a group of advisers I had called myself. The new construction of the Federal Chancellery, which had begun before my time and which I – by all honest respect for its functionality – never very much had a liking for aesthetically, was about to be completed. Plans were made for rooms and desks and machines. Art was never intended. And this had to be remedied. [...]

The said meetings dealt with several things, most particularly pictures for the walls.

The gigantic, paved forecourt surrounded by yew hedges was just one issue [...]. It took until March of 1977 until something concrete could be done. The spatial and architectonic situation was difficult: a massive stone-covered space in front of an extremely austere architecture, literally crushing everything in its vicinity, in a characteristic blackish-brown colour. The advisers quickly agreed that there were only few that were able to tame this situation, to form it and not to get lost in it. [...] One of the very few suggestions from the very beginning was Henry Moore, who we were confident could subdue this spatial mass.

At that time, I had not yet personally met Henry Moore, an amiable, gracious older man, whose appearance belied the sheer scope of the colossi he created. I had certain hesitations in writing him a letter – on 29 April 1977 – out of the blue [...] and asking him for his help in the form of a loan. [...]

On 29 May 1977, I received a handwritten reply in which Moore said he would come and have a look. He arrived on 13 June 1977, a short, slender individual on a large parade ground. [...] For the sake of completeness, I also led him to beautiful park of Palais Schaumburg situated on the other side of the new Federal Chancellery. After about an hour, Moore spontaneously said he would like to make a loan to the park, for a location about halfway between the Chancellery and the Chancellor's bungalow. The forecourt however was unsuitable. As far as I can remember, I took a short breath, expressed my gratitude, and said that didn't entirely solve my problem. We parted amicably. He promised to think out it and invited me and my wife to his residence in Much Hadham. [...]

There, in this splendid English landscape, filled with his own creations, [...] is where, although I had understood him before, I was fully and physically able to feel the reaction he had to my request in Bonn. [...]

In July of 1978, Moore celebrated his 80th birthday for which he was honoured with the famous outdoor exhibition in London's Kensington Gardens; and on 17 August he received my "emissaries". [...]

Moore first sent them to Kensington Gardens for them to have a look around, [...]. In terms of style and required volume, they essentially agreed on Large Two Forms. Having returned to Moore's residence, they learned that this sculpture, consisting of four editions and produced at the prestigious fine art foundry Noack in Berlin, was no longer available. Our rather delicately and diplomatically formulated request as to whether there was a possibility of an additional cast was, as expected, refused by Moore. [...]

Nevertheless, Moore consoled us by telling us that he would try to see whether one copy destined for a complex in Jeddah could still be returned. [...]

Moore called in September to let us know, to our great surprise, that the Jeddah sculpture was available. Much, much later, I asked the artist how he had managed to pull that off. He said that he was having reservations due to the anatomical, artistically reduced shapes integrated in the figure. Islam forbids such images. So he offered them a more suitable sculpture. [...]

43
—

Helmut Schmidt
Kunst im Kanzleramt
Speech on the occasion of the opening in:
"Festschrift for Gerhard Bott on his
60th birthday. 14 October 1987",
edited by Ulrich Schneider, 1987

It is the era of social-liberal government and so-called Ostverträge (a treaty with the countries of Eastern Europe). The existence of two German nations is regarded as inflexible, historically and in the long term. Schmidt's decision to install Henry Moore's sculpture in front of the Chancellery is also a cultural-political statement. Schmidt, who has works of art from German expressionists in offices and hallways, wants to present Germany as a country open to modernity and internationality. The decision is made for a pair of sculptures which were really intended for Saudi Arabia. The dependence on the physical form feeds Moore's suspicion that it does not belong in Islam's image-sceptical cultural sphere. For Jeddah it is not abstract enough; for Bonn and the taste of many contemporaries, it is too much so.

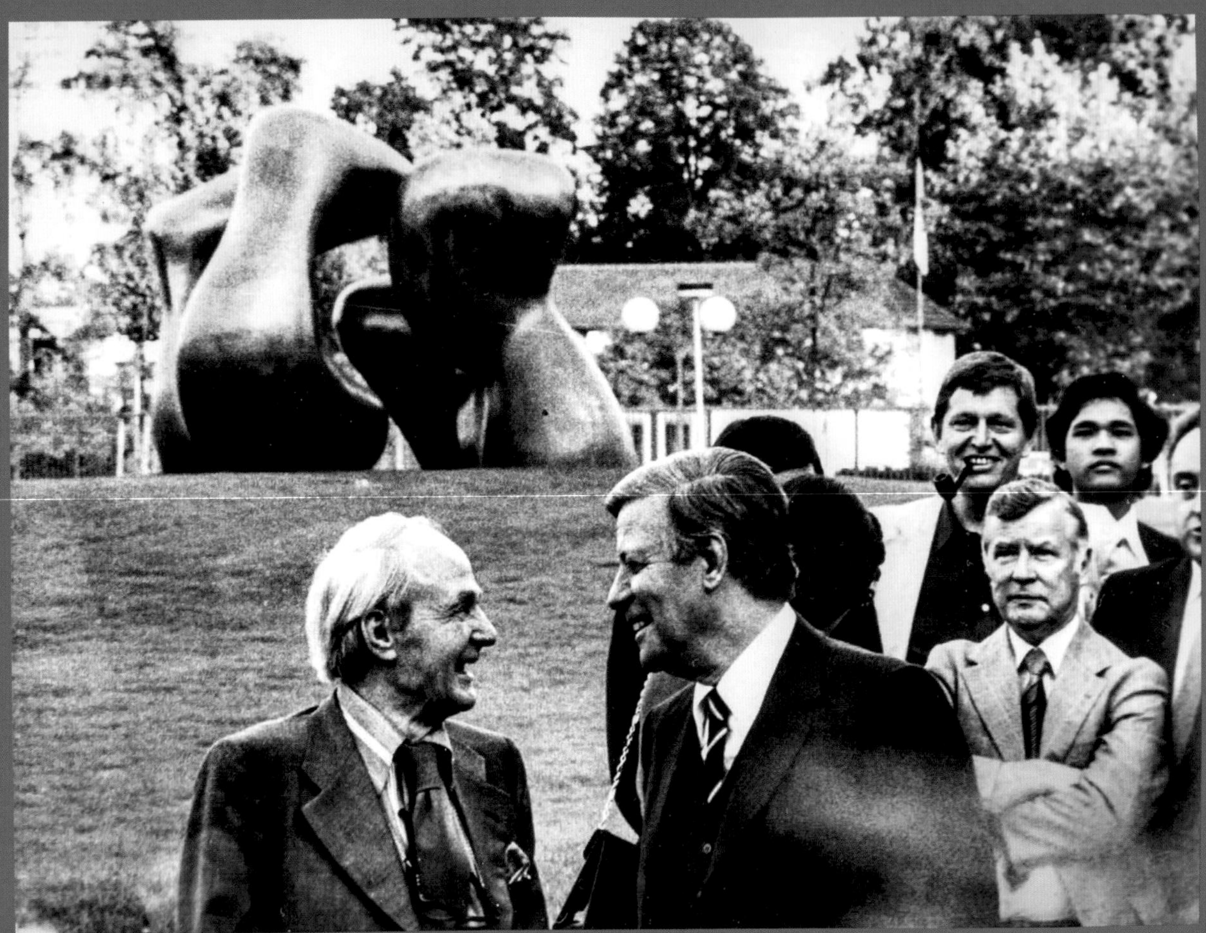

44

44

———

Henry Moore und
Helmut Schmidt in Bonn
1979
SW-Fotografie / Black and
white photograph
19,5 × 27 cm
Henry Moore Foundation,
Much Hadham

In medialen Auftritten bemüht sich Helmut
Schmidt, sein Naheverhältnis zur Kunst deutlich werden zu lassen. Er gibt sich als kulti-
vierte Persönlichkeit, die mit seiner Auswahl-
entscheidung persönlichen Empfindungen
und Neigungen folgt. Die Oldenburger Kunst-
wissenschaftlerin Silke Wenk schreibt dazu.
„Abgesehen von dem deutlich sexualisierenden
Ton ist der Gestus der Intimisierung bemer-
kenswert. ‚Privat‘, jeden in seiner intimen
Sphäre betreffend, erscheint nicht nur das, was

Moores Skulptur zeigt, sondern auch die Art
und Weise, wie der Bundeskanzler darüber
spricht." /
In the media, Helmut Schmidt made an effort
to explain his close relationship to art. He is
a cultivated person who follows his own incli-
nations and emotions when making decisions.
The Oldenburger-based art historian Silke
Wenk writes: "Irrespective of the clearly sexu-
alising tone, the gesture of intimacy is remark-
able. 'Private', in terms of everyone's intimate
personal sphere, is not merely what Moore's
sculpture depicts, but also the manner in
which the Chancellor speaks about it."

45

———

Henry Moore mit Large Two Forms
in der Bildgießerei Noack, Berlin
Henry Moore with Large Two Forms at
the Fine Art Foundry Noack, Berlin

Zwei SW-Fotografien / Two black and
white photographs
20 × 28 cm (oben / top)
20,5 × 28 cm (unten / bottom)
Henry Moore Foundation,
Much Hadham

Die große Version von *Large Two Forms* ließ
Henry Moore wie viele seiner weiteren Werke
in der Bildgießerei Noack in Berlin herstellen.
In den Augen Helmut Schmidts macht ihn
diese Tatsache zu einem „halben Bürger dieses
Landes". /
Henry Moore had the large version of *Large
Two Forms* produced at the fine art foundry
Noack in Berlin. According to Schmidt, this
makes him "half a citizen of this country".

Henry Moore
Large Two Forms
1979
Lithografie/Lithograph
20 × 28 cm
Henry Moore Foundation,
Much Hadham

Das Foto zeigt eine Zeichnung, die Henry
Moore als Lithografie publiziert. Sie stammt
aus den Jahren 1973 – 1974, am linken unteren
Rand findet sich die Signatur. In grobem Netz-
werk deutet Moore die Kontur der Figuren an,
unterstützt von starken Schraffuren, welche
die Schatten andeuten. Das Liniennetz findet
sich im Hintergrund in Landschaft und Himmel wieder. Es überzieht die hellbraunen und
bläulichen Töne mit teils heftig bewegten
Strichen. Die Skulptur im Vordergrund wirkt
wie eine Brandung gegen Landschaft und
Wetter. /
The photo depicts a drawing that Henry Moore
published as a lithographic print. It was made
in 1973 – 74; his signature is in the lower left-
hand corner. Moore outlines the contour of
the figures in rough meshwork, supported by
strong hatchings, which outline the shadows.
The line network is located in the background.
He covers the light brown and blueish shades
with often heavily placed strokes. The sculpture in the forefront is like a rock against the
landscape and the weather.

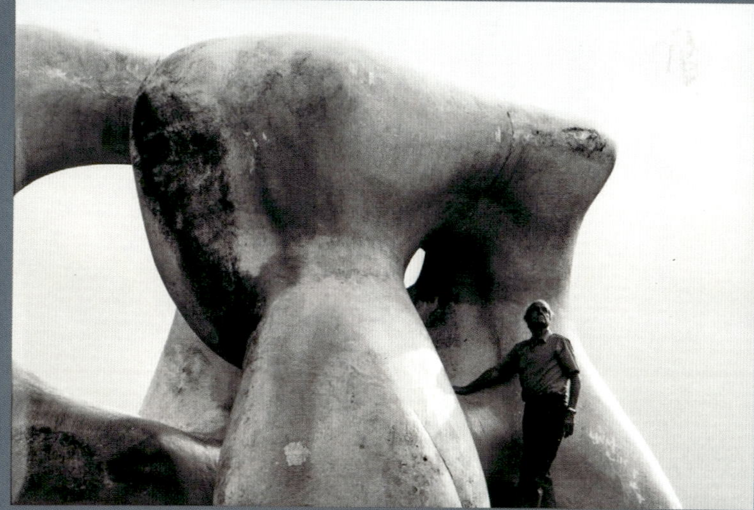

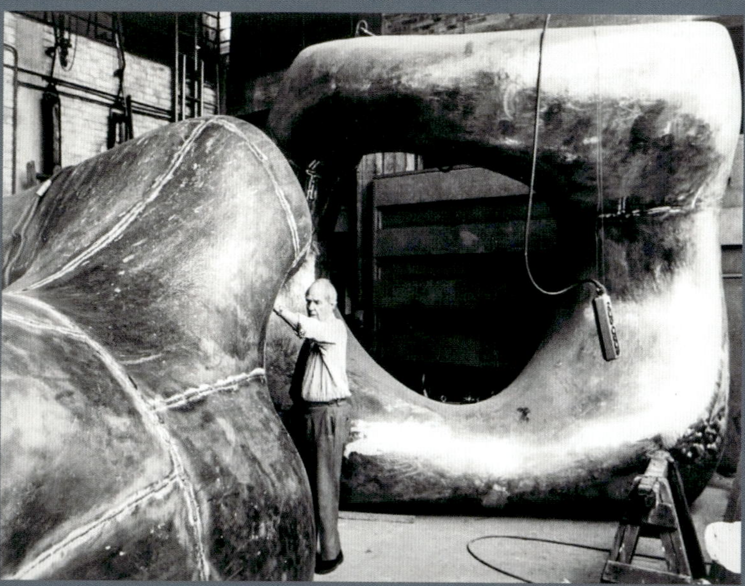

45

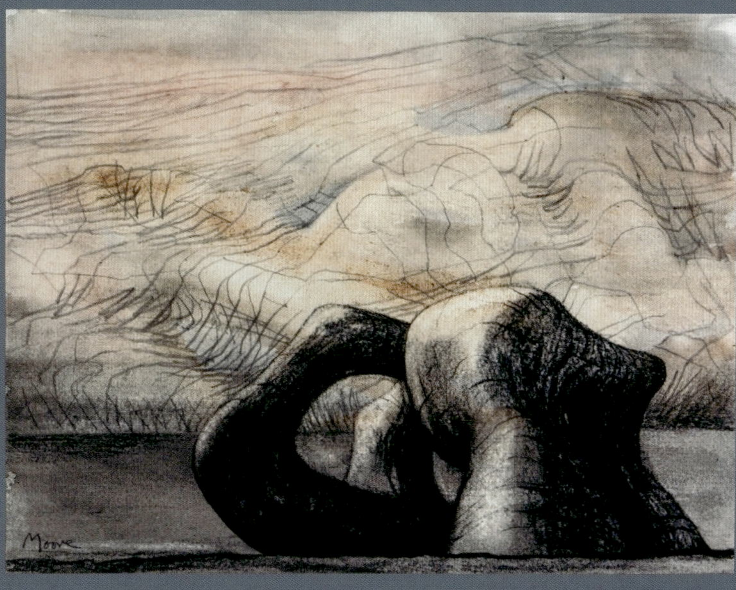

46

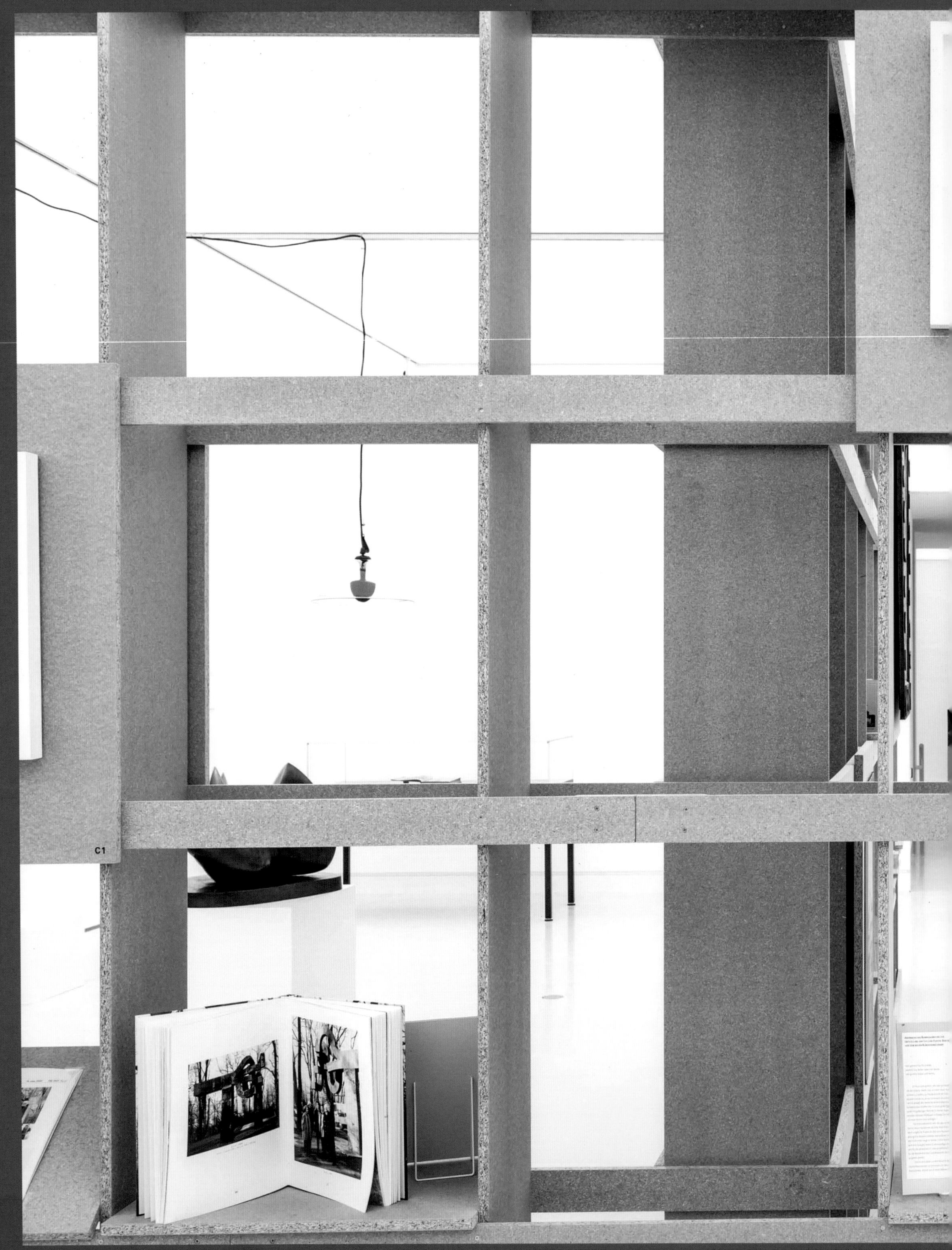
C1

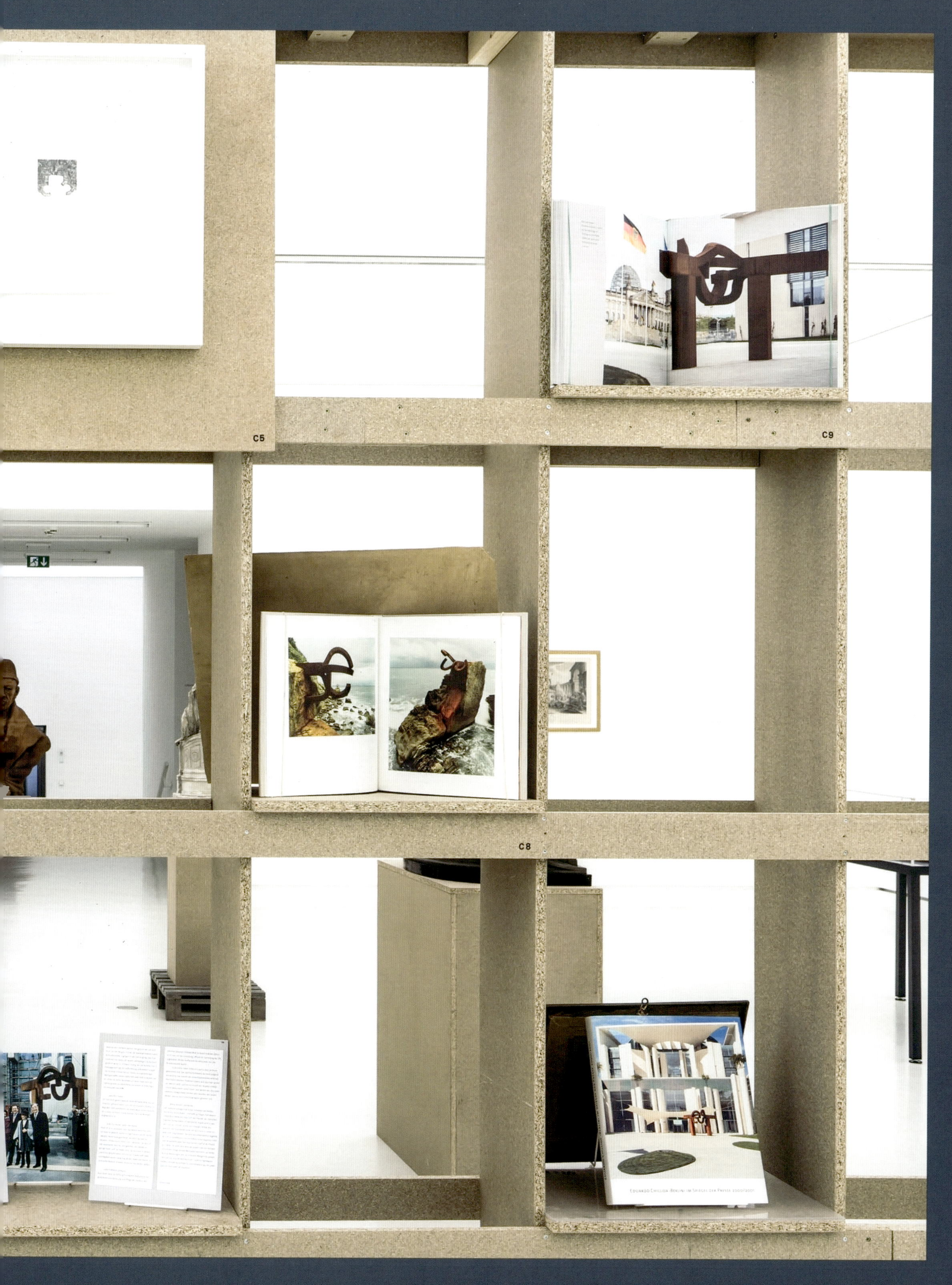

C5
C9
C8

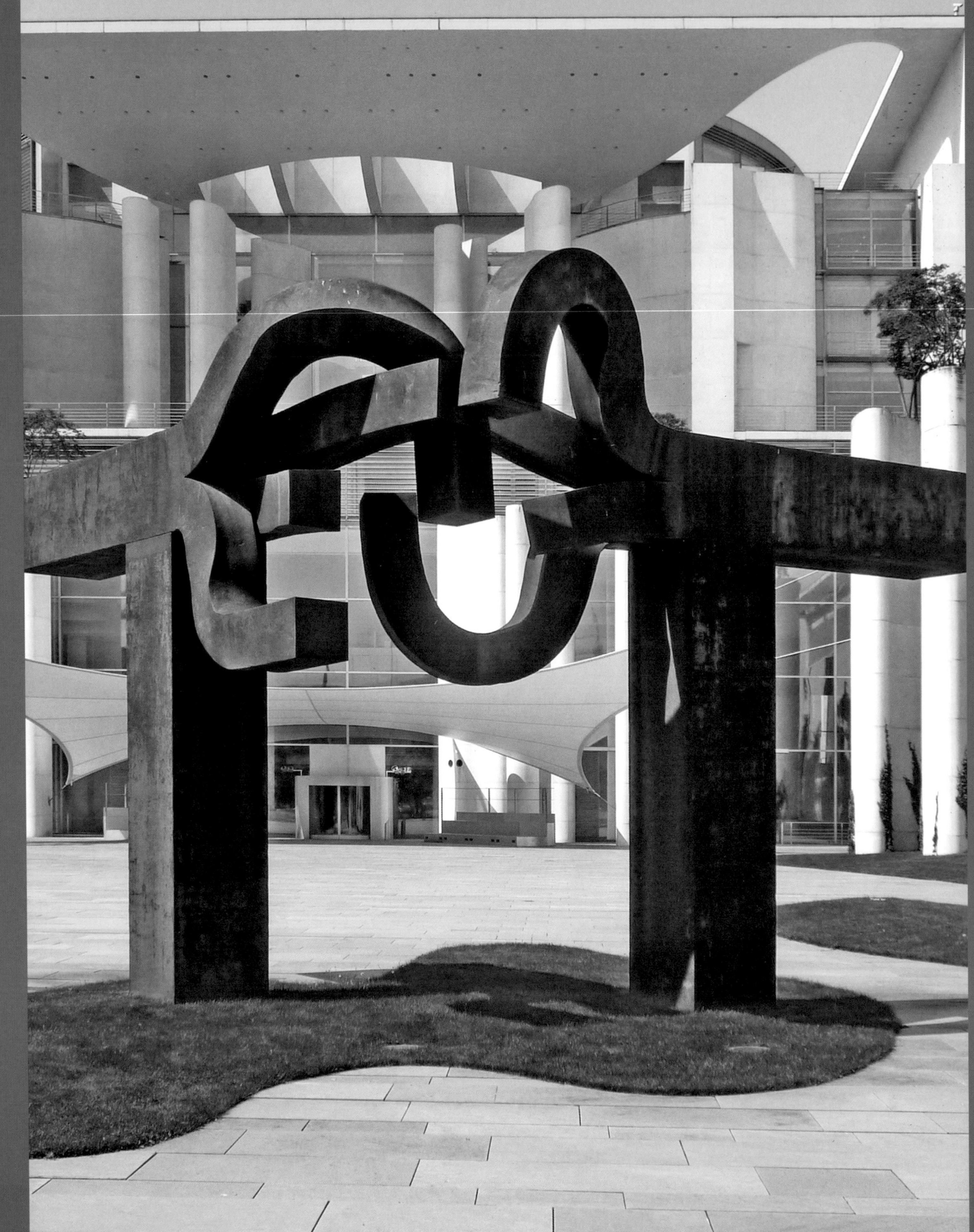

„Es wird sicher zur Bild-Ikone für das vereinigte Deutschland werden."

"It will surely become the icon of unified Germany."*

Berlin von/by Eduardo Chillida

47

———

Eduardo Chillida
Berlin
1999
Stahl/Steel
530 × 550 cm
Bundeskanzleramt Berlin
Foto/Photo: Fabienne Rosenbach

Zwei mächtige Zangen begegnen einander. Eduardo Chillidas Skulptur *Berlin* ist eine Fortführung der Idee von Zweiheit und skulpturaler Ebenbildlichkeit. Aufgerissene Stahlarme und strenge Gesten gehören zu den Kennzeichen des baskischen Bildhauers. Chillida errichtet ähnliche Zangen an den Klippen der Atlantikküste. Die *Windkämme* greifen nach Wellen, Gischt und Witterung. In Berlin setzt er diese archaisch inspirierten Formen auf monumentale Stahlträger. Aus den Querträgern werden durch die Prellung gebogene Rundungen. Fast berühren die Profile einander. Teils scheinen sie wie wuchtige Magneteisen angezogen, teils voneinander wie nach einem Aufprall ins Leere abgelenkt. Benutzte Henry Moore in Bonn weich wirkende Oberflächen und warmfarbige Bronze, so verwendet Chillida für *Berlin* das rohe Gusseisen in rostendem Zustand. Statt komplementäre werden antithetische Kräfte wirksam,

obwohl wiederholt von einem Symbol der Wiedervereinigung die Rede ist. Die Skulptur wird vor dem zahnweißen Bau von Axel Schultes und Charlotte Frank errichtet. Ein nierenförmiges Rasenstück dient als Standortareal. Dahinter ist ein weißes Sonnensegel angebracht, verschiedene Bepflanzungen sind zu sehen. Die Skulptur wird feierlich unter Anwesenheit von Bundeskanzler Schröder, der als Kunstfreund gilt, und der Frau des damals bereits betagten Künstlers eröffnet. Anwesend sind auch die Sponsoren, ein bayrisches Unternehmerehepaar. Das wieder vereinigte Deutschland wählt die sperrige Form und einen spanisch stämmigen Autor für den Staatsakt. Die prominenteste skulpturale Setzung des Landes wird im Unterschied zu Johannes Schillings *Germania* ohne öffentliches Geld finanziert. /

Two powerful pliers confront one another. Eduardo Chillida's sculpture *Berlin* is a continuation of the idea of duality and sculptural identity. Wide open steel arms and harsh gestures are characteristic of the Basque sculptor. Chillida installed similar pliers on the cliffs of the Atlantic coastline. The *Wind Combs* reach for the waves, spray and weather. In Berlin, he places the archaically inspired shapes on monumental steel columns. The profiles nearly touch. To some extent, it seems as if they are being attracted like massive magnets; on the other hand, they appear as if

they have been turned away from each other towards the emptiness, as if they had just collided. Whereas Moore makes use of soft-looking surfaces and warm-coloured bronze in Bonn, Chillida makes use of oxidising red cast iron for *Berlin*. Instead of complementary forces, antithetical forces become apparent, despite the fact that one speaks repeatedly of the symbolism of reunification. The sculpture is installed in front of the bright white building by Axel Schultes and Charlotte Frank.
A kidney-shaped lawn is the installation site. A white solar sail is installed in the back; various types of plants can be seen. The sculpture is festively inaugurated by Chancellor Schröder, a known friend of the arts, and the ageing artist's wife. Further guests were a Bavarian couple who had sponsored the work. Reunited Germany chooses the bulky shape and a Spanish artist for the state commission. Unlike Johannes Schilling's *Germania*, the most prominent sculptural installation in the country takes place without a contest and no public funding.

* Bundeskanzler Gerhardt Schröder Kat. 54
German Chancellor Gerhard Schröder, cat. 54

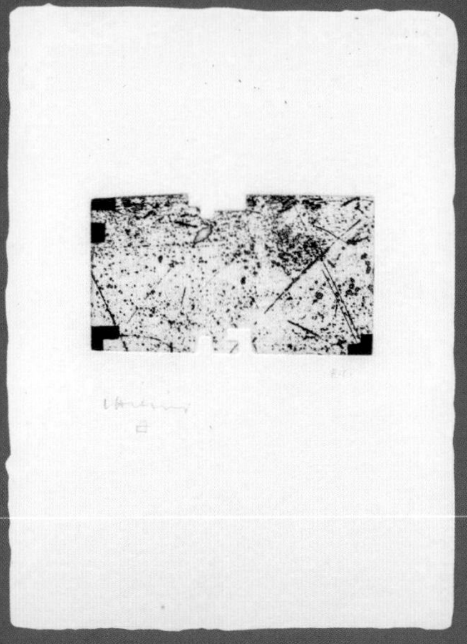

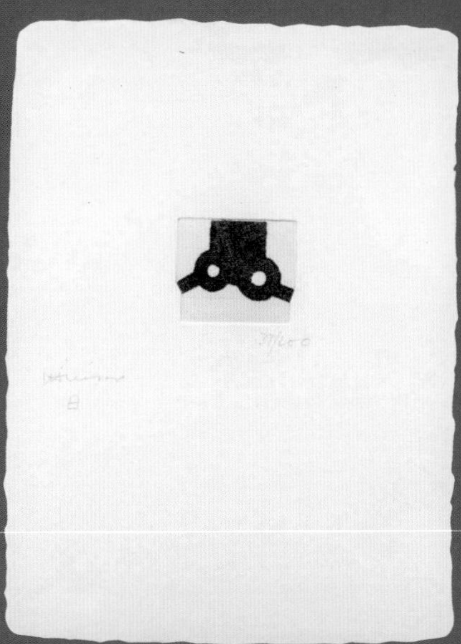

48

49

48

Eduardo Chillida
Ohne Titel
Untitled
1996
Radierung/Etching
31 × 23 cm
Dr. Dorothea van der Koelen, Mainz

Das Blatt zeigt die willkürliche Einwirkung von Säurespritzern. Wie fahrige Sternschnuppen verteilen sich Linien, Punkte und Flecken. An den Rändern bekundet sich Chillidas konstruktives Formprinzip. In den Ecken finden sich schwarze Felder wie Scharniere oder Halter. Am oberen und unteren Rand verdeutlichen eckige Formkanten das Eindringen des Äußeren in die Binnenwelt des Bildes. /
The sheet depicts the random impact of acid splatters. Lines, points, and spots are distributed like erratic falling stars. The edges express Chillida's constructive principle of form. The corners boast black fields such as hinges or brackets. At the upper and lower limits, the angular edges illustrate the penetration of the outer world into the inner world of the sculpture.

49

Eduardo Chillida
Ohne Titel
Untitled
1999
Radierung/Etching
31 × 23 cm
Dr. Dorothea van der Koelen, Mainz

Als Eduardo Chillida mit seinem grafischen Werk beginnt, ist sein Ruf als Bildhauer bereits gefestigt. Seine Grafiken sind dennoch keine Abbilder der Skulpturen. Weder rein konstruktiv noch spontan, wirken sie wie zeichenhafte Verdichtungen, in denen die Fremdartigkeit der Formen konzentriert wird. Ihre unbewegte Stille löst Nachdenklichkeit und archaische Erinnerung aus. /
When Eduardo Chillida started to work on his graphic pieces, his reputation as a sculptor had already been established. His graphic work, however, is not a copy of his sculptures. Neither purely constructive nor spontaneous, they have the appearance of symbolic consolidations, in which emphasis is placed on the foreignness of the forms. Their motionless silence triggers reflection and remembrances of the past.

50

Peter-Klaus Schuster
„Die Lesbarkeit der Kunst.
Zu Eduardo Chillidas Skulptur
für das Bundeskanzleramt"
in: *Die Zeit*, 19. April 2000
"The readability of art. On Eduardo
Chillida's sculpture for the Federal
Chancellery"
Die Zeit, 19 April 2000

Die Chillida-Plastik in Berlin bleibt nicht ohne Widerspruch, so ist sie in einem Artikel der *Süddeutschen Zeitung* vom 5. April 2000 zu „illustrativem Politkitsch" degradiert worden. Peter-Klaus Schuster, der damalige Direktor der Stiftung Preußischer Kulturbesitz, weist diese Kritik zurück. Schuster sieht Chillidas Skulptur stattdessen als „vieldeutig offenes Kunstwerk", welches ähnlich wie Henry Moores *Large Two Forms* als „Sinnbild der Teilung wie als mühevoller Versuch nach Nähe und Berührung" gelesen werden kann. Den Titel der Plastik *Berlin* hat Eduardo Chillida selbst gewählt, wodurch die sich nie berührenden Elemente seiner Plastik als Anspielung auf die Teilung sowie die „noch nicht abgeschlossene Einheit" Berlins gedeutet werden können. /
The Chillida sculpture in Berlin is not without opposition, as illustrated in an article in the newspaper *Süddeutsche Zeitung* on 5 April 2000, which demotes it to "illustrative political kitsch". Peter-Klaus Schuster, former Director of the Foundation for Prussian Culture (Stiftung Preußischer Kulturbesitz), dismisses the criticism. Instead, Schuster sees Chillida's sculpture as an "ambiguous and open piece of art", which, similar to Henry Moore's *Large Two Forms*, can be interpreted as a "symbol of separation and arduous attempt to establish closeness and contact". The title *Berlin* was chosen by Eduardo Chillida himself, whereby the non-touching elements of his sculpture could be interpreted as the reference to a state of division as well as the "still incomplete unity" of the city of Berlin.

Die Lesbarkeit der Kunst

Zu Eduardo Chillidas Skulptur für das Kanzleramt / Von Peter-Klaus Schuster

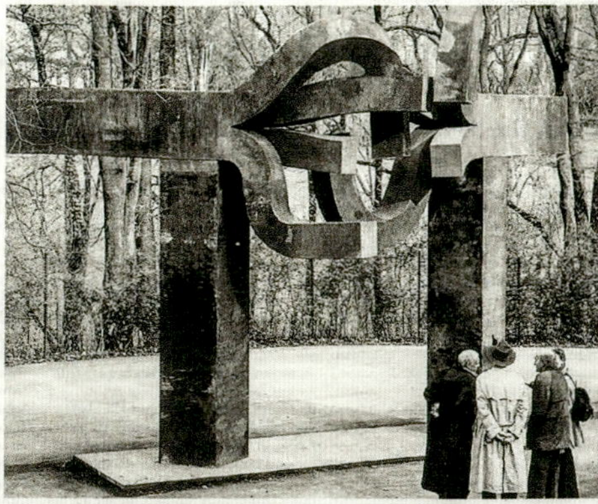

SPUKT DIE BERLINER REPUBLIK auch in der Skulptur des Spaniers Chillida? Foto: DZ

Kunstwerke können unter ihren Interpreten so verkümmern, dass sie nur noch als ihr Gegenteil wahrgenommen werden. Eine solche Hinrichtung erfuhr jüngst Eduardo Chillidas Skulptur für das neue Bundeskanzleramt (*Süddeutsche Zeitung* vom 5. 4.). Die Polemik verstand sich im Zusammenhang mit der Bundestagsdebatte über Hans Haackes Kunstprojekt *Der Bevölkerung* als ein Plädoyer für das Neue, das Kritische und das Vieldeutige im Bereich politischer Kunst.

Mit dem Übergang von der Bonner zur Berliner Republik, so wird behauptet, zeige sich ein tiefer Wandel im Verhältnis von Kunst und Politik. Statt des rätselhaften Vieldeutigen werde nun in Berlin das Affirmative und Erbauliche bevorzugt. Die *Large two forms* von Henry Moore, die vor dem Bonner Kanzleramt stehen, seien „wunderschöne, rätselhaft fließende Formen" gewesen, die sich nicht auf einen „simplen Bedeutungsgehalt" herunterschrauben lassen. Anders dagegen Chillidas Skulptur, die Gerhard Schröder „als Inkunabel der Berliner Republik" vor das neue Bundeskanzleramt stellen möchte. Bei ihr handle es sich um „illustrativen Politkitsch", der in einer „pubertär-pathetischen Dampfhammer-Mentalität die Einigung ins Bild" setzt.

Diese Kritik ist ein Meisterwerk der Desinformation. Sie ist verfasst, um das kulturelle Klima der so genannten Berliner Republik zu diffamieren und zugleich trifft sie einen der größten lebenden Bildhauer. Beides sollte man nicht durchgehen lassen. Um dem kunsthistorischen Kurzzeitgedächtnis abzuhelfen, sei erinnert, dass es mit Helmut Kohl immerhin ein prägender Kanzler der so genannten Bonner Republik war, mit dem sich auf dem Felde der politischen Kunst für Berlin ebenso wichtige wie unterschiedliche Entscheidungen verbinden: die posthume Vergrößerung einer Skulptur von Käthe Kollwitz als Mahnmal für die Opfer des Zweiten Weltkrieges und des Nationalsozialismus in der Neuen Wache, die erfolglose Ablehnung von Christos Reichstagsverhüllung sowie die Befürwortung des Stelenwaldes von Eisenman neben dem Brandenburger Tor als Denkmal für die ermordeten Juden in Europa. Wer die letztere Entscheidung für mutig hält, dem gelten die beiden ersteren möglicherweise als timide oder uninspiriert.

Bereits an dieser Gemengelage wird deutlich, wie hohl solche Begriffskonstruktionen sind, die eine Bonner Republik von einer Berliner Republik als kunstsinniger unterscheiden möchten. Im Falle von Chillida hat das umso weniger Sinn, als die Entscheidung für dessen Skulptur vor dem Berliner Bundeskanzleramt noch von einem Gremium zur Regierungszeit von Helmut Kohl getroffen wurde. Einer Umsetzung der *Large two forms* von Henry Moore, die der Altbundeskanzler Schmidt angeregt hatte, weil er die Skulptur auch als Sinnbild der Teilung Deutschlands auffasste und deshalb nach der Wiedervereinigung in der neuen alten Hauptstadt sinnvoll untergebracht fand, konnten weder Kohl noch Schröder etwas abgewinnen (von den Bonner Protesten gegen einen solchen Umzug einmal abgesehen). Chillida, so war allgemeiner Konsens, ist der einzige Bildhauer, der die von Moore in Bonn begonnene Tradition einer sprachmächtigen Skulptur vor dem Bundeskanzleramt fortsetzen könnte.

Offenes Kunstwerk – fixes Kritikerklischee

Unklar war nur, ob Chillida einem solchen Wunsch nachkommen würde. Seit der großen Ausstellung 1981 in Hannover ein großer Bewunderer des spanischen Bildhauers, hat Gerhard Schröder die schon getroffene Entscheidung für Chillida nachdrücklich befördert. Wenige Wochen nach der Ortsbesichtigung lieferte Chillida ein Modell mit dem Vorschlag, dieses als massive Stahlskulptur von über fünf Meter Höhe auszuführen. Die Skulptur sollte den Titel *Berlin* tragen.

Die fatale Eindeutigkeit, die der Kritiker an Chillidas Skulptur als „systemkonformer Einheitsplastik" glaubte beklagen zu müssen, diese allzu plakative Eindeutigkeit hat der Kritiker allerdings durch den von ihm selbst erfundenen Titel *Einheit* erst hergestellt. Aber nicht *Einheit*, sondern *Berlin* ist nach Chillidas wohlüberlegter Wortwahl der Titel seiner Skulptur. Kein abstrakter Begriff wird illustriert, sondern ein Ort und damit die Vorstellung von einem Raum ist Chillidas Gegenstand.

Dieser Raum wird bei Chillida ganz offensichtlich aus spannungsreichen Kräften geformt, die sich mit stählernen Fangarmen annähern, die sich verschlingen scheinen und doch stets Abstand halten. Zwischen den Tentakeln oder Fingern dieser beiden stählernen Baumgebilde, die kompliziert aufeinander zustreben, findet offensichtlich keinerlei Berührung statt. Chillidas Skulptur, die in ihrer Zweiteiligkeit auch eine deutliche Hommage an Henry Moores *Large two forms* ist, kann also ebenso als Sinnbild der Teilung oder unaufhebbaren Trennung wie als mühevoller Versuch nach Nähe und Berührung gelesen werden.

Den wie eine Hand aufgespreizten Stahlblock, ein wichtiges Grundmotiv seiner Skulpturensprache, das Wachstum ebenso wie Energie und Raum verdeutlicht, hat Chillida hier horizontal auf einen zweiten, vertikal stehenden Stahlblock aufgelegt. Die daraus entstehende Kreuzformation attackiert mit einem aufgerissen ausgreifenden Kreuzarm ein ebensolches Gegenüber. Zusammen bilden sie jenes expressive Raumgefüge, das an Passion erinnert und von Chillida als Großform aus zwei sich annähernden Teilen höchst anspielungsreich *Berlin* genannt wird. Berlin wird so bei Chillida zum Sinnbild eines noch offenen und schmerzhaften Prozesses, den manche Betrachter als Anspielung auf die Teilung und andere auf die noch nicht abgeschlossene Einheit beziehen werden.

Mehr ist dazu gegenwärtig nicht zu sagen. Denn im Unterschied zu Henry Moores abwandig gegossenem *Large two forms* kann die in ihrem ganzen Materialvolumen völlig wahrhaftig dastehende Skulptur Chillidas vor den ondulierenden Formen von Axel Schultes Berliner Kanzleramt zukünftig noch ganz andere Bedeutungen annehmen. Möglich sind Anspielungen auf geborstene oder noch zu vollendende Architekturen, auf Brücken, Tore oder Kräne. Chillidas Skulptur ist jedenfalls als vieldeutig offenes Kunstwerk ganz das Gegenteil zu jenem „aus dem Stahl heraus geprügelten Bild der Einheit", das erst die Kritik unter dem Pretext eines apokryphen Titels als plumpe Eindeutigkeit erzeugt hat.

Hinter einer solchen Kritik, nimmt man sie denn als Symptom, steht wohl die Furcht vor einer reglementierenden Vereinfachung durch Berlin. Weit weg von der neuen Metropole soll es noch wunderschöne, rätselhafte Formen geben wie bei Moore im Bonner Kanzlergarten. Gegenüber solcher Süßigkeit gilt Berlin als laut, eindeutig, plakativ und primitiv. So will es die geistige Topografie eines Vorurteils, vor dem man nicht nur Berlin in Schutz nehmen sollte. Denn so, wie die Berliner Republik nichts anderes als die Fortsetzung der Bonner Republik ist, hätte es früher Spree-Athen auch nie ohne Isar-Athen gegeben. Ludwig II. und seine Kunsthauptstadt München sind jedenfalls das erklärte Vorbild der Berliner Museumsinsel. Das komplementäre Gegenstück zu Chillidas *Berlin*-Skulptur von 1999 ist deshalb jene nicht weniger monumentale Skulptur, die Chillida in Gestalt dreier zum Licht aufstrebender Wachstumsformen als Hymnus auf die drei Pinakotheken 1998 für München geschaffen hat.

Dass sich im Spätwerk Chillidas zwei Monumentalskulpturen antithetisch auf zwei bedeutende Städte in Deutschland beziehen, auf die Schönheit und den Reichtum der Kunststadt München und auf die geschichtliche Passion Berlins, das ist vielleicht ein Appell an die Bevölkerung dieses Landes, der viel sublimer ist als alles, was andere politische Skulpturen oder deren Apologeten und Kritiker zu bewirken vermöchten. Es stimmt jedenfalls zuversichtlich für die Kultur dieser Berliner Republik, dass Mäzene wie München die Berlin-Skulptur Chillidas für das neue Bundeskanzleramt großherzig bezahlt haben.

Peter-Klaus Schuster ist Generaldirektor der Museen der Stiftung Preußischer Kulturbesitz

50

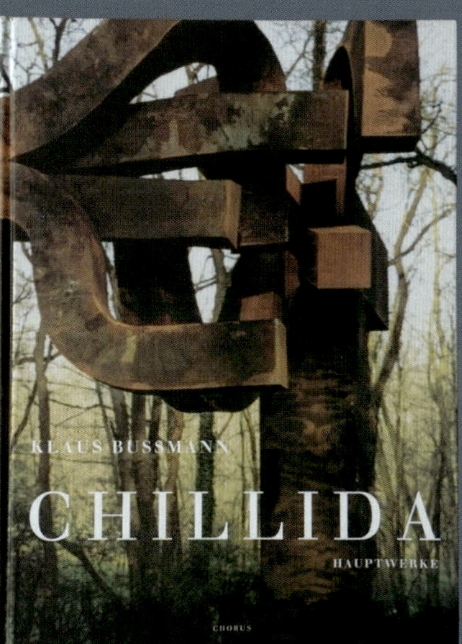

51

Klaus Bussmann (Hg.)
Eduardo Chillida Hauptwerke
Eduardo Chillida Main Works
Layout/Layout: Dorothea und Martin van de Koelen
Mainz/München Chorus Verlag/Publisher
2003
Kunsthalle Mainz

Die Skulptur entsteht durch Stauchung und die Eigendynamik inneren Widerstands. Wie ausrangierte Maschinenteile wenden sich die Greifarme zueinander, fassen jedoch ins Leere. Das Objekt ist nicht frei von martialischem Drängen. Ein dramatisches Licht- und Schattenspiel, das an kriegerisches Gefecht erinnert, vollzieht sich über der Kopfhöhe des Betrachters. Der Mitbegründer der *Skulptur Projekte Münster*, Klaus Bussmann, das Ehepaar Chillida und Dorothea und Martin van der Koelen sind unter dem Objekt in Spanien zu sehen. /
The sculpture is the result of compression and the momentum of inner resistance. Like discarded machine components, they extend their arms toward one another, yet reach into nothingness. The work is not free from martial urges. A dramatic interplay of light and shadows, reminiscent of a wartime battle, takes place above the head of the observer. Co-founder of the Sculpture Projects Münster, Klaus Bussmann on the right, Eduardo Chillida and his wife, and Dorothea and Martin van der Koelen are seen beneath the sculpture in Spain.

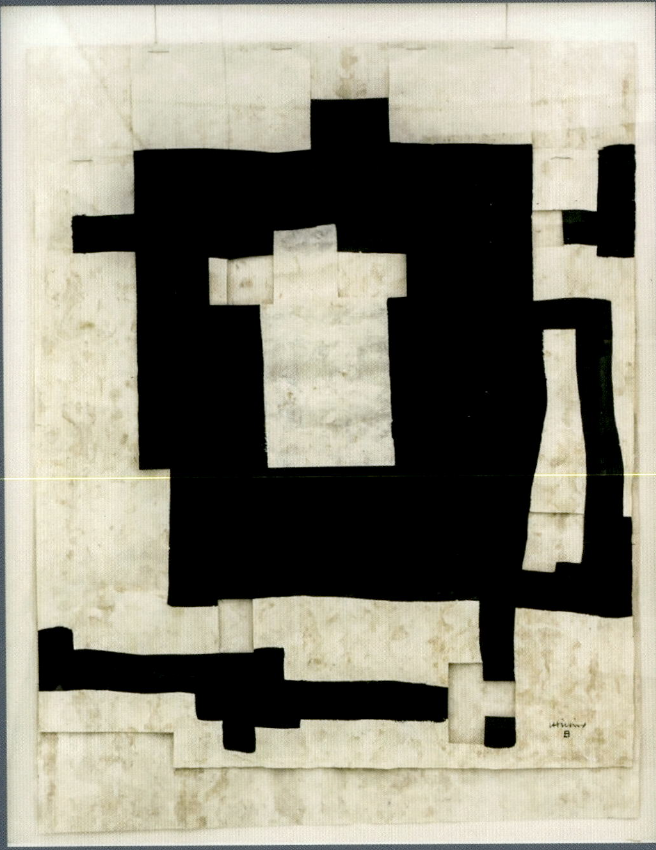

52

The image consists of several layers. Windows have been cut out, opening up empty space and allowing for a further look at the lower image layers. Like thin curtains, the opaque leaves hang down from seams. The elements of the image are influenced by real tractive forces. As in the sculpture and architecture, supports and weights are used. Accordingly, Chillida calls this series *Gravitations*. This *Gravitacion* dominates a black square. It is placed in the centre with much contrast, yet has a slight appearance. Some sides depict geometric stratifications of the black ink frame. The subject remains a mystery. It has the appearance of an archaeological excavation through sandy sediments. At the same time, the brownish paper is reminiscent of archaic masonry or the remainders of a faded fresco.

53
——

Eduardo Chillida
Ohne Titel
Untitled
1997
Radierung/Etching
31 × 23 cm
Dr. Dorothea van der Koelen, Mainz

Chillidas Grafiken konzentrieren den Raum. Im Kleinformat des Blattes besteht die Möglichkeit, Monumentalität zu erproben. Wie viel Raum und Leere braucht die Form, um sich als kraftvolle Setzung zu bewähren? / Chillida's graphic work concentrates on space. The small format of the sheet allows one to try monumentality. How much space and form does emptiness need in order to prove itself as a powerful expression?

54
——

Irene und Rolf Becker
Grusskarte 25. Oktober 2000/
Greeting card 10/25/2000
„Eduardo Chillida. Berlin. Im Spiegel der Presse 2000/2001", Hg./Ed. Wort & Bild Verlag Baierbrunn
22 × 18 cm
Beschriftung Rückseite:
„Vor dem Bundeskanzleramt wurde am 25. Oktober 2000 in Anwesenheit von Bundeskanzler Gerhard Schröder die Plastik ‚Berlin' der Öffentlichkeit vorgestellt. Diese wohl eindrucksvollste Arbeit des bedeutendsten lebenden europäischen Bildhauers Eduardo Chillida

52
——

Eduardo Chillida
Gravitación
1998
China Tusche auf Amate Papier/
Chinese ink on Amate paper
Dr. Dorothea van der Koelen, Mainz

Das Bild besteht aus mehreren Schichten. Aus ihm sind Fenster herausgeschnitten, die Leerstellen öffnen und Durchsicht auf untere Bildlagen ermöglichen. Wie dünne Vorhänge hängen die opaken Blätter an Nähten herab. Die Bildbestandteile werden durch reale Zugkräfte geprägt. Wie in Skulptur und Architektur kommen Tragen und Lasten ins Spiel. Entsprechend nennt Chillida diese Werkserie *Gravitationen*. Diese *Gravitacion* dominiert ein schwarzes Geviert. Es ist kontrastreich ins Zentrum gesetzt und doch karg an Erscheinung. An manchen Seiten finden sich geometrische Auslagerungen des schwarzen Tuscherahmens. Das Sujet gibt Rätsel auf. Es wirkt wie eine archäologische Grabung durch sandige Sedimente. Zugleich gemahnt das bräunliche Papier an archaisches Mauerwerk oder die Reste eines verblichenen Freskos. /

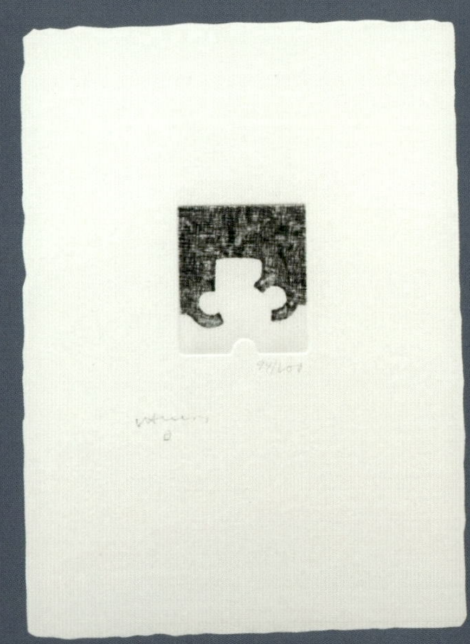

53

fand über die Grenzen Deutschlands hinaus begeisterte Zustimmung. Mit der beifolgenden Dokumentation, die im Buchhandel nicht erhältlich ist, möchten wir unseren Freunden eine besondere Freude bereiten. Irene und Rolf Becker"
Inscription on the reverse:
"In front of the Federal Chancellery, in the presence of Chancellor Gerhard Schröder, the sculpture *Berlin* was presented to the public on 25th October 2000. Probably the most impressive work of the most significant European sculptor alive, Eduardo Chillida, was received with great enthusiasm far beyond the borders of Germany. With the following documentation, which is not available in bookshops, we would like to give our friends a special treat. Irene and Rolf Becker"
Privatsammlung/Private collection, Baierbrunn

Der Verleger und Gründer des Wort & Bild Verlags Rolf Becker stiftete zusammen mit seiner Frau Irene Becker die Chillida-Plastik *Berlin*. Anlässlich der Enthüllung des Werkes wurde dieser Bildband mit Aufnahmen von Stephan Erfurt veröffentlicht. Der Titel *Berlin* gibt allein Auskunft über den Aufstellungsort. Der Skulptur selbst gegenüber bleibt er sprachlos. Die Medienberichte wiederholen den Wortlaut der offiziellen Pressestelle: Es sei ein „schlichter Titel". Darin zeigen sich die Grenzen öffentlicher Auftragskunst, die im Namen der Demokratie agiert. Anders als die pathetischen Kolosse des 19. Jahrhunderts, die unverhohlen von Sieg und Herrschaft erzählen, ist Chillidas Werk ob seiner Verhaltenheit und abstrakten Kargheit willkommen. /
The publisher and founder of the Wort & Bild publishing house, Rolf Becker and his wife Irene Becker, donated the Chillida sculpture *Berlin*. This illustrated book containing photographs by Stephan Erfurt was published on the occasion of the unveiling of the work. The title *Berlin* only reveals information about the location of the work. It says nothing about the sculpture. Media reports repeat the wording of the original press office: It is a "simple title". This is where publicly commissioned artwork in the name of Democracy has its limits. Unlike the pathos-laden colossuses of the 19th century that blatantly tell tales of victory and dominion, Chillida's work is welcome despite its reticence and abstract frugality.

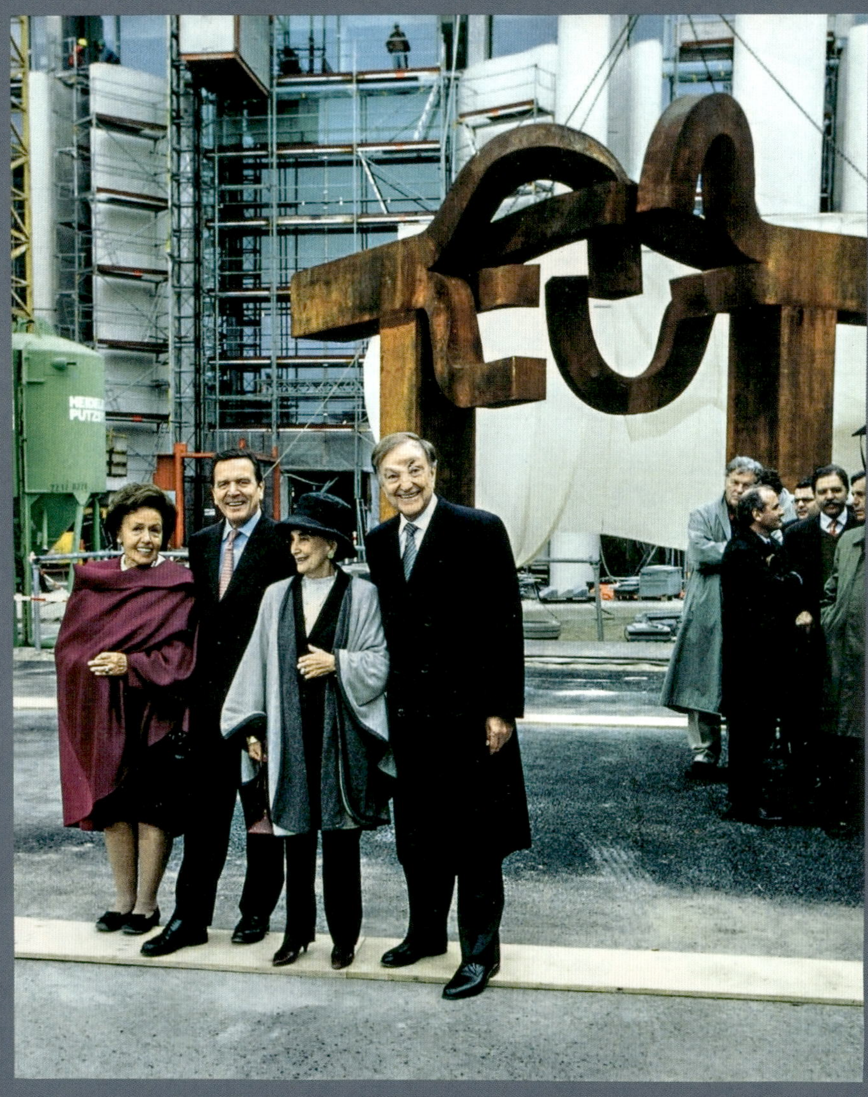

54

55
————

Bundeskanzler Gerhard Schröder
Öffentliche Ansprache 25. Oktober 2000,
Berlin Bundeskanzleramt
Abgedruckt in: „*Eduardo Chillida.*
Berlin. Im Spiegel der Presse 2000/2001",
hg. von Wort & Bild Verlag Baierbrunn
Privatsammlung, Baierbrunn

„[...] Für mich bedeutet es sehr viel, dass es die Kunst ist, die hier im neuen Kanzleramt als Erste ihren Platz einnimmt. Noch umgibt die Plastik das Bild einer Baustelle, das passt ganz gut zu Eduardo Chillidas Assoziationen zu Berlin – wird aber nicht mehr lange so bleiben. Schon bald wird das Kunstwerk eine Aufgabe haben: Es wird würdige Empfangskulisse sein für die zahlreichen in- und ausländischen Gäste wie auch für die Mitarbeiterinnen und Mitarbeiter, die hier ein- und ausgehen werden.

Und es wird sicher zur Bild-Ikone für das vereinigte Deutschland werden, verschmolzen mit dem Anblick des Kanzleramtes, ähnlich wie es Henry Moores Large Two Forms für die Bonner Republik waren. Und wenn die harmonischen, runden, weichen – fast bin ich geneigt zu sagen: die nach Konsens strebenden – Formen ein perfektes Symbol für die alte Bundesrepublik waren, so passt dieses kraftvolle, um Annäherung ringende, ja, dramatische Werk von Eduardo Chillida zur veränderten politischen Wirklichkeit der nunmehr von Berlin aus gestalteten vereinigten Republik.

Henry Moore hatte seine Plastik nicht für Bonn und nicht für die Politik konzipiert. [...] Auch Eduardo Chillida kam die Idee zu seiner

Skulptur nicht, weil er ein Werk für den politischen Raum vor Augen hatte. Gleichwohl ist sein erstes, klitzekleines Modell, die Vorarbeit zur Großplastik, ein künstlerischer Kommentar, der fast ideal den Aufbruch des vereinigten Deutschlands in einem neuen, offenen Europa versinnbildlicht. Anfang 1991 war Chillida hier, um seine große Ausstellung im Martin-Gropius-Bau zu eröffnen, gleich neben der eben abgeräumten Mauer. Tief beeindruckt von der Hoffnung und Freude über das wiedervereinte Deutschland, [...], schuf er nach seiner Rückkehr die ersten Skizzen.

Eduardo hat mir von diesem Gefühl berichtet, im März, als wir gemeinsam diesen Platz für die Berlin-Skulptur ausgesucht haben; [...]. Er sprach von dieser besonderen Stimmung, die er, der Baske aus dem äußersten Westen Europas, hier in Berlin, an der Nahtstelle zwischen Ost und West, damals hier gespürt hat: vom Aufbruch, von der Neugier, mit der die wieder gefundenen Landsleute aufeinander zugingen in der Überzeugung, dass man zusammen ein neues, ein wieder vollständiges Deutschland gestalten werde. Es ist dieser Dialog, den der Künstler hier in Eisen gegossen hat, die Aufforderung, aufeinander zuzugehen. [...]“

55

Federal Chancellor Gerhard Schröder
Public speech 25 October, 2000, Berlin
Federal Chancellery
Printed in: “*Eduardo Chillida. Berlin. In Spiegel der Presse 2000/2001*”, published by Wort & Bild Verlag Baierbrunn
Private collection, Baierbrunn

“[...] It is very important to me that it is this piece of art is the first to take its place here at the new Chancellery. The sculpture is still surrounded by a construction site, which generally fits in quite well with Eduardo Chillida’s associations with Berlin – but it will not stay like this for much longer. Soon the art work will assume its task: It will serve as a worthy backdrop when receiving guests from Germany and abroad as well as for the employees that come and go here.

And it is certain to become a visual icon for a unified Germany, merged with the view of the Chancellery, similar to that of Henry Moore’s *Large Two Forms* for the Bonn Republic. And if harmonious, round, soft – I am almost tempted to say: consensus-aspiring – forms were the perfect symbol for the old Federal Republic, this powerful work by Eduardo Chillida, dramatic and striving for

proximity, fits in perfectly with the changed political reality of a unified republic now orchestrated from Berlin.

Henry Moore did not make his sculpture for Bonn and not for the political world. [...] Neither did Eduardo Chillida base his work on a political setting. Nonetheless, his initial tiny miniature model, as a precursor to the large sculpture, was an artistic statement that virtually ideally symbolises the awakening of a unified Germany in a new and open Europe. Chillida visited Berlin early 1991 to open an exhibition at the Martin-Gropius-Bau right next to the just recently cleared away Berlin Wall. Deeply impressed by the hope and joy of a reunified Germany, [...], he created his very first sketches upon his return.

Eduardo told me about his feelings back then, in March, as we chose this location for the *Berlin* sculpture; [...]. He spoke of the special atmosphere, that he, the Basque from the western-most part of Europe felt while visiting Berlin, the junction between east and west: of the sense of awakening, the inquisitiveness with which compatriots approached one another, convinced that they would rebuild a unified Germany. This is the dialogue that the artist has cast in iron, the call for everyone to join together. [...]“

56

Eduardo Chillida
Windkamm
Peine del Viento
1977
Bucht von San Sebastian, Eisen

Kantige Zangen greifen in die Gischt. Sie stemmen sich gegen Wind, Wetter und Gezeiten. Die rostigen Arme, die horizontal gegen die Wellen ausgreifen, sind archaische Zeichen, die direkt im Fels verankert sind. Chillida setzt seine Windkämme direkt mit der Natur in Beziehung. Die rostroten Elemente werden angesprochen und der ewige Fluss von Zeit und Vergehen. Das geschmiedete Eisen und der klobige Fels bilden den harten Widerstand gegen die weichen Energien von Wasser und Wind. Für Berlin übernimmt Chillida die Formen, die er an der baskischen Küste und in der Natur erprobt. Anstatt jedoch sie aus unbehauenen Felsen vorragen zu lassen, setzt er sie auf Stelen. Das Kampfgeschehen spielt sich kopfüber in ungreifbarer Höhe ab. Die Horizontalen erhalten zwei schlanke Sockel. Zugleich verlieren die Berliner Windkämme ihr symbolisches Gegenüber, die Witterung, und beginnen gegeneinander und ineinander zu arbeiten. /

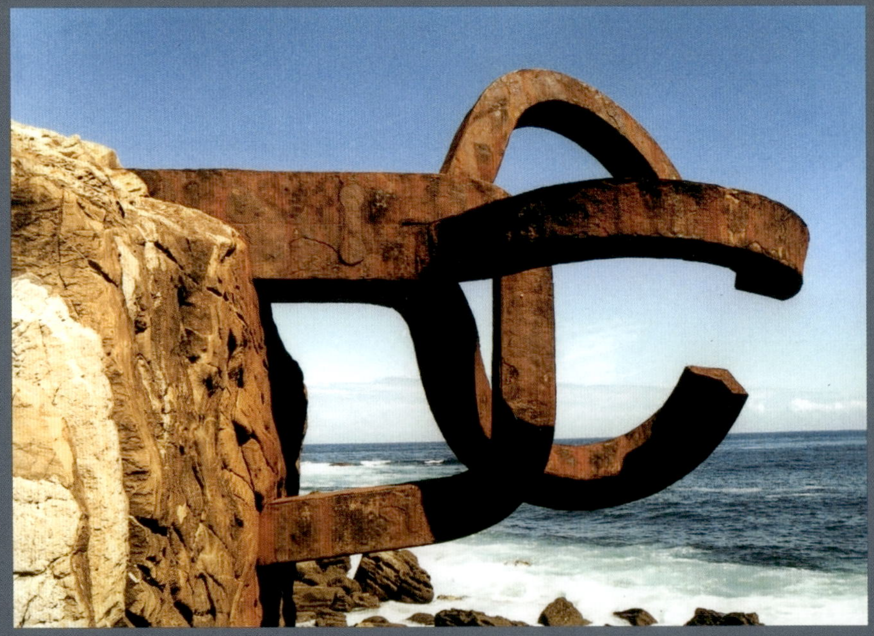

56

58

Eduardo Chillida
Parmenides – Le Poeme
1999
Serie von sechs Grafiken /
A series of six graphic works
50 × 40 cm
Dr. Dorothea van der Koelen, Mainz

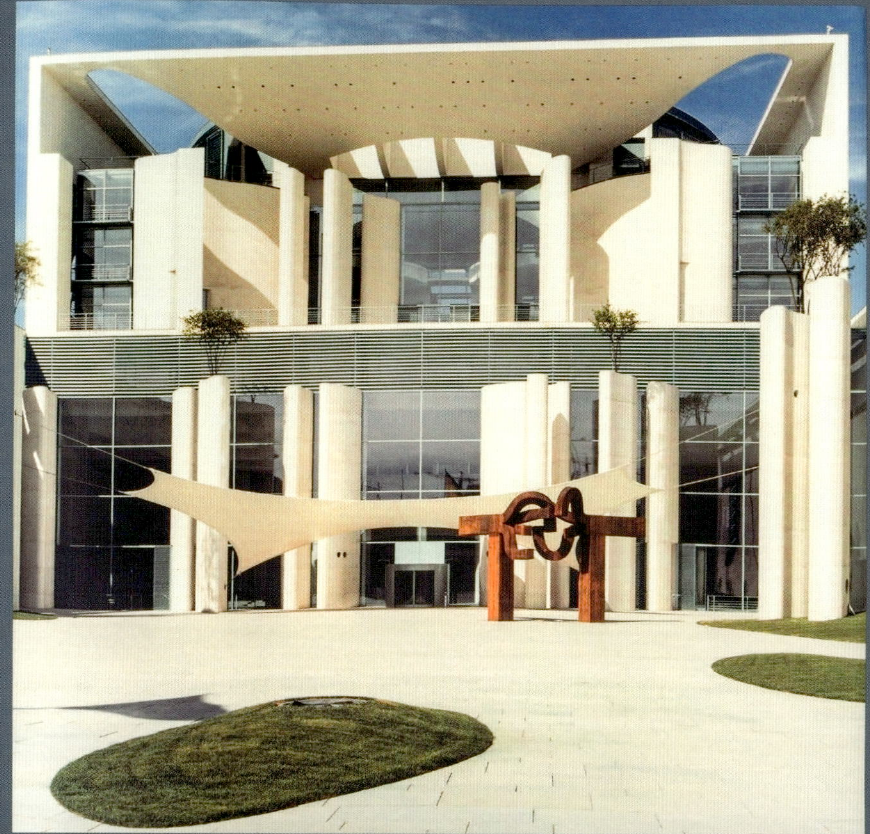

57

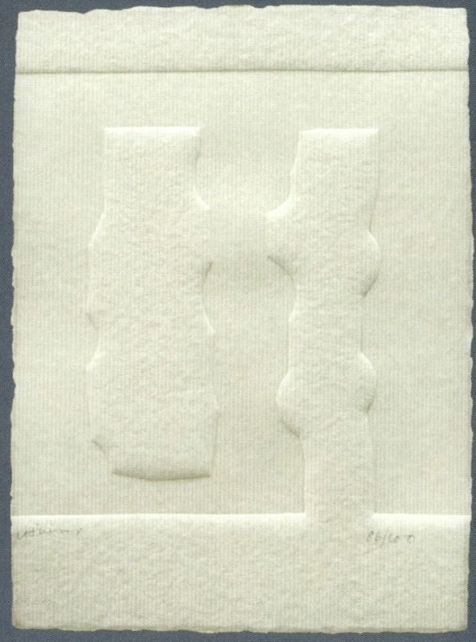

58.1

Angular pliers reach into the spray. They are
fighting against the wind, the weather and the
seasons. The rusty arms that reach horizontally
toward the waves are archaic symbols directly
connected to the cliffs. Chillida establishes a
direct relationship between his *Wind Combs*
and nature. The rusty red elements, as well as
the eternal flow of time and decay. The forged
iron and bold cliff form a hard resistance
against the soft energies of water and wind.
Chillida uses the shapes that he had tested on
the Basque coast and in nature in Berlin.
However, instead of having them protrude
from natural cliffs, he places them on columns.
The battle takes place overhead and at a reach-
able height. The horizontal objects receive two
slim pedestals. At the same time, the wind
combs in Berlin lose their opposite positioning,
the weather and start working against each
other and within one another.

Colour photograph on book cover
Privatsammlung / Private collection,
Baierbrunn

Eduardo Chillida entwirft die Stabformen
seines abstrakten Gebildes vor dem Bundeskanzleramt mit Andeutungen an die Skulptur von Henry Moore in Bonn. Die formalen
Beziehungen zwischen den zwei Segmenten
und der Dialog mit der Architektur sind
offenkundige Referenzen. Chillida, der wie
Moore an der für die moderne Skulptur
maßgeblichen documenta 2 (1959) in Kassel
beteiligt war, ersetzt die schwellenden Massen
Moores durch kantige und spröde Stabformen. Er zeigt monumentale Rohlinge aus
Schmiedeeisen, die sich in ihren lagernden
Waagrechten zu kräftigen Krallen auswach-
sen. /
Eduardo Chillida designed the rod-shaped
forms of his abstract sculpture in front of the
Federal Chancellery with references to the
sculpture by Henry Moore in Bonn. The formal relationship between the two segments
and the dialogue with the architecture are
obvious references. Chillida who, like Moore,
was significantly involved in documenta 2
(1959) in Kassel, an event which proved to be

57

*Eduardo Chillida. Berlin. Im Spiegel der
Presse 2000 / 2001*
Wort & Bild Verlag (Hg. / Ed.)
Farbfotografie auf Buchumschlag /

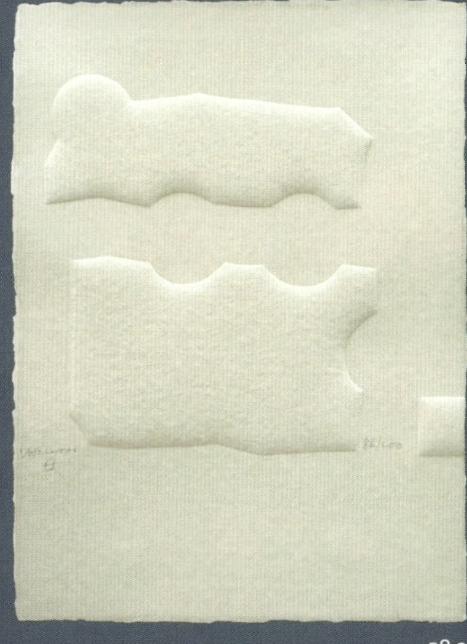

58.2

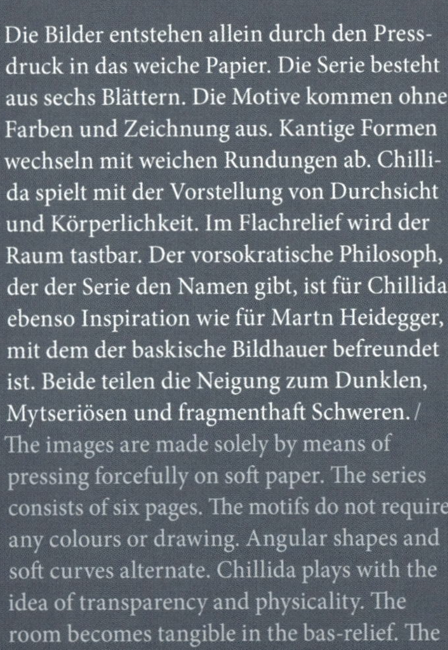

59

Die Bilder entstehen allein durch den Press-druck in das weiche Papier. Die Serie besteht aus sechs Blättern. Die Motive kommen ohne Farben und Zeichnung aus. Kantige Formen wechseln mit weichen Rundungen ab. Chilli-da spielt mit der Vorstellung von Durchsicht und Körperlichkeit. Im Flachrelief wird der Raum tastbar. Der vorsokratische Philosoph, der der Serie den Namen gibt, ist für Chillida ebenso Inspiration wie für Martn Heidegger, mit dem der baskische Bildhauer befreundet ist. Beide teilen die Neigung zum Dunklen, Mytseriösen und fragmenthaft Schweren. / The images are made solely by means of pressing forcefully on soft paper. The series consists of six pages. The motifs do not require any colours or drawing. Angular shapes and soft curves alternate. Chillida plays with the idea of transparency and physicality. The room becomes tangible in the bas-relief. The pre-Socratic philosopher, who lends the se-ries his name, is just as much an inspiration for Chillida as for Martin Heidegger, a friend of the Basque sculptor. Both share a disposi-tion towards dark, mysterious, and heavy fragments.

59

—

Postkarte / Postcard
10,5 × 14,6 cm
Fotografie / Photograph:
Jürgen Henkelmann
Skoworonski & Koch Verlag,
Berlin
Privatbesitz / Private Collection, Mainz

Dies ist eine kommerzielle Postkarte, deren kommerzieller Erfolg jedoch ausbleibt. Sie wird eingestellt. Der Verleger übermittelt den Lagerrestbestand von fünf Stück. Das Motiv ermangelt der Nachfrage.

In Deutschland wird Chillidas Werk von öffentlichen Auftraggebern geschätzt. Vor der Nationalgalerie in Berlin steht die Skulptur *Krieger* (1975), die eine ähnliche Konstruktion wie *Berlin* aufweist. Für die Frankfurter Taunusanlage entwirft Chillida eine Skulptur mit dem Titel *Toleranz durch Dialog* (1986). Es ist ein begehbares Objekt aus Beton. Auf dem Platz des Westfälischen Friedens in Münster (1993) errichtet er zwei formalisierte Bänke aus Eisen. Auf dem Rasen vor der Pinakothek der Moderne in München steht die dreistrahlige Skulptur *Buscando la Luz* (1997), ebenfalls eine Spende von Rolf Becker. /
This is a commercial postcard, which however did not achieve any commercial success. It

Z
HO

BERLIN
RO
WIT
© KARTENEDITION PAWLOWSKI SOUVENIRS & POSTKARTEN BERLIN · Foto: G. Schneider
Deutschland
5 JAHR 06
Naturschutz www.de
Joseph von Fraunhofer
www.Die-Marke-BERLIN.de
www.berlin-tourist-information.de

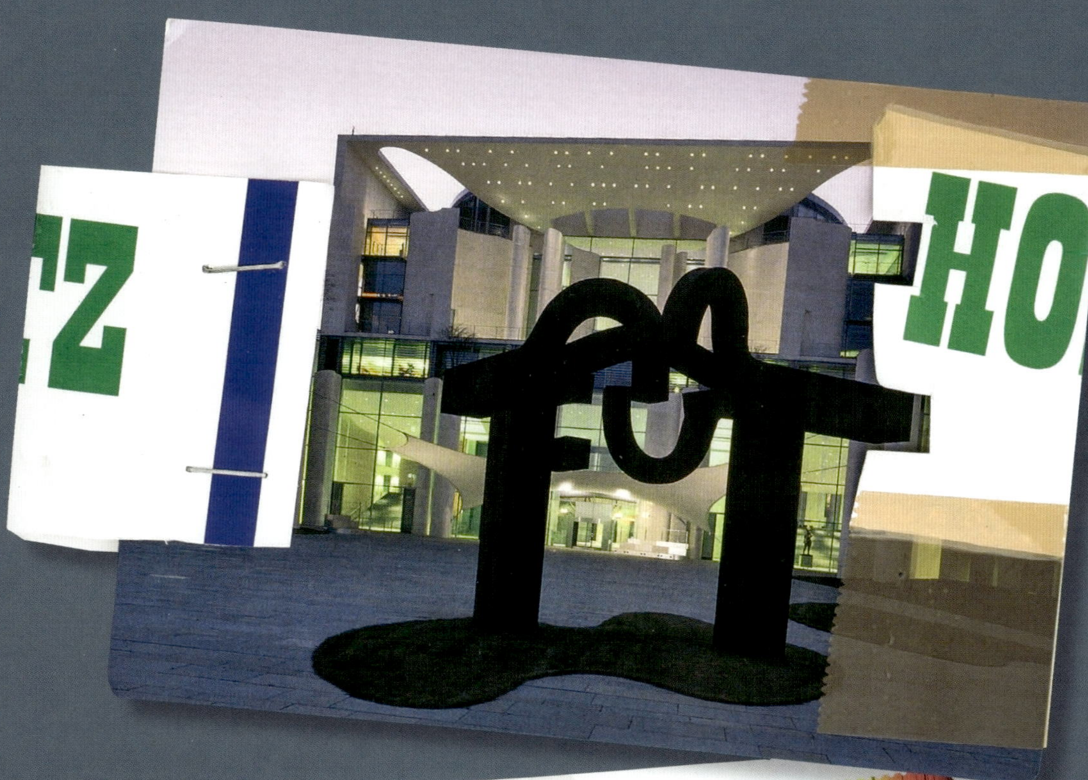

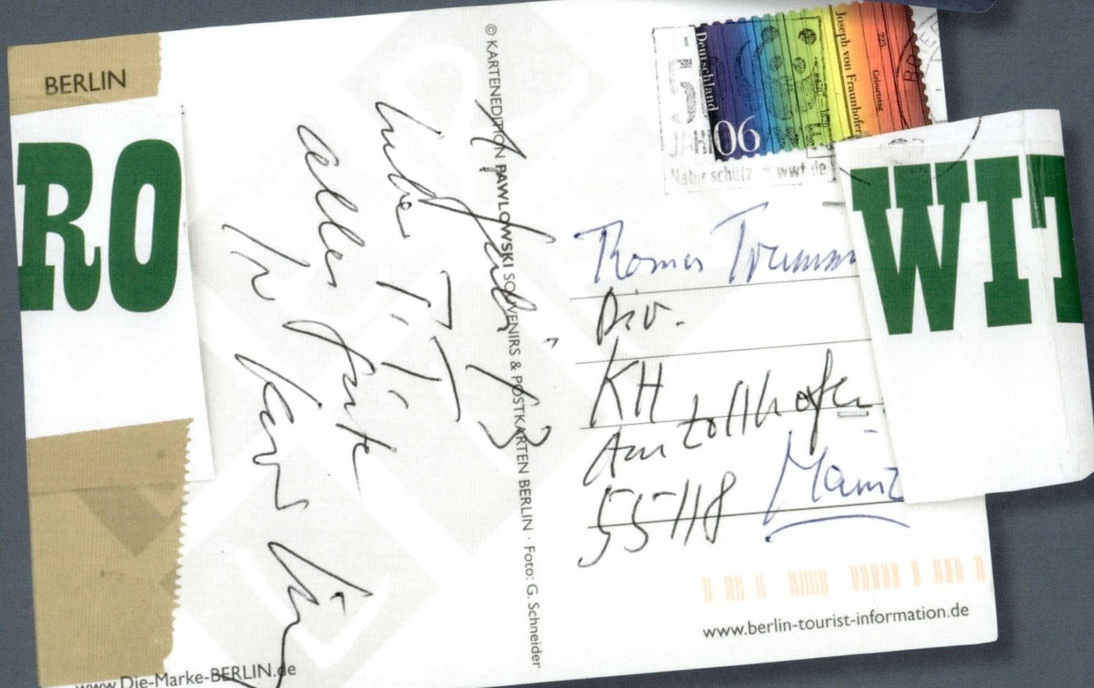

60

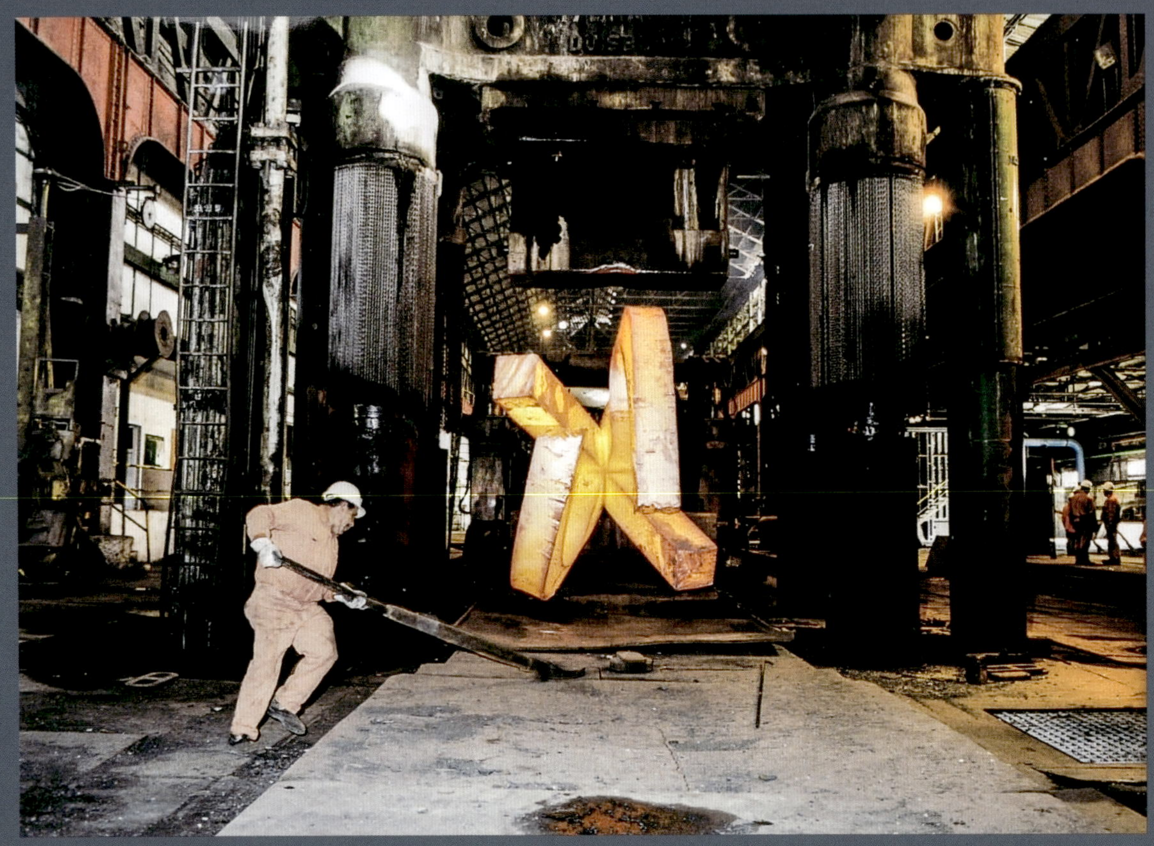

61.1

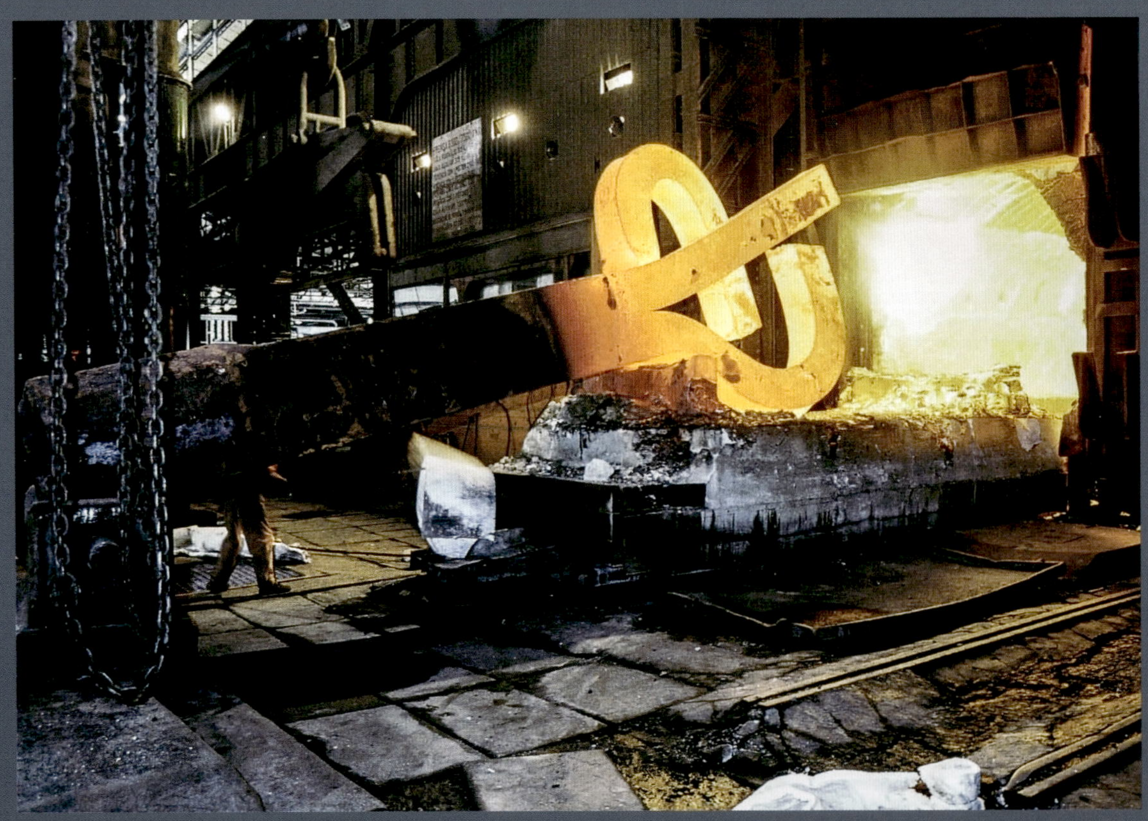

61.2

was discontinued. The publisher passes on the remaining stock of five pieces. There is no demand for the image.

In Germany, Chillida's work is highly esteemed by public commissioning bodies. His sculpture *Warrior* (1975), which is in the Nationalgalerie in Berlin, has a structure similar to that of *Berlin*. For Frankfurt's Taunusanlage he designed a sculpture entitled *Tolerance through Dialogue* (1986). It is an accessible object made of concrete. He created two formalised benches made of iron on the Platz des Westfälischen Friedens in Münster (1993). On the lawns of the Pinakothek of Modern Art in Munich stands the triple sculpture *Buscando la Luz* (1997), also donated by Rolf Becker.

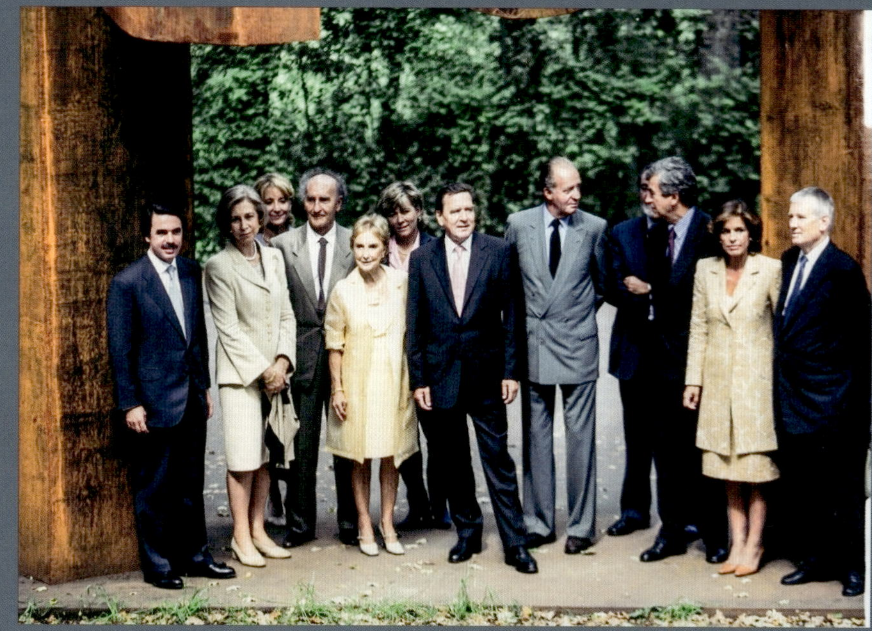

62

60

Kasper König
Collage, Ansichtkarte adressiert an Thomas D. Trummer 2. Juli 2013
Collage, postcard addressed to Thomas D. Trummer, 2 July 2013
Privatbesitz / Private Collection, Mainz

Kasper König verschickt häufig selbst gestaltete Postkarten. Die vorliegende wurde als Glückwunschkarte zu dieser Ausstellung verschickt. Sie zeigt die Fassade des Kanzleramtes mit der Skulptur von Chillida. An den Schmalseiten ist eine Textschleife eingeklebt. Sie ist mit *HOR* und *WITZ* zu lesen. Dies ist als eine Anspielung auf die Geschichte monumentaler Plastik und Auftragskunst zu deuten, deren Horror nicht selten in Komik umschlägt. Es ist auch Verweis auf den New Yorker Künstler Jonathan Horowitz (geb. 1966), der sich in seinem Werk mit den Zeichen von Politik und Macht auseinandersetzt. /
Kasper König frequently sends self-made postcards. This postcard was sent to congratulate on this exhibition. It depicts the façade of the Chancellery with Chillida's sculpture. A band of text is glued onto the narrow sides. It is to be read as *HOR* and *WITZ*. It is a reference to the history of monumental sculptures and commissioned art, where interpretations of horror have been known to turn comedic. It is also a reference to New York artist Jonathan Horowitz (born 1966), whose work deals with the symbolism of politics and power.

61

Schmieden der Plastik „Berlin"
Forging of the sculpture "Berlin"
Farbfotografien / Colour Photographs
je 21 × 30 cm
Dr. Dorothea van der Koelen, Mainz

Die Aufnahmen aus dem Hochofen zeigen den aufwändigen Herstellungsprozess. Chillida fertigt weder Vorzeichnungen noch Modelle an. Seine plastischen Ideen entwickeln sich aus einer prozesshaften Raumvorstellung und der Substanzialität des Materials Eisen, das im Zustand extremer Erhitzung biegsam wird. So werden die beiden stählernen Kanteisen wie Schmiedezangen in den Ofen eingeführt, um noch in glühendem Zustand mit einem schweren Bolzen zu rundlichen Gliedern gekrümmt zu werden. /
The photos of the furnace depict the elaborate manufacturing process. Chillida neither produces preliminary sketches nor models. His sculptural ideas are developed on the basis of a process-related idea of space and the substantiality of iron, which becomes malleable when extremely hot. Thus, square iron bars are inserted into the furnace and, while still in a glowing state, are bent into curved elements with forging tongs.

62

„Berlin" in Hernani, Spanien
"Berlin" in Hernani, Spain
Farbfotografie 12. September 2000 /
Colour photograph 9/12/2000
21 × 29,4 cm
Frank Ossenbrink

Auf dieser Fotografie sieht man Eduardo Chillida mit seiner Frau Pilar neben Gerhard Schröder, König Juan Carlos sowie Felipe Gonzales und das Stifterehepaar Irene und Rolf Becker unter Chillidas Skulptur *Berlin*, bevor sie nach Deutschland und an ihren endgültigen Aufstellungsort gebracht wurde. /
This image depicts Eduardo Chillida with his wife, Pilar, standing next to Gerhard Schröder, King Juan Carlos, Felipe Gonzales, and donors Irene and Rolf Becker beneath Chillida's sculpture *Berlin*, before it was shipped to its final destination in Germany.

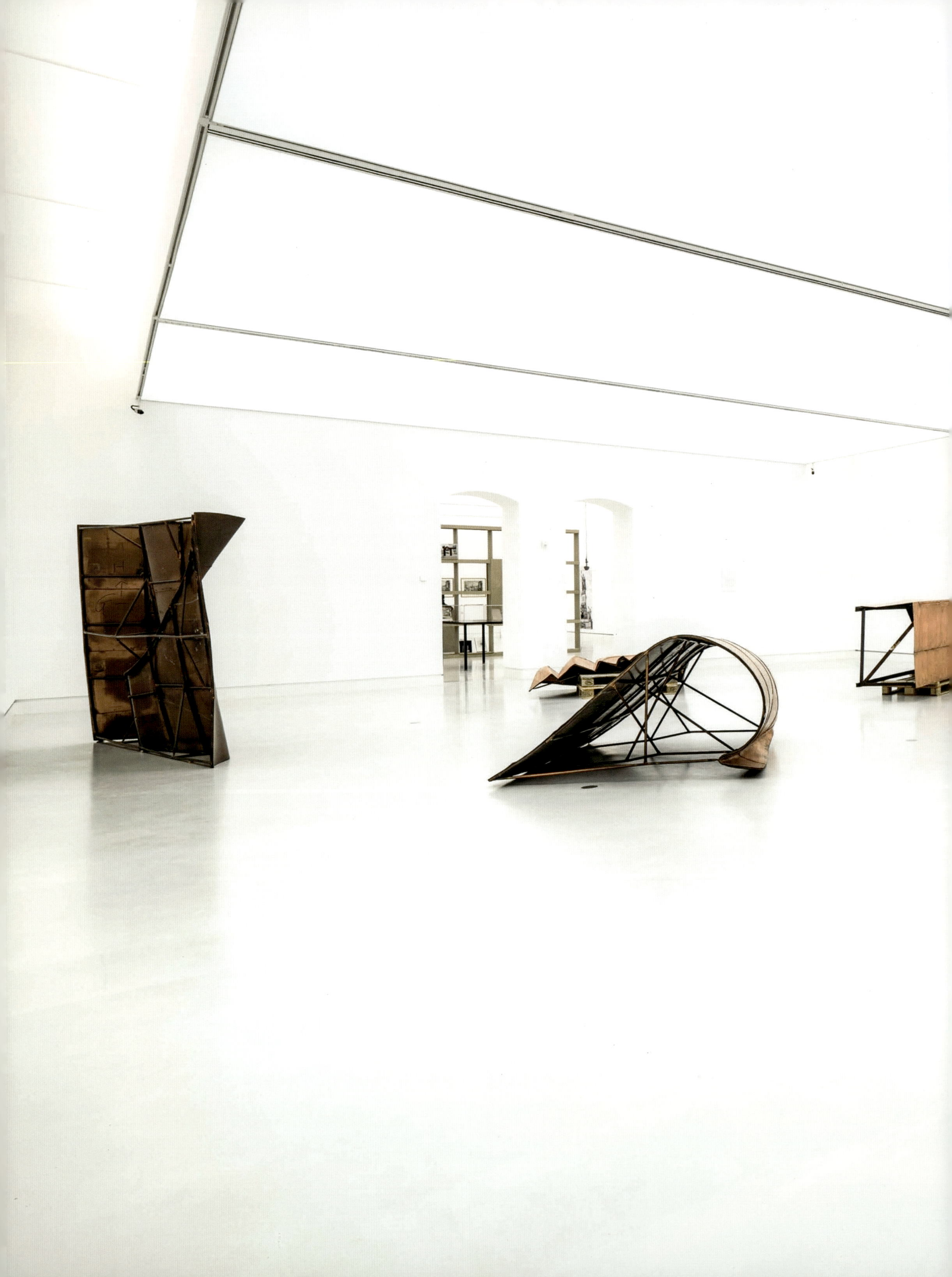

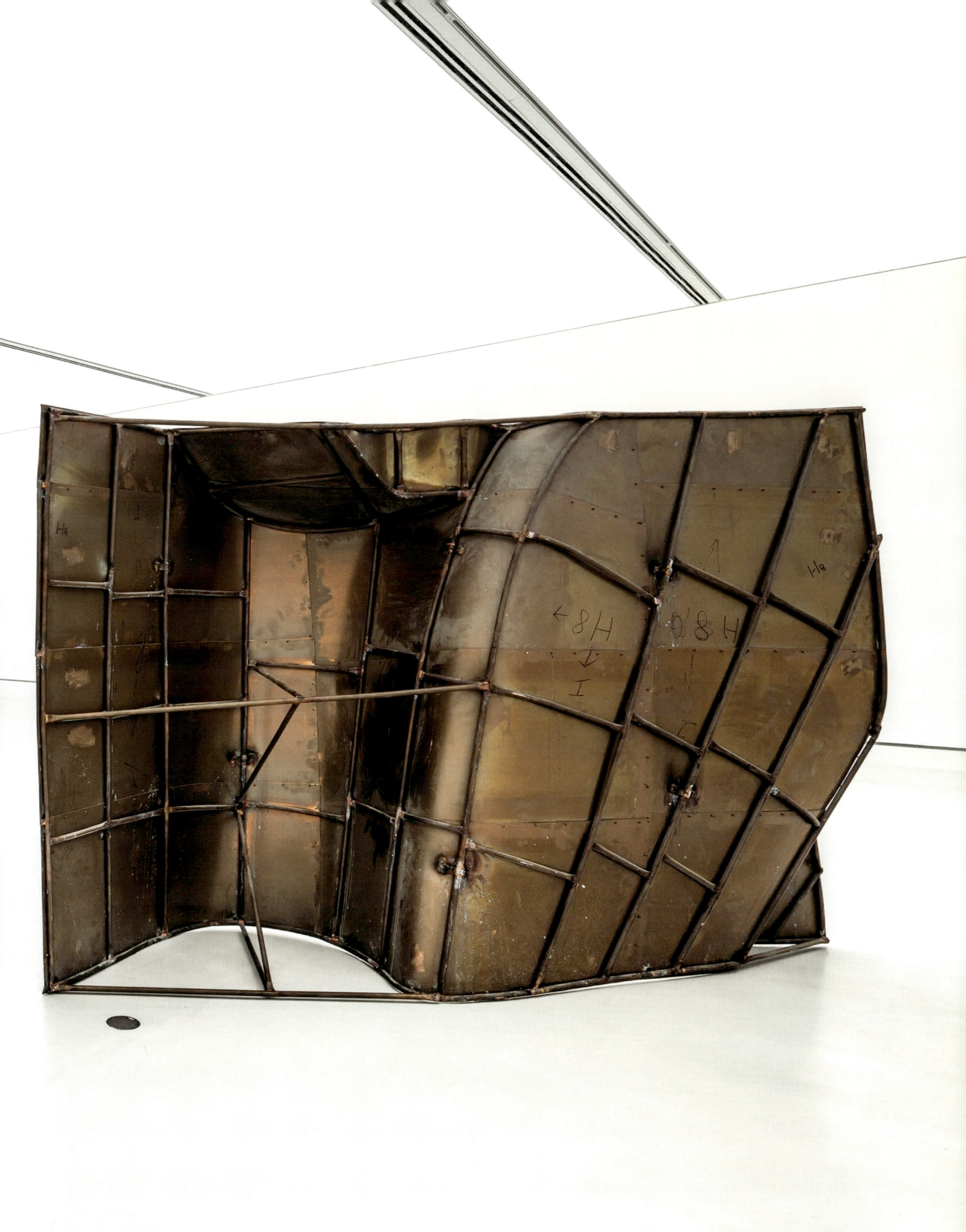

Danh Vo
We the people

——

2011 – 2013, Kupfer, verschiedene Maße/
Copper, variable dimensions

ca. 200 × 200 × 100 cm

Courtesy: Danh Vo, Chantal Crousel Gallery, Paris

We the people … sind die ersten Worte der Präambel der Verfassung der Vereinigten Staaten (Abb. Seite 74, 75/77 – 81). In ihr wird die Grundordnung der Gewaltentrennung festgelegt. Danh Vo, 1975 geboren, stammt ursprünglich aus Vietnam. Im Kindesalter kommt er als Bootsflüchtling nach Europa, wächst in Dänemark auf und lebt heute in London. Seine monumentalen Skulpturen aus Kupfer sind maßstabsgetreue Nachbildungen einzelner Teile der amerikanischen Freiheitsstatue. Die *Statue of Liberty* des aus Colmar stammenden Frédéric Auguste Bartholdi ist etwa gleich alt wie die *Germania*. Die Kupferfragmente von Danh Vo beziehen sich auf die historischen Ideen der *Freiheitsstatue*, wie Grundrecht, Mündigkeit und Demokratie. In der Kunsthalle Mainz sind sie auf Paletten gelegt oder an Wände gelehnt. Lose liegen sie in den weißen Räumen wie in einem sterilen Lager. Ursprünglich stammen sie aus Shanghai. Seitdem sind sie auf Reisen. Danh Vo legt sie an vielen Orten in der Welt ab. Herkunft, Gebrauch und Abnutzung sind ihnen abzulesen. An manchen finden sich Abdrucke von Spanngurten, an vielen die Spuren von Schweißnaht und Bearbeitung. Die Vorderansichten zeigen die Faltenwürfe des berühmten Vorbildes. Große Wölbungen treten hervor. Ursprünglich wurde die *Freiheitsstatue* in Teilen von Frankreich nach New York verschifft und neben Ellis Island, der historischen Sammelstelle für Immigranten, aufgestellt. Danh Vo erinnert an Asyl, Migration und die symbolischen Zeichen der Selbstbestimmung. Er zeigt sie jedoch nicht siegesgewiss, sondern als zerbrechliche Wesen. Es geht um Heimatlosigkeit, Entfremdung, Waren- und Menschenverkehr im Zeitalter von Entrechtung und Globalisierung. Dabei bekommen die Skulpturen konkrete politische Aktualität. Die Ausstellung in Mainz wird am 4. Juli 2013 eröffnet, dem amerikanischen Nationalfeiertag und Tag der Erinnerung an die Unabhängigkeit im Jahr 1776. Nur wenige Tage zuvor steigert sich die Affäre um den ehemaligen Geheimdienstmitarbeiter, Edward Snowden, zu beunruhigender Brisanz. Snowden hat Hongkong verlassen, sitzt jedoch, von den amerikanischen Behörden gesucht, im Transitbereich des Moskauer Flughafens fest. Er ist eine staatenlose Existenz ohne Ort, Gesetz und Gemeinschaft.

We the people … are the first words of the preamble to the Constitution of the United States (Ill. pp. 74, 75/77 – 81). It defines the basic principles of the separation of power. Danh Vo, who was born in 1975, is originally from Vietnam. He came to Europe as a child as one of the boat people, grew up in Denmark, and currently lives in London. His monumental sculptures made of copper are true-to-scale copies of the individual parts of the American *Statue of Liberty*. The *Statue of Liberty*, by Frédéric Auguste Bartholdi of Colmar, is about the same age as *Germania*. Danh Vo's copper fragments are a reference to the historical principles of the *Statue of Liberty*, such as fundamental rights, responsibility, and democracy. At Kunsthalle Mainz, they are placed on pallets or lean against walls. There are lots of them in the white rooms, like in a sterile storage hold. The fragments originally came from Shanghai. They have been travelling ever since. Danh Vo installs them at many locations around the world. They show signs of their origin, usage, and wear. Some have impressions made by lashing straps; many have traces of welding joints and processing. The front views depict the folds of the original statue. Large bulges protrude. Originally, the *Statue of Liberty* was shipped from France to New York in parts and then installed adjacent to Ellis Island, the historical immigrant inspection station. Danh Vo evokes asylum, migration, and the symbols of self-determination. Yet, his rendition is not one of confident victory, but of a fragile being. It is about homelessness, alienation, the movement of goods and people in an age of disfranchisement and globalisation. In this sense, the sculptures obtain a concrete political topicality. The exhibition opened on the 4th of July 2013, the American national holiday and day of remembrance of the nation's independence in 1776. Just a few days earlier, the affair concerning former CIA employee Edward Snowden developed to disturbing proportions. Snowden had left Hong Kong, and, being persecuted by US authorities, was stuck in the transit area of Moscow Airport. His is a stateless existence without place, law, and community.

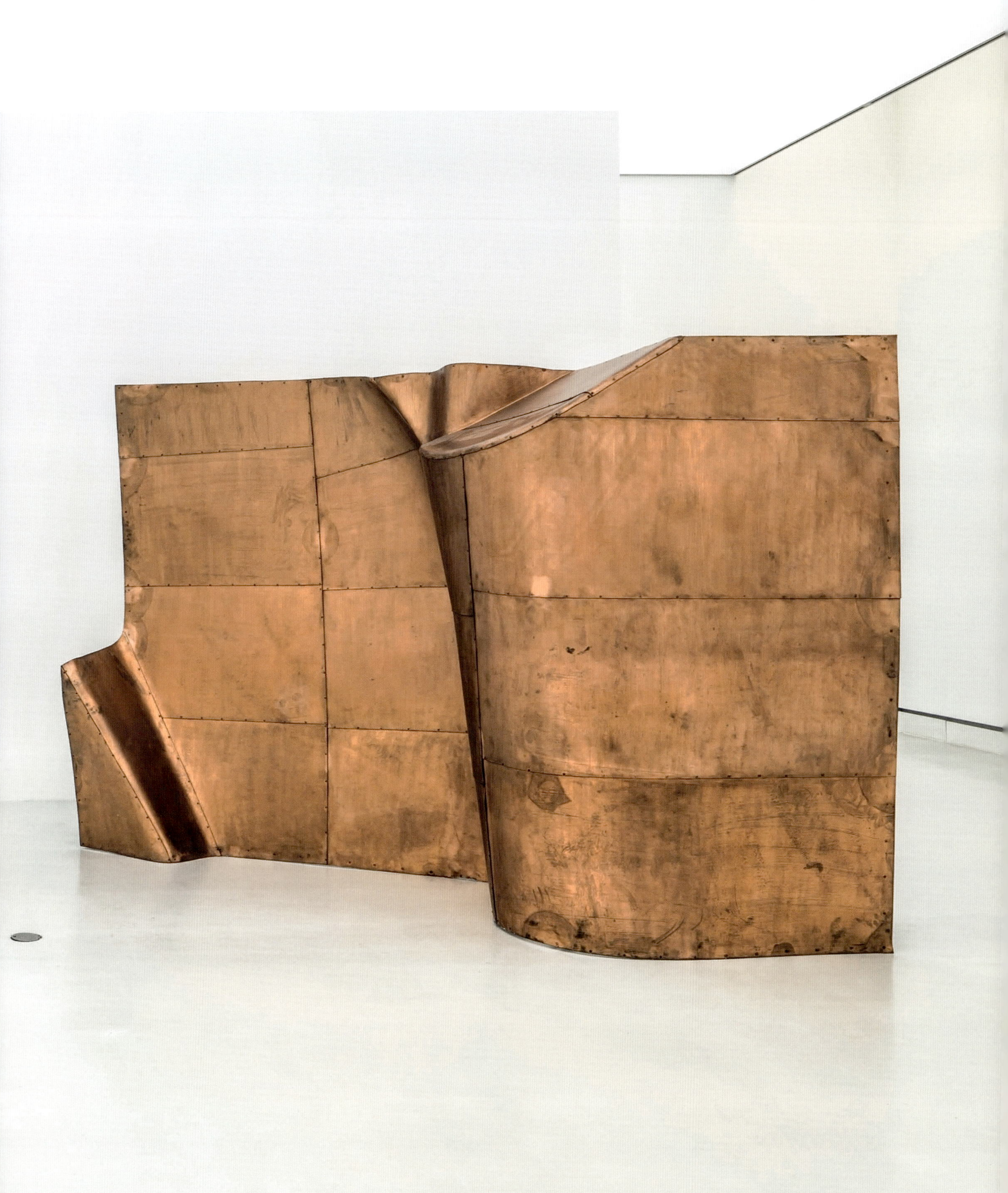

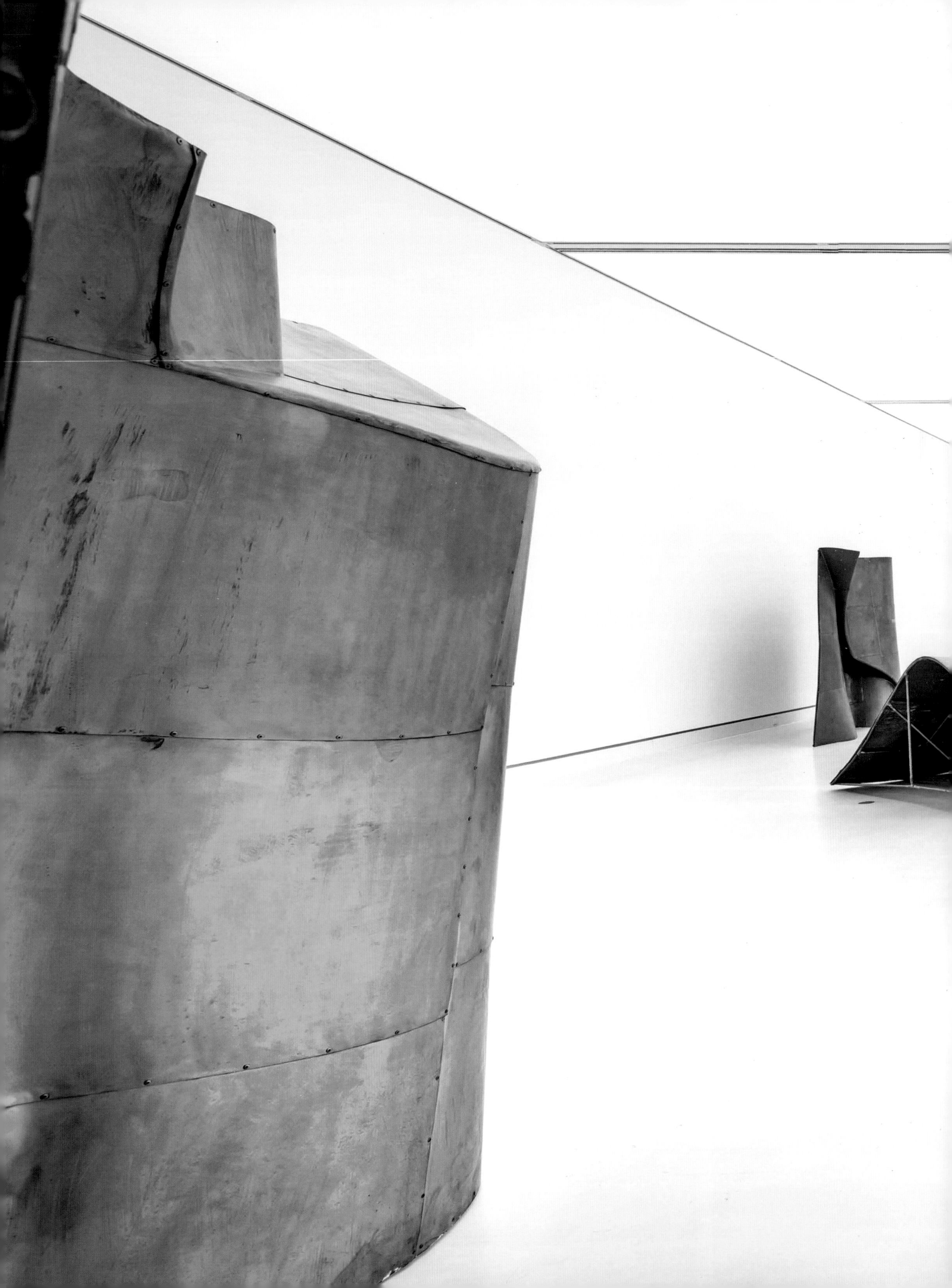

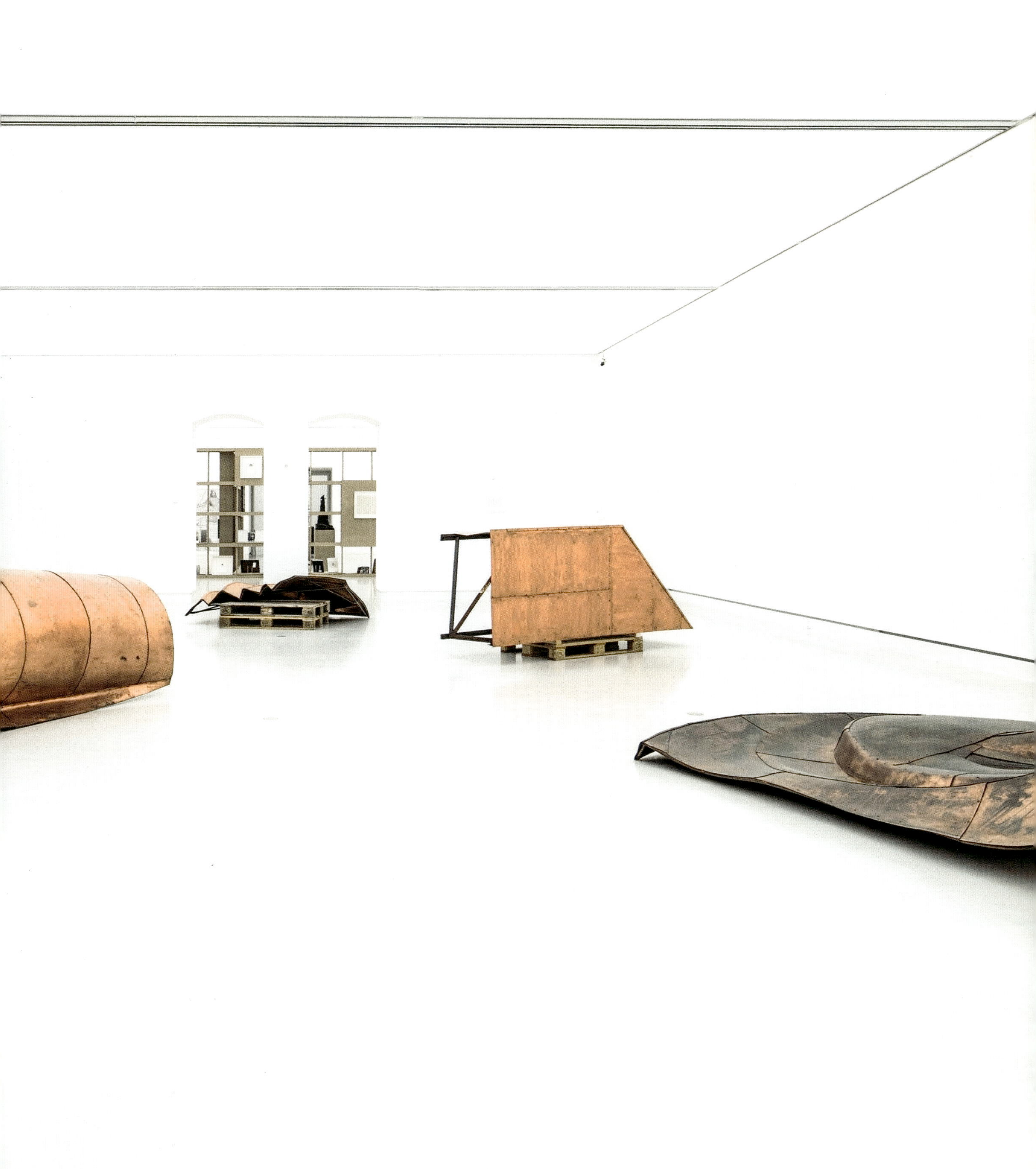

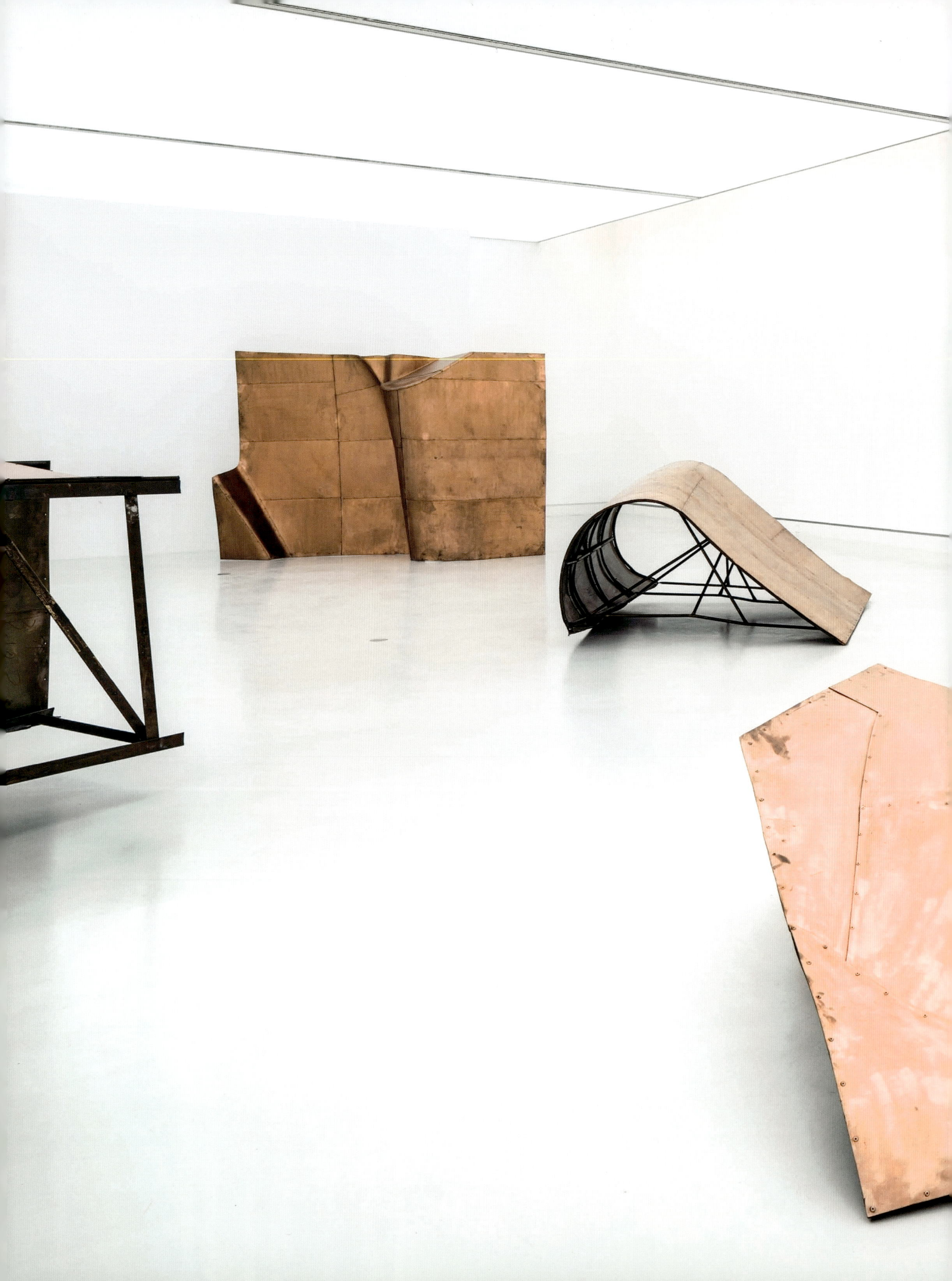

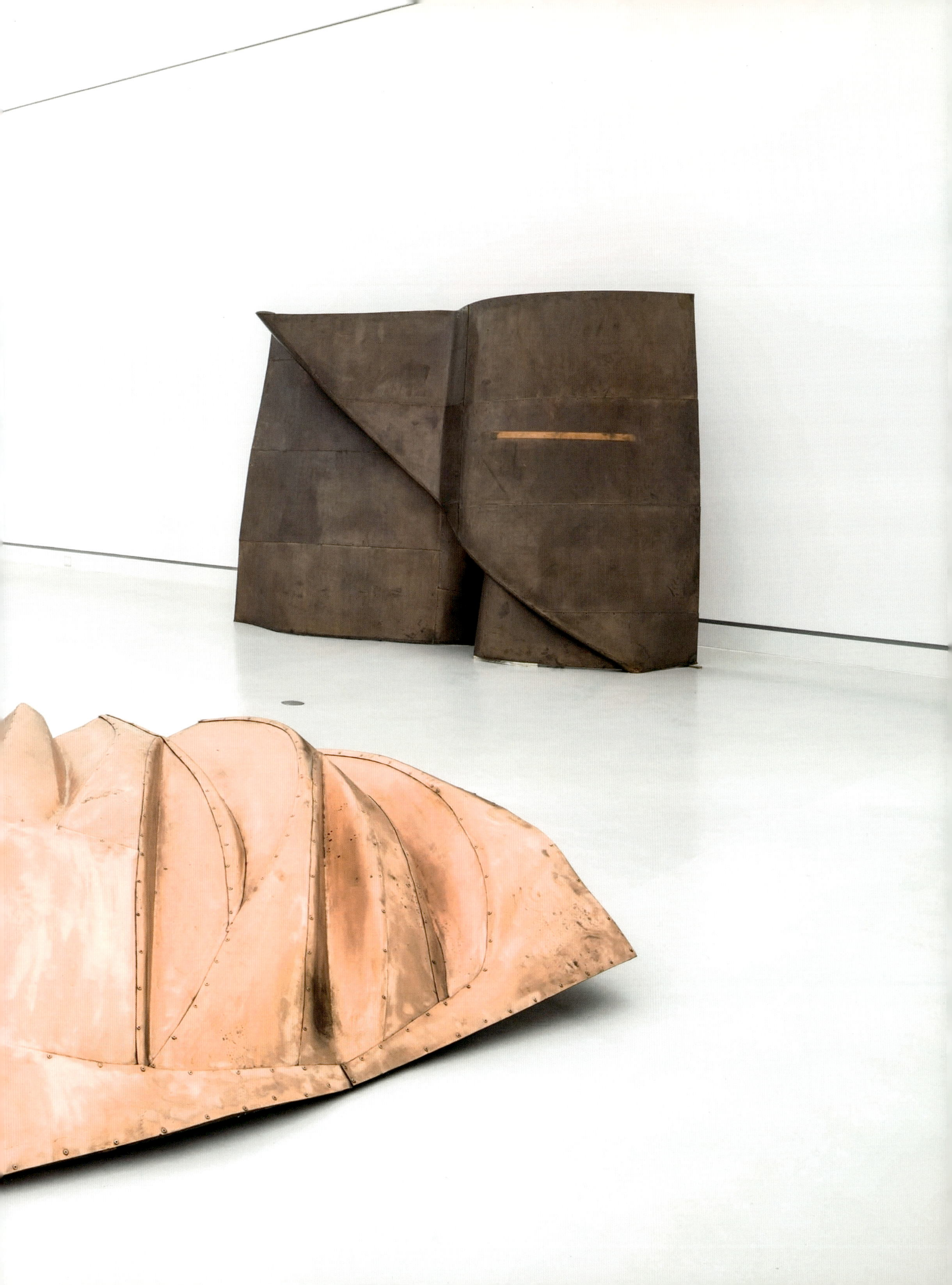

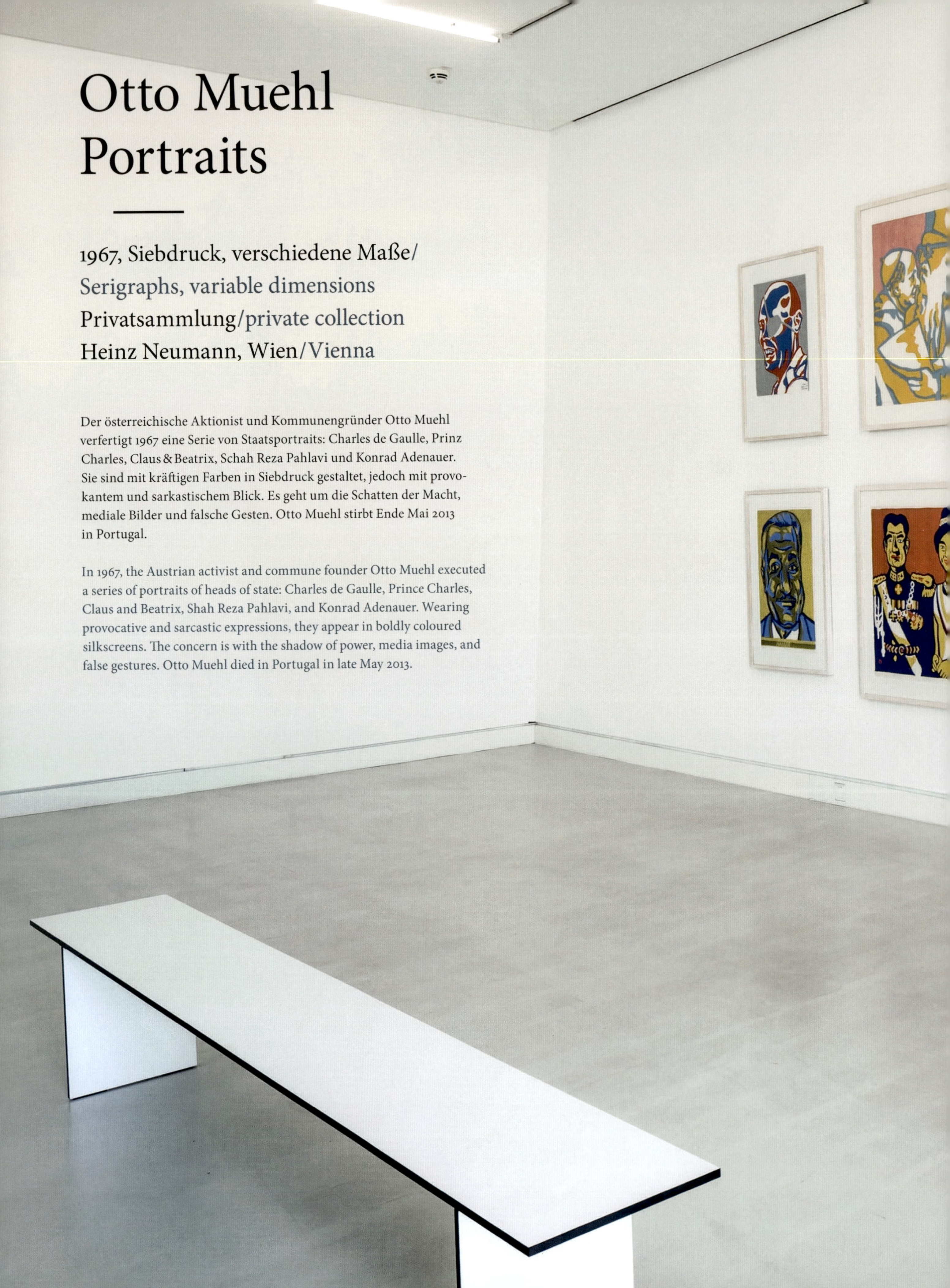

Otto Muehl
Portraits

1967, Siebdruck, verschiedene Maße/
Serigraphs, variable dimensions
Privatsammlung/private collection
Heinz Neumann, Wien/Vienna

Der österreichische Aktionist und Kommunengründer Otto Muehl
verfertigt 1967 eine Serie von Staatsportraits: Charles de Gaulle, Prinz
Charles, Claus & Beatrix, Schah Reza Pahlavi und Konrad Adenauer.
Sie sind mit kräftigen Farben in Siebdruck gestaltet, jedoch mit provo-
kantem und sarkastischem Blick. Es geht um die Schatten der Macht,
mediale Bilder und falsche Gesten. Otto Muehl stirbt Ende Mai 2013
in Portugal.

In 1967, the Austrian activist and commune founder Otto Muehl executed
a series of portraits of heads of state: Charles de Gaulle, Prince Charles,
Claus and Beatrix, Shah Reza Pahlavi, and Konrad Adenauer. Wearing
provocative and sarcastic expressions, they appear in boldly coloured
silkscreens. The concern is with the shadow of power, media images, and
false gestures. Otto Muehl died in Portugal in late May 2013.

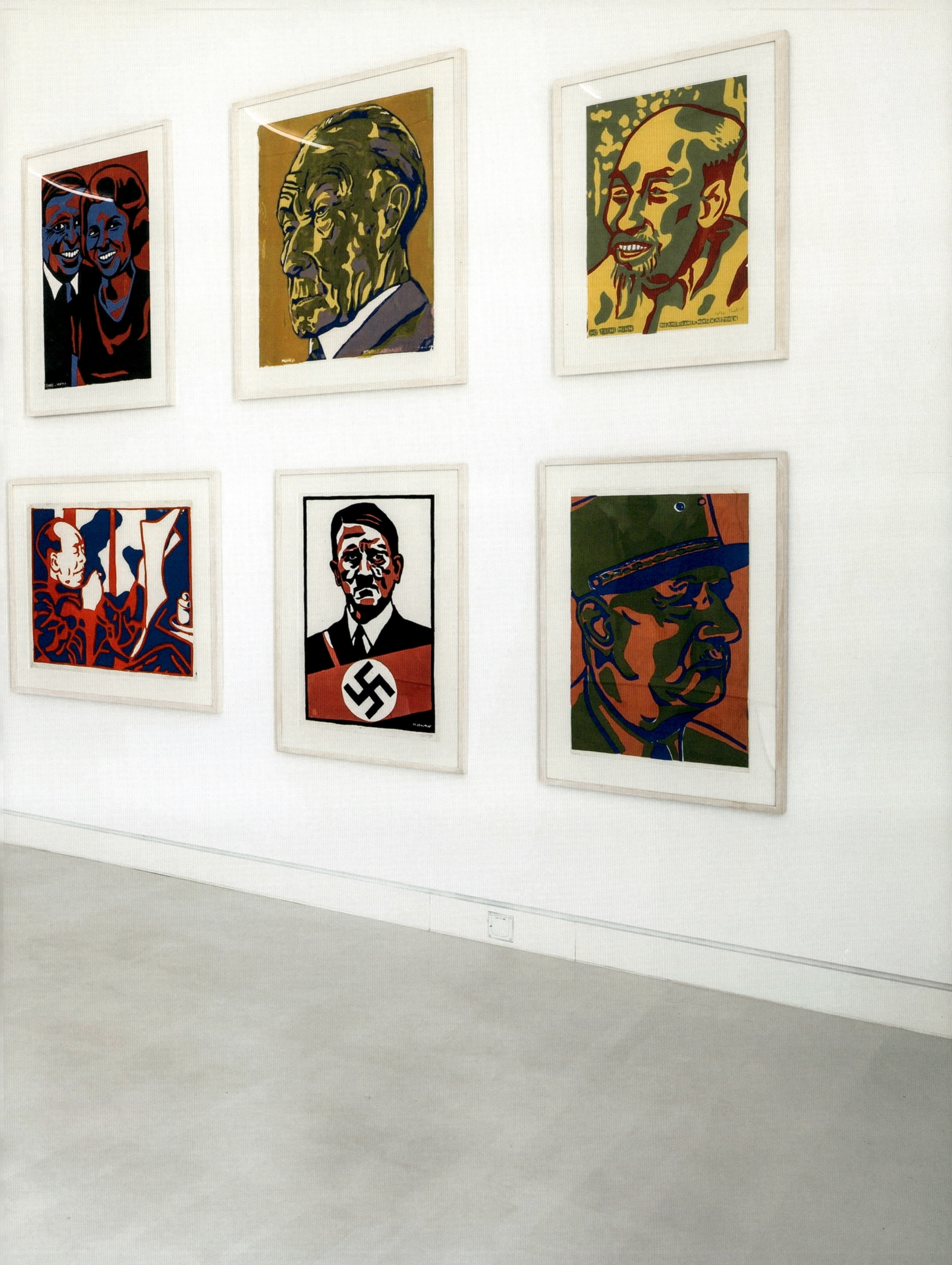

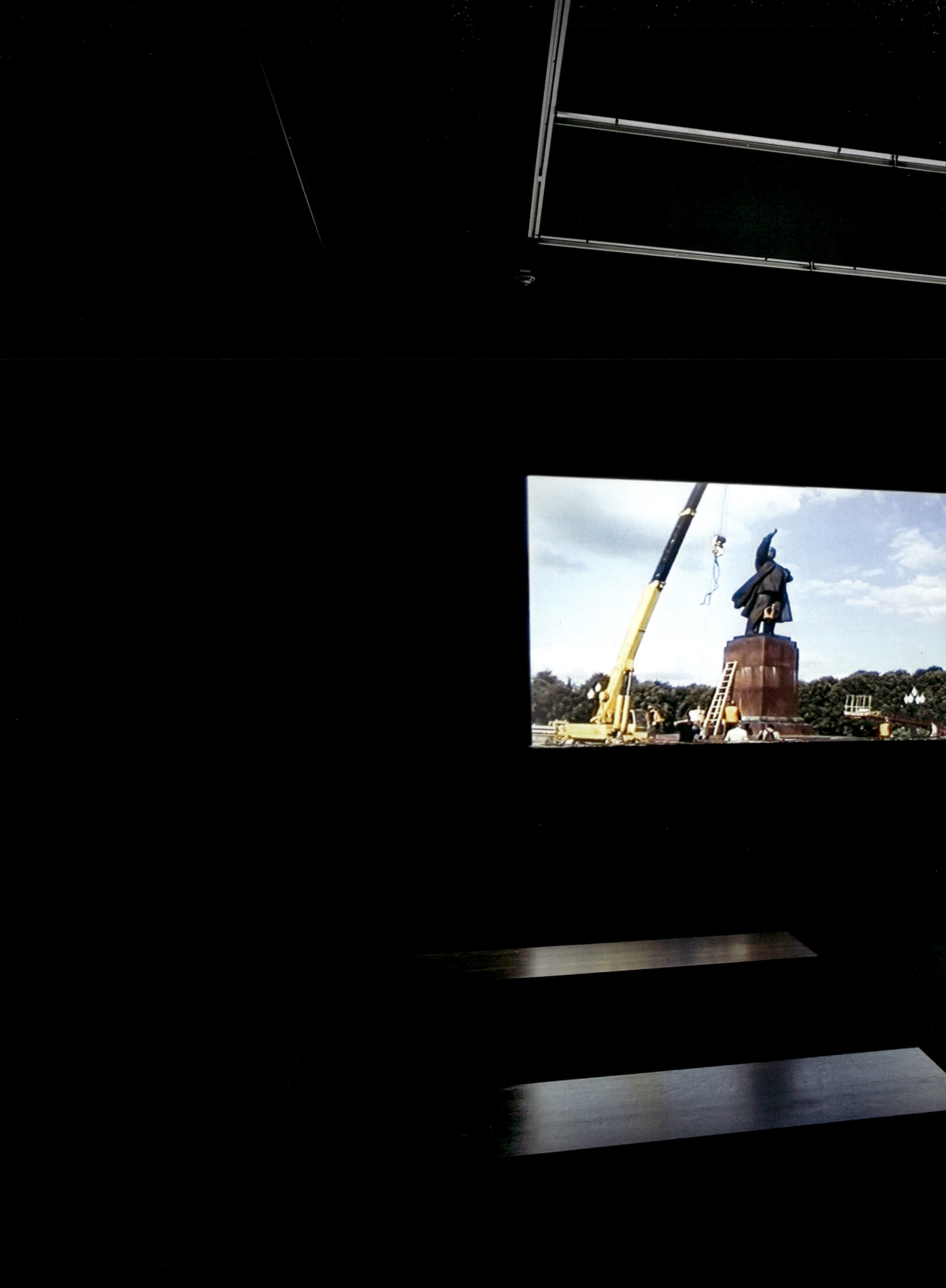

Deimantas Narkevičius
Once in the XX Century

———

2004, Video, 7 Min. Loop
Courtesy Deimantas Narkevičius,
Barbara Weiss Galerie, Berlin

Es ist schwer zu sagen, in welchem Land sich die Menschen versammelt haben. Der Film bleibt ohne Kommentar. Wir sehen einen schönen Sommertag in der Stadt. Aufgeregt verfolgt die Menge ein vorerst unbekanntes Schauspiel. Nach einiger Zeit tritt ein mächtiger Sockel ins Bild. Zwei barocke Kirchtürme erscheinen vor dem blauen Himmel, danach die unteren Beine einer fragmentierten Figur. Ein schweres Fahrzeug trägt einen Torso einer Lenin-Statue an seinem ausfahrbaren Arm. Jubelrufe sind zu hören. Der LKW hält in der Mitte der Menge. Manche erklettern auf die Figur, Geheul flammt auf und Begeisterung. Die Statue wird von ihrem Thron gestürzt. Allmählich wird klar. Der Film läuft rückwärts. Das Geschehen der Geschichte wird umgekehrt. Der Kran erhebt den metallischen Torso über die Menge. Lenins Arm schwingt so als würde er in einer Geste der Vergebung die Menschen grüßen. Schließlich kommt er auf seinen eigenen Beinen wieder zu stehen. Die Ganzheit des Monuments ist wieder hergestellt. Lenin überblickt als Souverän seine Untertanen.

It is difficult to say which country the people are assembled in. No commentary accompanies the film. We see a beautiful summer day in the city; a crowd excitedly watches a drama initially not disclosed to us. After a while, an immense pedestal enters the picture. Two Baroque church spires appear in the blue sky, then the lower legs of a fragmented figure. A heavy-duty vehicle carries the torso of a Lenin statue in its extendible crane arm. Cheering is heard. The lorry stops in the middle of the crowd. People climb onto the figure; howling and enthusiasm erupt. The statue is toppled from its throne. Gradually it becomes clear. The film is running backwards. The crane lifts the metallic torso over the heads of the crowd. Lenin's arm swings as if to greet the people with a gesture of forgiveness. Finally, he is once again standing on his feet. The monument's integrity has been restored. Lenin, the sovereign, looks out over his subjects.

Ausgewählte Biografien
Selected Biographies

Sabine Idstein, Anina Huck

Ottomar Anschütz

Geboren 1846 in der westpolnischen Stadt Lissa (damals Preußen), gestorben 1907 in Berlin; Fotograf; nach seiner Ausbildung übernimmt er 1868 das Geschäft seines Vaters. Zunächst entsteht ein Fotoatelier auf Rädern, dann ermöglicht ihm das neue Trockenplattenverfahren erste Momentaufnahmen. Die von ihm geschaffene Handkamera mit Rolltuch-Schlitzverschluss schafft kurze Belichtungszeiten und damit scharfe Einzelbilder von bewegten Objekten. In Fachkreisen werden seine Fotografien mit jenen Muybridges und Mareys verglichen. 1883 erhält er auf der *Photographischen Ausstellung* in Brüssel die Bronzemedaille. Im gleichen Jahr entstehen Aufnahmen der *Enthüllungsfeier auf dem Niederwald*. Ein Jahr später beginnen die Experimente mit den Chronophotographien, deren Höhepunkt die Aufnahmen von 1886 aus Hannover sind. 24 elektrisch miteinander verbundene Kameras lichten die Bewegungsabläufe der Pferde der *Königlichen Militärakademie* exakt ab. 1887 öffentliche Präsentation der Serie mit dem so genannten elektrischen Schnellseher: auf einer Drehscheibe werden die Bilder in Rotation gebracht und im richtigen Moment kurzzeitig beleuchtet, sodass die Bewegung animiert zu sein scheint, die Vorstufe der Kinematographie ist erreicht.

Born in 1846 in the western Polish city of Lissa (then Prussia), died 1907 in Berlin; photographer and pioneer of photo technology; after training as a photographer, he takes over his father's business in 1868. He first establishes a mobile photo studio, then the new dry plate method enables him to take his first snapshots. The hand-held camera he develops with a focal-plane shutter curtain allows for short exposure times and sharp still images of moving objects. Experts compare his photographs to those of Muybridge and Marey. In 1883 he awarded, at the *Photography Exhibition* in Brussels, he is awarded a bronze medal. That same year, he takes pictures of the *unveiling ceremony of the Niederwald* monument. The festive inauguration takes place on 28 September 1883 in the presence of the Emperor. One year later, he starts to experiment with chronophotography, the climax of which was to be the photographs made in 1886 in Hanover. There, 24 electrically connected cameras took pictures of the motion sequences of the horses of the *Imperial Military Academy*. In 1887 he makes a public presentation of the series with his so-called electrical "Schnellseher": images are rotated on a rotary disk and lighted for a brief moment so that the images appear to be animated; the precursor to cinematography has been realized.

Eduardo Chillida

Geboren 1924 in San Sebastián, 2002 ebendort gestorben; Bildhauer und Grafiker; ab 1943 Beginn eines Architekturstudiums in Madrid, kurze Zeit später Wechsel an eine private Kunstakademie. 1948 Umzug nach Paris. Es entstehen erste Plastiken aus Gips und Ton. 1949 Berufung als Kurator an das Musée National d'Art Moderne. 1951 Rückkehr nach Spanien, wo er sich in Hernani ein Atelier mit Schmiede einrichtet. Eisen und Granit werden seine favorisierten Materialien. „Ich habe gemerkt, dass ich mit diesen Materialien den leeren Raum formen, das Vakuum provozieren und den Horizont umarmen kann", sagt er. Eine der zahlreichen im öffentlichen Raum aufgestellten Eisenskulpturen ist jene, die im Jahr 2000 unter dem Titel *Berlin* vor dem neuen Bundeskanzleramt ihren Platz findet. Bereits 1958 erhält er den internationalen Preis für Bildhauerei der Biennale von Venedig. Chillida wie auch Moore gehören zu den wenigen Künstlern, die mehrmals in Kassel vertreten sind: Chillida bei der documenta 2 (1959), der documenta 3 (1964), der documenta 4 (1968) und der documenta 6 (1977). Die Präsenz der beiden Bildhauer in Kassel wird zum Klassiker. Auffällig ist ihre Abwesenheit bei der von Harald Szeemann kuratierten documenta 5 (1972). Zahlreiche weitere Ausstellungen, u. a. im Guggenheim Museum in New York.

Born (1924) and died (2002) in San Sebastián; sculptor and graphic artist; pursues a degree in architecture in Madrid in 1943, later changing to a private art academy. In 1948 Chillida moves to Paris, where he makes his first sculptures out of plastic and ceramics. In 1949, he assumes a position as curator at Musée National d'Art Moderne. In 1951, he returns to Spain where he sets up a studio with a forge in Hernani. Iron and granite are his favourite materials. "I realised that with this material I could form empty space, provoke a vacuum and embrace the horizon", he says. One of his many publically exhibited iron sculptures is that installed in front of the new Chancellery in the year 2000 and entitled *Berlin*. In 1958, he receives the International Sculpture Award at the Venice Biennale. Chillida, like Moore, is one of the few artists who have been shown in Kassel on several occasions: Chillida at the documenta 2 (1959), documenta 3 (1964), documenta 4 (1968) and documenta 6 (1977). The presence of both sculptors in Kassel had become a classic event. Against this backdrop, they were noticeably absent at the documenta 5 (1972) curated by Harald Szeemann. He had many other exhibitions, including at the Guggenheim Museum, New York.

Eugène Delacroix

Geboren 1798 als Ferdinand Victor Eugène Delacroix in Charenton-Saint-Maurice (Île-de-France), 1863 in Paris gestorben; 1815 Beginn seiner künstlerischen Ausbildung im Atelier des Malers Pierre-Narcisse Guérin und Studium der alten Meister im Louvre. 1816 Wechsel an die École nationale supérieure des Beaux-Arts de Paris. In den folgenden Jahren entstehen *La Barque de Dante* oder *Dante et Virgile aux Enfers* (1822), inspiriert durch Géricaults *La Redeau de La Méduse* (1818–19), und *Les Scènes des Massacres de Scio* (1824). Beide Werke erregen bereits zur Zeit ihrer Entstehung großes öffentliches Aufsehen. 1825–1827 Studienreise nach London; es entstehen Lithografien zu Goethes *Faust* und Shakespears *Hamlet*. Zurück in Paris wird der englische Einfluss unter anderem in *La Grèce sur les ruines de Missolonhi* (1827) deutlich. Im Pariser Salon wird er als Vorreiter der Romantik und Gegenspieler des Klassizisten Ingres gefeiert. Ab 1830 arbeitet Delacroix unter dem Eindruck der Julirevolution an *La Liberté guidant le peuple* (1830). Das heute im Louvre-Lens befindliche Gemälde wurde zunächst vom Bürgerkönig Louis-Philippe gekauft. Nachhaltig wirkt sich schließlich seine Reise nach Marokko 1832 auf Farbigkeit, Thematik und Duktus aus.

Born 1798 as Ferdinand Victor Eugène Delacroix in Charenton-Saint-Maurice (Île-de-France), died in 1863 in Paris. In 1815, Delacroix starts his artistic training in the atelier of the painter Pierre-Narcisse Guérin and studies the old masters at the Louvre. In 1816, he goes to study at École nationale supérieuere des Beaux-Arts de Paris. In the years to follow, he produces *La Barque de Dante or Dante et Virgile aux Enfers* (1822), inspired by Géricault's *La Redeau de La Méduse* (1818–19) and *Les Scènes des Massacres de Scio* (1824). At the time of their production, both works attract major public attention. From 1825–27 he takes a study trip to London; here he produces lithographs for Goethe's *Faust* and Shakespeare's *Hamlet*. Back in Paris, the English influence becomes apparent, for example in *La Grèce sur les ruines de Missolonhi* (1827). He is celebrated by the Salon as the precursor of the romantic style and the opponent of classical painter Ingres. From 1830, Delacroixs work is influenced by the July Revolution: *La Liberté guidant le peuple* (1830). Currently located in Louvre-Lens, the painting was first purchased by the citizen king Louis-Philippe. His trip to Morocco in 1832 has a lasting effect on colouration, subject matter and style.

Thomas Hobbes

Geboren 1588 in Westport bei Malmesbury, gestorben 1679 in Derbyshire auf Hardwick Hall; englischer Staatstheoretiker und Philosoph; vierzehnjährig beginnt Hobbes ein Studium am renommierten Magdalen Hall Collage der Universität Oxford. 1608 tritt er als Privatlehrer in den Dienst Sir William Carvendish of Hardwicks, des späteren 1st Earl of Devonshire. Diese Tätigkeit beinhaltet die Möglichkeit ausgedehnter Studienreisen, bei welchen er in Kontakt mit Francis Bacon, Herbert of Cherbury und Ben Jonson kommt. Er trifft René Descartes in Paris und Galileo Galilei in Pisa. Mit dem Vorwort der englischen Übersetzung des *Thukydides* (1628) wird erstmalig sein ausgeprägtes politisches Interesse nachweisbar. Ab 1629 wird die Beeinflussung durch Euklids Elementa auffällig, die sich in der Parteischrift *Elements of Law* (1640) und in dem dreiteiligen Werk *Elementa Philosophiae* nachvollziehen lässt. 10 Jahre verbringt er im Exil in Frankreich und lernt Ludwig XIV. kennen. Nachdem 1649 King Charles I. verurteilt und hingerichtet wird, herrscht in England die Militärdiktatur Oliver Cromwells. Hobbes beginnt mit seinem Hauptwerk, dem *Leviathan*, das 1651 in London veröffentlicht wird. Den berühmten Frontispiz des *Leviathan* gibt er bei dem niederländischen Stecher Abraham Bosse in Auftrag. 1651 kehrt er nach England zurück und unterwirft sich der Republik.

Born 1588 in Westport near Malmesbury, died 1679 in Derbyshire at Hardwick Hall; English political theorist and philosopher; at the age of fourteen, Hobbes begins to study at the prestigious Magdalen Hall at the University of Oxford. In 1608, he assumes a position as tutor for Sir William Cavendish of Hardwick, later to become the 1st Earl of Devonshire. This employment gives him the opportunity to travel extensively, during which he meets the likes of Francis Bacon, Herbert of Cherbury, and Ben Jonson. He meets René Descartes in Paris and Galileo Galilei in Pisa. In the preface of the English translation of *Thukydides* (1628) his pronounced political interest becomes detectable for the first time. From 1629 he is influenced by Euclid's *Elements*, as found in his *Elements of Law* (1640) and in his three-part work *Elementa Philosophiae*. He spends ten years as an exile in France and meets Louis XIV. After King Charles I. was charged and executed in 1649, England is ruled by the military dictatorship of Oliver Cromwell. Hobbes starts his magnum opus *Leviathan*, which is published in London in 1651. The famous frontispiece of *Leviathan* was commissioned from Dutch engraver Abraham Bosse. In 1651, Hobbes returns to England and acquiesces to the republic.

Udo Jürgens

Geboren 1934 in Klagenfurt als Udo Jürgen Bockelmann; Unterhaltungs-
musiker, Komponist, Pianist und Sänger, 2014 in Münsterlingen in der
Schweiz gestorben; am Konservatorium Klagenfurt studiert er Klavier,
Harmonielehre, Komposition und Gesang. 1949 schreibt Jürgens seine
ersten Lieder. Im Alter von 16 Jahren gewinnt er mit dem Lied *Je t'aime*
beim Komponisten-Wettbewerb des Österreichischen Rundfunks den
1. Preis. 1960 den Presse-Preis *Bester Einzelsänger* des Festivals im belgi-
schen Knokke mit *Jenny*. Nun komponiert er für Shirley Bassey *Reach
For the Stars*. 1964 erstmalige Teilnahme am *Grand Prix Eurovision de la
Chanson* für Österreich (Platz 5). Ein Jahr später landet er auf Platz 4, 1966
schließlich mit *Merci Chérie* den 1. Platz. Die Komposition *Siebzehn Jahr,
blondes Haar* gewinnt den Goldenen Löwen. 1970 erhält er den ersten
Bambi und verkauft fortan seine Platten in Zehnmillionenauflagen. Um
das Lied mit dem Titel *Lieb Vaterland* (1971), dessen Text der Satiriker
Eckard Hachfeld geschrieben hat, kommt es zur öffentlichen Diskussion.
Jürgens Fassung versteht sich als Anklage des Staates im Namen der aufbegehrenden Jugend und des Widerstands der 68er Generation gegen das
Establishment.

Born Udo Jürgen Bockelmann in Klagenfurt (1934), died in Münsterlingen,
Switzerland (2014); entertainer, composer, pianist and singer; studied
piano, harmonics, composition and singing at the Carinthian State Con-
servatorium in Klagenfurt. In 1949, Jürgens writes his first songs. At the
age of sixteen, he wins the first prize at the composers' contest held by
the Austrian Broadcasting Corporation (ORF) with the song *Je t'aime*. In
1960, he wins the Press Prize for Best Solo Singer at the Festival in the
Belgian town of Knokke with the song *Jenny*. Then he composes *Reach for
the Stars* for Shirley Bassey. In 1964, he takes part in the Eurovision Song
Contest for the first time, representing Austria (fifth place). One year later,
he makes it to fourth, and then finally in 1966 he manages to come in first
with the song *Merci Chérie*. He wins the Golden Lion (Goldener Löwe)
with the composition *Siebzehn Jahr, blondes Haar*. In 1970 he receives his
first Bambi Award after which his record sales skyrocket to double-digit-
million figures. He sparks a public debate with the song entitled *Lieb Vaterland* (Dear Fatherland) (1971), the lyrics of which were penned by satirist
Eckard Hachfeld. Jürgen's version, however, is a denouncement of the
state from the point of view of the youth involved in the protests of 1968
and their resistance against the establishment.

Kaspar König

Geboren 1943 als Rudolf Hans König in Mettingen (Westfalen); Kurator,
lebt in Berlin; bereits 1966 kuratiert der damals 23-jährige Student seine
erste Museumsaustellung *Claes Oldenburg* in Stockholm, zwei Jahre später
die Schau *Andy Warhol*. 1977 ist König Mitbegründer der internationalen
Ausstellungsreihe *Skulptur-Projekte* in Münster, deren Leitung er bis 2007
viermal übernimmt. Ab 1981 Organisation von Großausstellungen wie
Westkunst (1981) in den Kölner Messehallen, *Von hier aus* (1984) in Düsseldorf, *Der zerbrochene Spiegel* (1993) in Wien und Hamburg, sowie das
Kunstprojekt der EXPO Hannover *In-Between-Architecture* (2000). 1985
Berufung an die Kunstakademie Düsseldorf für den neu gegründeten
Lehrstuhl „Kunst und Öffentlichkeit". Gefolgt von einer Professur an der
Städelschule Frankfurt am Main, die er später 11 Jahre lang leitet. König
ist Gründungsdirektor der Ausstellungshalle Portikus in Frankfurt am
Main, 2000 – 2012 Direktor des Museums Ludwig in Köln. 2011 kuratierte
er zusammen mit Thomas D. Trummer *Vor dem Gesetz*, wo auch Thomas
Schüttes Vater Staat zu sehen ist. Für sein Lebenswerk erhält er unter
anderem den First Annual Art Award des New Yorker Guggenheim-
Museums. 2014 ist er Chefkurator der Manifesta 10 in St. Petersburg.

Born Rudolf Hans König in 1943 in Mettingen (Westphalia); curator, resides
in Berlin; as a 23-year-old student, he curates his first museum exhibition
of the work of Claes Oldenburg in Stockholm, two years later he curates
an Andy Warhol exhibition. In 1977, König is co-founder of the international
exhibition series *Sculpture Projects Münster*, which he headed four times
up to 2007. From 1981, he organises large-scale exhibitions such as *Westkunst* (1981) at the Cologne exhibition grounds, *Von hier aus* (1984) in
Düsseldorf, *Der zerbrochene Spiegel* (1993) in Vienna and Hamburg, as well
as the art project of the EXPO Hanover *In-Between-Architecture* (2000).
In 1985, he becomes professor for the newly established institute "Kunst
und Öffentlichkeit" (Art and the Public) at the Art Academy in Düsseldorf. This is followed by a professorship at the Städelschule Frankfurt am
Main, which he later heads for eleven years. König is the founding director
of the exhibition hall Portikus in Frankfurt am Main. Between 2000 and
2012 he is the director of the Museum Ludwig in Cologne. In 2011 he curated
with Thomas D. Trummer *Vor dem Gesetz* where Schütte's Vaterstaat was
also presented. For his life's work, he also receives the First Annual Art
Award of the Guggenheim Museum in New York. In 2014, he becomes head
curator of Manifesta 10 in St. Petersburg.

Henry Moore

Geboren 1898 in Castleford, Yorkshire, gestorben 1986 in Much Hadham; Bildhauer, Grafiker und Zeichner; mit 18 Jahren zum Militärdienst eingezogen, erhält er als Kriegsteilnehmer 1919 ein Stipendium und beginnt sein Kunststudium am Leeds College of Art. 1921 wechselt er an das Royal College of Art in London. Unter dem Eindruck von afrikanischen und mexikanischen Skulpturen, seiner Studienaufenthalte in Italien, und unter dem Einfluss der Pariser Avantgarde verlässt Moore den klassischen Formenkanon. 1924 Beginn der Lehrtätigkeit am Royal College of Art, 1932 Wechsel an die Chelsea School of Art als leitender Dozent der Bildhauerklasse. Während des Zweiten Weltkriegs ist Moore *Official War Artist*. Es entsteht ein beachtliches grafisches Oeuvre. Das Grundthema seines skulpturalen Schaffens bildet der Mensch im Zwischenspiel zwischen Abstraktion und Figuration. Bronze wird sein bevorzugtes Material und die Steigerung ins Monumentale seine Passion. Auf Betreiben des Bundeskanzlers Helmut Schmidt wird die Bronzeskulptur *Large Two Forms* 1979 auf dem neu gestalteten Vorplatz des Bundeskanzleramtes in Bonn platziert. Die erste große Retrospektive erfolgt 1946 im Museum of Modern Art, New York; die Biennale in Venedig ehrt ihn – wie Chillida – mit ihrem Skulpturpreis. Moore nimmt an der documenta 1 (1955), der documenta 2 (1959), der documenta 3 (1964) und der documenta 6 (1977) teil.

Born in 1898 in Castleford, Yorkshire, died 1986 in Much Hadham; sculptor, graphic artist and draughtsman; drafted at the age of 18, he receives a scholarship for ex-servicemen and pursues a degree in art at the Leeds College of Art. In 1921, he goes on to study at the Royal College of Art in London. Impressed by African and Mexican sculptures, his study visits to Italy, and the influence of the Parisian avant garde, Moore departs from the classic artistic canon. In 1924, he begins teaching at the Royal College of Art, and assumes a position as head of sculpture at the Chelsea School of Art in 1932. Moore is an official war artist during the Second World War. He produces an extensive graphic oeuvre. The fundamental theme of his sculptural art is the human being, in an interaction between abstraction and figuration. Bronze becomes his material of choice and the escalation of the monumental his passion. Due to the efforts of Federal Chancellor Helmut Schmidt, the bronze sculpture *Large Two Forms* (1979) is installed on the newly built forecourt of the Federal Chancellery. His first large retrospective is held in 1946 at The Museum of Modern Art, New York; the Venice Biennale pays tribute to him – like Chillida – with their sculpture award. Moore takes part in documenta 1 (1955), documenta 2 (1959), documenta 3 (1964) and documenta 6 (1977).

Otto Muehl

Geboren 1925 in Grodnau (Burgenland), gestorben 2013 in Olhão in Portugal; bildender Künstler; 1940 zum Landdienst in der Steiermark eingezogen, meldet er sich freiwillig zur Deutschen Wehrmacht. Nach dem Krieg Abschluss eines Lehramtsstudiums, Besuch der Akademie der bildenden Künste in Wien und Arbeit als Maltherapeut mit Kindern. Mitbegründer des Wiener Aktionismus. Mit Günter Brus Gründung des *Instituts für Direkte Kunst*. Mit Nitsch, Kurt Kren und Peter Weibel Reise nach London zum *Destruction in Art Symposium DIAS*. Ein Jahr später initiiert er mit dem Dichter und Philosophen Oswald Wiener unter dem Titel ZOCK eine Plattform für agitativ-öffentliche Aktionen. In dieser Zeit entsteht die Serie von Staatsporträts in Siebdruck. Nach mehrfachen Konflikten mit der Polizei emigriert er nach Berlin. 1970 Teilnahme an der von Harald Szeemann kuratierten Ausstellung *Happening und Fluxus*, 1972 an der documenta 5 (1972). Die *Muehl-Kommune Friedrichshof* verspricht alternative, freiere Lebensformen, entwickelt aber sektenähnliche Züge, deren übelste Auswirkung der Kindesmissbrauch ist. Trotz der Missstände entstehen von Beginn an Kunstprojekte mit namhaften Künstlern, Schriftstellern und Ausstellungsmachern. 1991 wird Muehl wegen *strafbaren Handlungen gegen die Sittlichkeit und Verstoßes gegen das Suchtgiftgesetz* zu sieben Jahren Haft verurteilt und die Kommune geschlossen.

Born 1925 in Grodnau (Burgenland), died 2013 in Olhão in Portugal; artist; drafted 1940 in Styria, he volunteers to join the German Wehrmacht. After the war, he completes his teacher's training, attends the Academy of Fine Arts in Vienna and works as an art therapist with children. Co-founder of Viennese Actionism. Establishes with Günter Brus the Institut für Direkte Kunst. He joins Nitsch, Kurt Kren, and Peter Weibel on a trip to London to the Destruction in Art Symposium DIAS. One year later, in collaboration with poet and philosopher Oswald Wiener, he establishes a platform for agitative public actions entitled ZOCK. During this period, he creates a series of screen-printed state portraits. After several conflicts with the police, he immigrates to Berlin. In 1970, he takes part in the exhibition curated by Harald Szeemann, *Happening und Fluxus*, and in 1972 in documenta V (1972). The Muehl commune Friedrichshof promises an alternative, more liberal way of life, yet develops sect-like characteristics, the direst consequences of which are child abuse. Despite irregularities that are apparently from the very beginning, several art projects are developed with renowned artists, writers, and curators. In 1991, Muehl is sentenced to seven years imprisonment for illegal acts against morality and violation of narcotics laws and the commune is closed.

Deimantas Narkevičius

Geboren 1964 in Utena (Litauen); Film- und Videokünstler, lebt und arbeitet in Vilnius. Anfang der 1990er Jahre Studium der Bildhauerei an der Kunstakademie in Vilnius. Er reflektiert in seinem Werk die Bedingungen seines Heimatlandes Litauen als Sowjetrepublik und nach dem Zusammenbruch des Ostblocks. Narkevičius experimentiert mit konzeptueller Objektkunst, Installationen, Tonprojekten und arbeitet zunehmend im Medium Film. Sein erster Film entsteht 1997 unter dem Titel *54° 54′ – 25° 19′*. Die Koordinaten geben eine Stelle nördlich Vilnius wieder, die 1989 laut dem französischen Institut Géographique National den Mittelpunkt Europas bezeichnet. 2004 wird *Once in the XX Century* fertiggestellt. Durch einfache Montage, indem die Bilder rückwärts laufen, stürzt das Leninstandbild in Vilnius nicht vom Podest, sondern wird unter Applaus aufgerichtet. *The Head* (2007) zeigt Reaktionen von Passanten im Lauf der Zeit – auf das 1971 errichtete monumentale Denkmal von Karl Marx in Karl-Marx-Stadt (Chemnitz). 2001 ist Narkevičius auf der Biennale in Venedig vertreten, 2007 bei Skulptur Projekte Münster. 2008 stellt er bei U-Turn, Quadriennale für Zeitgenössische Kunst in Kopenhagen aus.

Born 1964 in Utena (Lithuania); film and video artist, lives and works in Vilnius. In the early 1990s, Narkevičius studies sculpting at the Art Academy in Vilnius. His work predominantly reflects the conditions of his home country Lithuania as a part of the Soviet Union and, after the collapse of the Eastern bloc, as a society in transition. Yet his work focuses on the complicated mechanisms of society's capacity for remembering, even when it is confronted with the painful processes of history. Narkevičius experiments with conceptual object art, installations, audio projects, and increasingly with the medium of film. His first film, in 1997, is entitled *54° 54′ – 25° 19′*. The coordinates specify a location north of Vilnius, which according to the French Institut Géographique National is the centre of Europe. In 2004, he completes *Once in the XX Century*. Simple cutting techniques enable the film to run backwards; thus the statue of Lenin in Vilnius does not topple down from the pedestal; it is erected while onlookers applaud. *The Head* (2007) shows the reactions of passers-by – over the course of time – to the monument of Karl Marx erected in 1971 in Karl-Marx-Stadt (Chemnitz). In 2001, Narkevičius's work is represented at the Biennale in Venice, and in 2007 at Sculpture Projects Münster. In 2008, he exhibits his work at U-TURN Quadrennial for Contemporary Art in Copenhagen.

Johannes Schilling

Geboren 1828 in Mittweida, gestorben 1910 in Dresden; Bildhauer; mit 14 Jahren Beginn des Studiums an der Kunstakademie in Dresden, ab 1845 einer der Meisterschüler des Bildhauers Ernst Rietschel. Nach einer Forschungsreise nach Rom richtet er sich in Dresden ein eigenes Atelier ein; erste Aufträge u. a. für Bauten Gottfried Sempers. Zu seinem Durchbruch als Bildhauer verhilft ihm der Auftrag zur Figurengruppe *Vier Tageszeiten* am nördlichen Aufgang der Brühlschen Terrasse in Dresden. Seine Werke orientieren sich an klassischen Vorbildern, mit denen er auf seiner Romreise in Kontakt kommt. Nach einem Wettbewerb reicht Schilling im April 1874 seinen dritten und endgültigen Entwurf für das Niederwalddenkmal ein. Die Architektur und Terrassenbauten stammen von dem Architekten Karl Weißbach. Sowohl die Grundsteinlegung 1877, als auch die Einweihung 1883 wird unter Anwesenheit des Kaisers gefeiert, allein dies ist Hinweis auf die enorme politische Bedeutung des Denkmals. Weitere Aufträge folgen, so für das *Reformationsdenkmal* in Leipzig, das Schillerdenkmal in Wien oder das Denkmal für Kaiser Wilhelm I. in Wiesbaden. Bereits 1868 Berufung als Professor an die Dresdner Kunstakademie, wo er bis kurz vor seinem Tod unterrichtet.

Born 1828 in Mittweida, died in 1910 in Dresden; sculptor; studies at the Art Academy in Dresden at the age of fourteen; starting in 1845 he becomes a master pupil under sculptor Ernst Rietschel. Following a research trip to Rome, he sets up his own studio in Dresden and among his first commissions are buildings for Gottfried Semper. He achieves his breakthrough as a sculptor with the group of figures entitled *Four Times of Day* (Vier Tageszeiten), set up on the northern steps of Brühl's Terrace. His work is based on classical models that he had encountered during his trip to Rome. Following a contest, Schilling submits his third and final draft of the Niederwald monument in April of 1874. The architecture and terraces were designed by architect Karl Weißbach. The laying of the foundation stone in 1877, like the inauguration in 1883, is performed in the presence of the Emperor, which alone is evidence of the enormous political significance of the monument. Further commissions follow, such as for the *Reformation memorial* (Reformationsdenkmal) in Leipzig, the Schiller memorial in Vienna, and the Emperor Wilhem I monument in Wiesbaden. In 1868, he becomes a professor at the Academy, a position he held until his death.

Helmut Schmidt

Geboren 1918 in Hamburg als Helmut Heinrich Waldemar Schmidt, gestorben 2015; Altbundeskanzler, lebte in Hamburg-Langenhorn; 1937 Abitur, danach Arbeitsdienst in Hamburg-Reitbrook und Einzug zum Wehrdienst. Er zeigt sich dem NS-Regime kritisch gegenüber, bleibt aber von Abstrafungen verschont. Nach der Kriegsgefangenschaft Studium der Staatswissenschaften und Volkswirtschaftslehre. 1953 wird er Mitglied des Deutschen Bundestags, ab 1961 Innensenator der Stadt Hamburg. 1967–1969 Vorsitz der SPD-Bundestagsfraktion und 1969–1972 Bundesminister der Verteidigung. Gefolgt vom Bundesministerposten für Wirtschaft und Finanzen. 1974 wird er zum fünften Bundeskanzler der Bundesrepublik Deutschland gewählt und bleibt bis 1982 im Amt. Schmidt sorgt dafür, dass trotz Protesten vor seinem Amtssitz in Bonn die Plastik *Large Two Forms* von Henry Moore aufgestellt wird. Während seiner Zeit im Kanzleramt lässt Schmidt das Gebäude mit zahlreichen Kunstleihgaben ausstatten. Er schätzt die Malerei des Deutschen Expressionismus und erklärt diesbezüglich in einem Interview: „Pechstein, Schmidt-Rottluff, Nolde, andere Brücke-Maler, aber auch Barlach und Käthe Kollwitz: Mit ihnen bin ich in der Schule groß geworden, (…). Viele meiner Mitschüler kamen, wie ich, nicht aus begüterten Familien, wir hatten kein Geld für Museumsbesuche. Aber wir hatten einen Lehrer, der uns Kunstpostkarten mitbrachte und zeigte". Nach seiner Zeit als Bundeskanzler wird Schmidt Mitherausgeber der Wochenzeitung *Die Zeit*.

Born Helmut Heinrich Waldemar Schmidt in 1918 in Hamburg; died in 2015 former Federal Chancellor, lives in Hamburg-Langenhorn; completes his Abitur advanced secondary school exams in 1937, followed by labour service in Hamburg-Reitbrook and is then drafted into the Wehrdienst. He is critical toward the NS regime, yet is spared any punishment. After his return from being a prisoner of war, he studies political science and economics. In 1953, he becomes a member of the Lower House of German Parliament, and in 1961 Interior Senator of the city of Hamburg. From 1967 to 1969 he is Chair of the SPD parliamentary group. Between 1969 and 1972 he is Federal Minister of Defence, followed by the position of Minister of Economics and Finance. In 1974, he becomes the 5th Federal Chancellor of the Federal Republic of Germany and remains in this position until 1982. Despite protests, Schmidt ensures that the sculpture *Large Two Forms* by Henry Moore is installed in front of his official residence. During his tenure at the Chancellery, Schmidt has the building equipped with several works of art that were loaned to him. He appreciates the paintings of the German expressionists, saying during an interview: "Pechstein, Schmidt-Rottluff, Nolde, other 'Brücke' painters but also Barlach and Käthe Kollwitz: I grew up with them at school, (…). Like me, many of my fellow students did not come from well-to-do families; we didn't have the money for trips to the museum. But we did have a teacher who brought along art postcards." Following his term as Chancellor, Schmidt becomes co-editor of the weekly newspaper *Die Zeit*.

Gerhard Schröder

Geboren 1944 in Mossenberg; Altbundeskanzler, lebt in Waldhausen (Hannover). Während seiner Zeit als Einzelhandelskaufmann holt Schröder die Mittlere Reife nach. 1963 Eintritt in die SPD. Auf dem Zweiten Bildungsweg besteht er 1966 das Abitur und beginnt mit dem Studium der Rechtswissenschaften. Zunächst angestellt in einer Kanzlei, wird er schließlich Sozius einer Anwaltskanzlei in Hannover, in der er bis 1990 tätig ist. Ab 1979 Mitglied des SPD-Parteirates. 1990–1998 Ministerpräsident des Landes Niedersachsen. 1998–2005 ist Gerhard Schröder siebter Bundeskanzler der Bundesrepublik Deutschland. Mit dem Umzug des Kanzleramtes von Bonn nach Berlin kommen neue Kunstwerke hinzu. Die Plastik *Berlin* des baskischen Bildhauers Eduardo Chillida entsteht im Auftrag der Bundesrepublik und wird vor dem Regierungspalast aufgestellt. Der Auftrag wird noch während der Amtszeit von Helmut Kohl angeregt und durch Schröder letztendlich realisiert. Eine starkfarbige Wandbemalung im Eingang des Baus von Axel Schulte führt Markus Lüpertz aus, der Pressesaal wird mit Ernst Wilhelm Nays berühmten Augenbildern ausgestattet. Jörg Immendorff rühmt Schröder als „ersten Kanzler, der die zeitgenössische Kunst als wesentlichen Teil des deutschen Selbstverständnis erkannt und gefördert hat." Seit 2005 ist er wieder als Rechtsanwalt tätig und besetzt unter anderen den umstrittenen Posten bei der Nord Stream AG, einem Tochterunternehmen des russischen Energiekonzerns Gazprom.

Born 1944 in Mossenberg; former Federal Chancellor, lives in Waldhausen (Hanover). While working in the retail trade, Schröder completes his intermediate secondary school exams. He joins the SPD in 1963. He later attends evening school to complete his Abitur / advanced secondary school exams and goes on to pursue a degree in law. Initially employed by a law firm, he becomes a partner in a firm in Hanover, where he remains until 1990. He becomes a member of the SPD Party Council in 1979 and from 1990 to 1998 serves as Prime Minister of Lower Saxony. Between 1988 and 2005, Gerhard Schröder is the 7th Federal Chancellor of the Federal Republic of Germany. With the relocation of the Chancellery from Bonn to Berlin, new works of art are added. The sculpture *Berlin* by the Basque artist Eduardo Chillida is commissioned by the Federal Republic of Germany and is installed in front of the Federal Chancellery. The commission dates back to Helmut Kohl's term of office and is ultimately brought to fruition by Schröder. A vibrant wall mural in the lobby of the building designed by Axel Schulte is realised by Markus Lüpertz. The press room is adorned with Ernst Wilhelm Nay's paintings. Jörg Immendorff commends Schröder as "the first Chancellor who appreciates contemporary art as part of the German self-perception and promotes it accordingly." Since 2005, he has resumed his career in law and also has a controversial position with Nord Stream AG, the subsidiary of Russian energy provider Gazprom.

Thomas Schütte

Geboren 1954 in Oldenburg; Bildhauer und Zeichner, lebt und arbeitet in Düsseldorf; 1973 Beginn des Studiums an der Kunstakademie Düsseldorf als Schüler Fritz Schweglers und Gerhard Richters. Im Wintersemester 1985/1986 bereits Gastprofessur an der Hochschule für Bildende Künste in Hamburg. 1987 Teilnahme an der documenta 8 in Kassel und an den *Skulptur Projekten* in Münster. Mit *Die Ankunft der Fremden* zeigt Thomas Schütte auf dem Portikus des ehemaligen Roten Palais 1992 anlässlich der documenta 9 die ersten lebensgroßen Skulpturen. Auch 1997 ist Schütte auf der documenta und in Münster bei den Skulptur Projekten vertreten. 2005 Auszeichnung mit dem *Golden Lion Arward* auf der 51sten Biennale in Venedig. Sammlungen, die seine Werke bewahren, sind das Hirshhorn Museum in Washington, die Arco Foundation in Madrid, die Kunsthalle Bern, das K21 in Düsseldorf und das Centre Pompidou in Paris. Schütte erhält zahlreiche Preise, etwa den Hamburger Lichtwark-Preis (2004), den Kunstköln-Preis (2005) für seine Verdienste um die grafischen Künste und den Kunstpreis der Landeshauptstadt Düsseldorf zum Start der Quadriennale (2010). Für sein komplexes Oeuvre seit den 1980er Jahren, in dem „er formal traditionelle Kunstgenres neu[interpretiert]".

Born 1954 in Oldenburg; sculptor and draughtsman, he lives and works in Düsseldorf; in 1973 he studies at the Art Academy in Düsseldorf as a pupil of Fritz Schwegler and Gerhard Richter. During the winter semester of 1985 – 86, he assumes a position as visiting professor at the Hochschule für Bildende Künste in Hamburg. In 1987, he takes part in documenta 8 in Kassel and in *Skulptur Projekte Münster*. With *Die Ankunft der Fremden* (The Arrival of the Strangers), Thomas Schütte exhibits his first life-size sculptures on the portico of the former Roten Palais on the occasion of documenta 9 in 1992. Schütte is once again at documenta in 1997, as well as at Sculpture Projects Münster. In 2005, he receives the Golden Lion Award at the 51st Biennale in Venice. His artwork is found in the collections of Hirshhorn Museum in Washington, the Arco Foundation in Madrid, Kunsthalle Bern, K21 in Düsseldorf, and Centre Pompidou in Paris. Schütte has received several awards such as the Hamburger Lichtwark-Preis (2004) and Kunstköln-Preis (2005) for his contribution to graphic arts , as well as the Kunstpreis der Landeshauptstadt Düsseldorf at the start of the Quadriennale (2010), for his complex oeuvre since the 1980s, in which "he re[interprets] formal traditional art genres".

Johannes Mario Simmel

Geboren 1924 als Sohn eines jüdischen Chemikers und einer Lektorin in Wien, gestorben 2009 bei Zug in der Schweiz; Schriftsteller; während der NS-Zeit Flucht des Vaters nach London. Johannes Mario Simmel wächst in Österreich und England auf. Ausbildung zum Chemie-Ingenieur. Nach dem Krieg Dolmetscher für die amerikanischen Besatzer. Ab 1948 als Journalist für die Zeitung *Welt am Abend* tätig. Sein erster Roman *Mich wundert dass ich so fröhlich bin* erscheint 1949 und wird ein Erfolg. 1950 Übersiedlung nach München, Tätigkeit als Journalist für die Quick. Er verfasst Drehbücher für Filme wie *Es geschehen noch Wunder* (1951) mit Hildegard Knef und *Tagebuch einer Verliebten* (1953) mit Maria Schell. 1960 wird sein Roman *Es muss nicht immer Kaviar sein* veröffentlicht, 1961 verfilmt. 1965 erscheint sein Roman *Lieb Vaterland magst ruhig sein.* Simmel lässt stets in seinen Büchern eine antifaschistische, demokratische Haltung durchblicken. Ein Schuss Erotik ist immer inbegriffen und so ordnet der Literaturbetrieb sein Werk der Trivialliteratur zu. Dennoch lobt ihn Marcel Reich-Ranicki für seinen „fabelhaften Blick für Themen, Probleme, Motive".

Born 1924, the son of a Jewish chemist and a lecturer in Vienna, died 2009 near Zug in Switzerland; writer; during the NS regime, father flees to London. Johannes Mario Simmel grows up in Austria and England. Trains as a chemical engineer. After the war, works as an interpreter for the American occupying forces. From 1948, works as a journalist for the newspaper *Welt am Abend* (Evening World). His first novel, *Mich wundert dass ich so fröhlich bin* (I am puzzled to be so happy), is published in 1949 and becomes a success. In 1950, Simmel moves to Munich, works as a journalist for *Quick*. He writes screenplays for films such as *Es geschehen noch Wunder* (1951) with Hildegard Knef and *Tagebuch einer Verliebten* (1953) with Maria Schell. In 1960, his novel *Es muss nicht immer Kaviar sein* (It doesn't always have to be Caviar) is published and filmed in 1961. In 1965, his novel *Lieb Vaterland magst ruhig sein* (Dear Fatherland, no fear be thine) is published. Simmel's works always display an anti-fascist, democratic demeanour. The topics he deals with are often political or socially delicate, based on very extensive research. A pinch of sexuality is also always included, which is why his work is considered to be a part of the popular fiction genre. Nevertheless, Marcel Reich-Ranicki commended him for his "wonderful feel for issues, problems and motives".

Danh Vo

Geboren 1975 auf der vietnamesischen Insel Phu Quoc; bildender Künstler, lebt und arbeitet in Berlin; in einem selbstgebauten Boot flüchten der 4-Jährige und seine Familie über den Pazifik, wo sie von einem dänischen Frachtschiff gerettet werden. So erhält Danh Vos Familie durch Zufall die dänische Staatsbürgerschaft. In Kopenhagen ist er bis 2002 an der *Det Kongelige Danske Kunstakademi* eingeschrieben und schließt 2005 seine akademische Ausbildung an der Städelschule in Frankfurt bei Tobias Rehberger ab. Vos installative Arbeiten aus Dokumenten, Fotos und angeeigneten Arbeiten anderer Künstler sind von Beginn an mit der eigenen Biografie verknüpft. Bereits 2007 gewinnt er den Blauorange-Preis, 2012 den *Hugo Boss Prize der Solomon-R.-Guggenheim-Stiftung* mit einer Einzelschau im Guggenheim Museum in New York 2013. Ebenfalls 2013 Teilnahme an der Biennale in Venedig mit der Installation *The Encyclopedic Palace*. Kunstsammlungen wie die Tate Modern in London, das MoMA in New York, das Centre Pompidou in Paris und die Sammlung zeitgenössischer Kunst der Bundesrepublik Deutschland in Bonn bewahren seine Arbeiten auf. 2014 steht er auf der 8. Berlin Biennale als künstlerischer Berater dem Kurator Juan A. Gaitán zur Seite.

Born 1975 on the Vietnamese island of Phu Quoc; lives and works in Berlin; artist. At the age of four, he flees from Vietnam across the Pacific with his family in a home-made boat and is saved at sea by a Danish cargo ship. In this manner, Danh Vo's family obtains Danish citizenship by mere chance. In Copenhagen, he is a student at Det Kongelige Danske Kunstakademi until 2002 and completes his academic education in 2005 at Städelschule in Frankfurt under Tobias Rehberger. Vo's installation-style works, consisting of documents, photos and works appropriated from other artists, are linked to his life story from the very beginning. In 2007, he wins the blueorange award and in 2012 the Hugo Boss Prize of the Solomon R. Guggenheim Foundation with a one-man exhibition at the Guggenheim Museum, New York, in 2013. He also takes part in the Venice Biennale in 2013 with the installation *The Encyclopedic Palace*. Art collections such as the Tate Modern in London, MoMA in New York, Centre Pompidou in Paris, and the Sammlung zeitgenössischer Kunst der Bundesrepublik Deutschland (The Federal Collection of Contemporary Art) in Bonn have his work in their collections. In 2014, he participates in the 8th Berlin Biennale as an artistic advisor for curator Juan A. Gaitán.

Karl Weißbach

Geboren 1841 als Johann Karl Robert Weißbach in Dresden, gestorben 1905 ebendort; als Architekt verwirklicht Karl Weißbach zusammen mit Johannes Schilling zwischen 1877 – 1883 das Nationaldenkmal auf dem Niederwald bei Rüdesheim. Weißbach absolviert eine Lehre im Bauhandwerk und besucht die Baugewerkschule. In den Diensten des Dresdener Hofbaumeisters Krüger arbeitet Weißbach bis er ein Studium der Architektur an der *Kunstakademie in Dresden* antreten kann. Mithilfe eines Reisestipendiums begibt er sich 1863 auf Italienreise. Mitarbeit an der Publikation *Die Bauwerke der Renaissance in Toskana*. 1866 zurück in Dresden, Arbeit als Bauführer (Bauleiter) für Hermann Nicolai. Er verwirklichte vor allem Bauwerke des öffentlichen Lebens, etwa die *Villa Meyer* in Dresden (1867/1868). Später wird er selbst Professor an der Kunstakademie Dresden. Aus eigenen Stücken gibt er die Position des Professors auf und wird ab 1875 Lehrer an der *Hochbauabteilung des Königlichen Polytechnikums Dresden*. Er entwirft die Architektur des *Niederwalddenkmals* in Zusammenarbeit mit dem Bildhauer Johannes Schilling, welcher für die künstlerische Ausgestaltung des 25 Meter hohen, in Terrassen aufsteigenden Sockels sorgt und das Standbild der 10,5 Meter großen, in Bronze gegossenen *Germania* schafft.

Born Johann Karl Robert Weißbach in 1841 in Dresden, died 1905 in Dresden; as an architect, Karl Weißbach collaborates with Johannes Schilling to realise the Niederwald national monument near Rüdesheim between 1877 and 1883. Weißbach completes an apprenticeship in the construction industry and attends the building trades school (Baugewerkschule). Weißbach remains in the employment of the Dresden-based court architect Krüger until he is able to assume his studies at the Art Academy in Dresden. Having been granted a travel scholarship, he visits Italy in 1863. He then contributes to the publication *Die Bauwerke der Renaissance in Toskana* (The Buildings of the Renaissance in Tuscany). In 1866, back in Dresden, he works as a foreman (construction manager) for Hermann Nicolai. He predominantly works on public buildings, such as Villa Meyer in Dresden (1867–68). He later becomes a professor at the Art Academy in Dresden. He resigns from this position of his own accord and in 1875 assumes a teaching position at the building construction department of the Imperial Polytechnic Institute in Dresden. He designs the architecture for the Niederwald monument in collaboration with sculptor Johannes Schilling, who is responsible for the artistic realisation of the 25-metre high terraced pedestal and the statue of the 10.5 metre large, bronze-cast *Germania*.

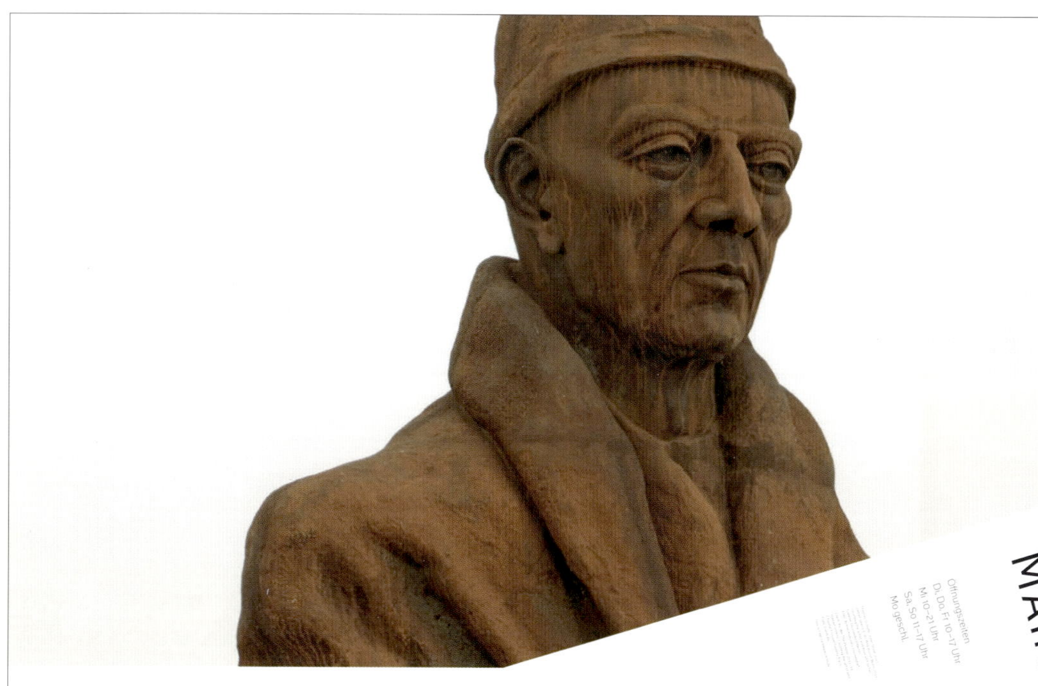

Kunsthalle Mainz
Am Zollhafen 3–5
55118 Mainz
www.kunsthalle-mainz.de
Öffnungszeiten
Di. Do. Fr 10–17 Uhr
Mi 10–21 Uhr
Sa. So 11–17 Uhr
Mo geschl.
KUNSTHALLE
MAINZ
Thomas Schütte
Danh Vo
Das Reich ohne Mitte 5/7 – 6/10/13
KULTURSOMMER
RHEINLAND-PFALZ

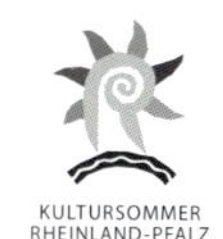

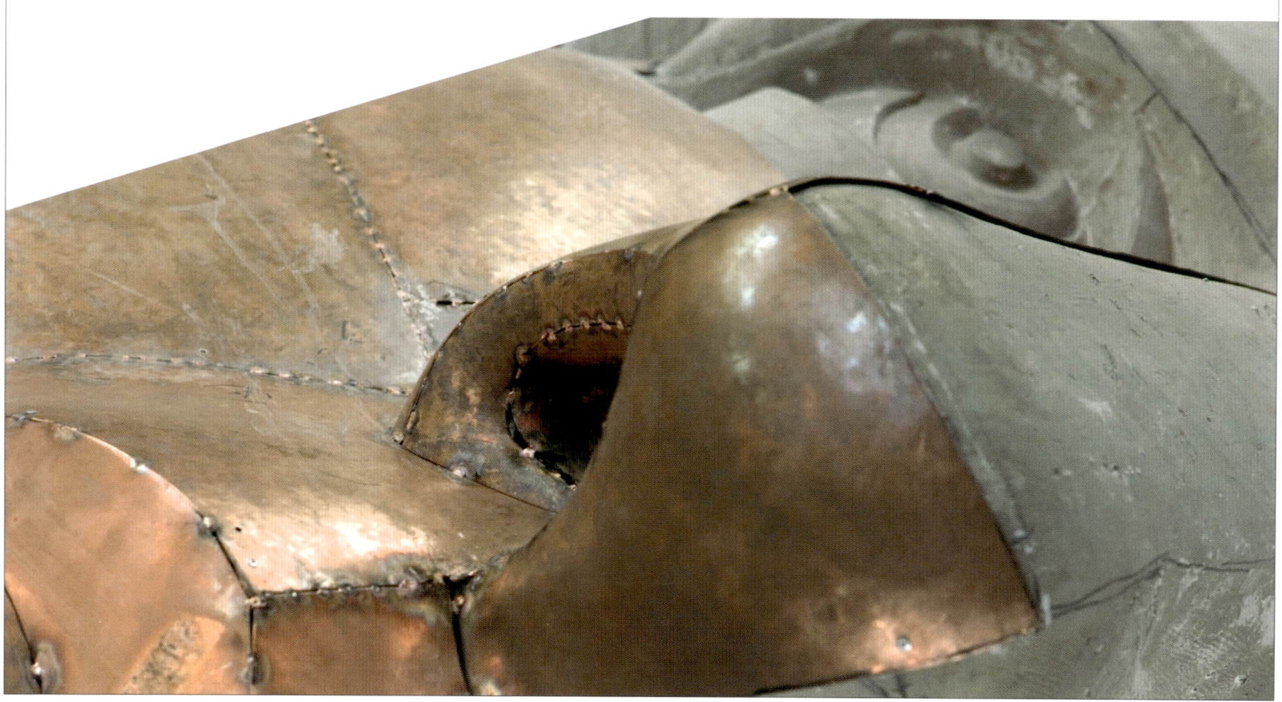

Impressum/*Imprint*

Ausstellung/*Exhibition*
Das Reich ohne Mitte
5 July – 6 October, 2013

Kunsthalle Mainz

Direktor/Kurator
Director/Curator
Thomas D. Trummer

Assistenz/*Assistance*
Fabienne Rosenbach
Isabelle Hammer

Ausstellungsorganisation/
Organisation of exhibition
Sabine Idstein

Kunstvermittlung/*Art mediation*
Angelika Klessinger

Ausstellungsaufbau/
Exhibition construction
Johanna Bodis
Samuel Fath
Thomas Hombach
Oliver Kelm
Lappiyul Park
Philipp Schneider
Katrin Trost
Stephan Truschel

Leihgeber/*Lenders*
AGO Art Gallery of Ontario, Toronto
Archive rbb, Berlin
Archive WDR, Cologne
Gallery Chantal Crousel, Paris,
    Frankreich
Gallery Konrad Fischer, Düsseldorf
Gallery Barbara Weiss, Berlin
General-Anzeiger Bonn/Heinz Engels
Henry Moore Foundation,
    Much Hadham, England
Johannes Schilling House, Mittweida
Musée de la Révolution française,
    Vizille, France
National and university library of
    Lower Saxony, Göttingen
Otto von Bismarck Foundation,
    Friedrichsruh
Private collection Berlin
Collection Rolf Beckers, Baierbrunn
Collection Günter Höhmann, Wiesbaden
Collection Dr. Dorothea van der Koelen, Mainz
Collection Heinz Neumann, Vienna
The city of Rüdesheim am Rhein

Statens Museum for Kunst, Copenhagen,
    Denmark
Thomas Schütte

Die Ausstellung wurde gefördert durch:/
The exhibition has been supported by:
Kultursommer Rheinland-Pfalz

Katalog/*Catalog*
Das Reich ohne Mitte
Zur politischen Skulptur in Deutschland.
Mit Werken von Eduardo Chillida,
    Thomas Hobbes, Henry Moore, Otto Muehl,
    Deimantas Narkevičius, Johannes Schilling,
    Thomas Schütte, Danh Vo.

Herausgeber/*Editor*
Thomas D. Trummer

Texte/*Texts*
Isabelle Hammer, Anina Huck,
    Sabine Idstein, Thomas D. Trummer

Übersetzung/*Translation*
Matthew Harris

Buchgestaltung und Herstellung/
Book Design and Production
FINE GERMAN DESIGN, Frankfurt am Main
    Larissa Pelka, Lilly Hummel, Carsten Wolff,
    Alyona Leonovich, Wim Schafspelz

Fotografien/*Photo Credits*
Norbert Miguletz
Fabienne Rosenbach

Lektorat/*Review*
Anina Huck (dt.)
Jane Calverley (engl.)

Druck/*Print*
Sigert GmbH Druck- und Medienhaus

Bildrechte/*Corporate rights*
Berliner Festspiele GmbH, Berlin
Dr. Dorothea van der Koelen, Mainz
General-Anzeiger Bonn, Heinz Engels
Kunsthalle Mainz, Mainz
Henry Moore Foundation, Much Hadham,
    England
Politikfoto, Frank Ossenbrink, Berlin
Deutscher Bundestag/Julia Nowak, Berlin
Luise Heuter, © VG Bild-Kunst, Bonn 2016

Besonderer Dank an/
Special thanks to
Manuela Alexejew-Brandl und Carlos Brandl,
    Berlin
Rolf Becker, Munich
Penelope Curtis, London
Véronique Despine, Vizille
Nicole Dietrich, Vienna
Jürgen Hardeck, Mainz
Günter Höhmann, Wiesbaden
Detlev Höhne, Mainz
Sibylle Karsch, Mittweida
Georg und Rita Kretkowski, Mainz
Dorothea van der Koelen, Mainz
Johann König, Berlin
Ulrich Lappenküper, Friedrichsruh
Philippe Manzone, Paris
Volker Mosler, Rüdesheim am Rhein
Heinz Neumann, Vienna
Karsten Otte, Göttingen
Thomas Rieger, Düsseldorf
Thomas Schütte, Düsseldorf
Danh Vo, Berlin
Regina Wyrwoll, Cologne

Dank an/*Thanks to*
Jean-Christophe Ammann, Frankfurt am Main
Anita Beckers, Frankfurt am Main
Wolfgang Bickl, Mainz
Gabriele Bohm, Berlin
Rainer Brenner, Mainz
Burkhard Brunn, Frankfurt
Arvid Brunnemann, Berlin
Klaus Bussmann, Paris
Giovanni Carmine, St. Gallen
Elisabeth Gram Christensen, Copenhagen
Jens Cording, Munich
Chantal Crousel, Paris
Thibaut de Champris, Mainz
Melanie Dankbar, Zurich
Anja Dötsch, Bad Homburg v.d.H.
Annette Doms, Munich
Berthold Ecker, Vienna
Edmund Elsen, Mainz
Oliver Elser, Frankfurt am Main
Leonhard Emmerling, Munich
Karl-Albert Engel, Mainz
Stephan Erfurt, Berlin
Ulrike Fassbender, Mainz
Ariane Fellbach-Stein, Mainz
Bärbel Fixemer, Cologne
Reinhold Forschner, Geisenheim
Sandra Frank, Berlin
Wolfgang Frank, Bad Kreuznach
Ferdinand Fürst von Bismarck, Friedrichsruh
Clara Garcia, Toronto
Joachim Gerstmeier, Munich
Laszlo Glozer, Hamburg

Sabine Grabner, Vienna
Susann Gramm, Mittweida
Daniela Gregori, Karlsruhe
Marianne Grosse, Mainz
Susanne Hennche, Bonn
Luise Heuter, Düsseldorf
Wilhelm Huber, Mainz
Anita Hübner, Künzelsau
Werner Huthmacher, Berlin
Christian Janecke, Offenbach
Silke Janßen, Frankfurt am Main
Debbi Johnson, Toronto
Anja Junge, Berlin,
    Schultes Frank Architekten
Wolfgang Kaiser, Mainz-Kastel
Stefan Kleinknecht, Mainz-Kastel
Michaela Klevers, Bonn
Olga Klymovych, Berlin
Knab GmbH, Düsseldorf
Paul Georg Knapstein, Mainz
Kasper König, Berlin
Walter Konrad, Mainz
Axel Kralik, Nuremberg
Mario Kramp, Cologne
Nicole Krapat, Hamburg
Andreas Kübler, Berlin
Achim Kukulies, Düsseldorf
Karsten Löckemann, Munich
Thomas Macho, Berlin
Christoph Mai, Vienna
Heike Maier-Rieper, Vienna
Rainer Metzger, Karlsruhe
Tino Michalski,
    Frankfurt am Main
Nelly Michel, Mainz
Norbert Miguletz,
    Frankfurt am Main
August Moderer, Mainz
Christoph Mücher, Munich
Thomas Mumbächer, Heidesheim
Heike Munder, Zurich
Deimantas Narkevičius, Wilna
Tobias G. Natter, Vienna
Angelika Nollert, Nuremberg
Margot Notarius, Bonn
Raphael Oberhuber, Berlin
Maik Ohnezeit, Friedrichsruh
Frank Ossenbrink, Berlin
Michael Palmen, Kloster Eberbach
Michael Phipps, Hertfordshire
Gerda und Kuno Pieroth,
    Bingen am Rhein
Philippe Pieroth, Berkeley
Andreas Prinzing, Cologne
Martin Reihl, Mainz
Christian Richter, Mainz
Sebastian Rupp, Berlin
Ingeborg Ruthe, Berlin

Eva Schmidt, Siegen
Karl Gerhard Schmidt,
    Nuremberg
Hemma Schmutz, Salzburg
Stefan Schröder, Wiesbaden
Michael Schultz, Moscow
Walter Schumacher, Mainz
Geraldine Sievers, Mainz
Elizabeth Smith, Toronto
Trevor Smith, Salem, MA
Gabi Spindler, Linz
Eva M. Stadler, Munich
Andreas Stopp, Cologne
Birol Teke, Cologne
Frederic Thelen, Wiesbaden
Kerstin Thomer, Mainz
Pauline und Emily Trummer,
    Vienna
Andreas Tyrock, Bonn
Victoria Ubiria, Mainz
Wolfgang Ullrich, Karlsruhe
Bjanka Varmaz, Mainz
Vitus Veh, Vienna
Kirsten Wandschneider,
    Berlin
Grit Weber, Frankfurt
Gregor Wedekind, Mainz
Sylvia Weber, Künzelsau
Silke Wenk, Oldenburg
Peter Weibel, Karlsruhe
Barbara Weiss, Berlin
Renate Wiehager, Stuttgart
Cornelia Willius-Senzer, Mainz
Matthias Winzen, Saarbrücken
Bettina Witte, Wiesbaden
Clara Marie Wörsdörfer, Mainz
Carsten Wolff,
    Frankfurt am Main
Rein Wolfs, Bonn
Reinhold Würth, Salzburg

Abbildung Nachsatz/
    illustration endpapers last page
    Danh Vo
    We the people, (Detail)
Abbildung Vorsatz/
    illustration endpapers first page
    Thomas Schütte
    Vater Staat, (Detail)
Abbildung Nachsatz/
    illustration endpapers last page
    Henry Moore
    Architectural Project, (Detail)
Abbildung Vorsatz/
    illustration endpapers first page
    Ausstellungsansicht Kunsthalle Mainz

Verlagsangaben/*Publisher's imprint*

Erschienen im/*Published by:*
Vfmk Verlag für moderne Kunst GmbH
Salmgasse 4a
A-1030 Wien/*Vienna*
hello@vfmk.org
www.vfmk.org

ISBN 978-3-903153-58-5
Alle Rechte vorbehalten/*All rights reserved*
Gedruckt in Deutschland/*Printed in Germany*

Vertrieb/*Distribution*
Europa/*Europe*: LKG, www.lkg-va.de
CH: AVA, www.ava.ch
UK: Cornerhouse Publications,
    www.cornerhousepublications.org
USA: D.A.P., www.artbook.com

Bibliografische Information der
    Deutschen Nationalbibliothek
Die Deutsche Nationalbibliothek verzeichnet
    diese Publikation in der Deutschen
    Nationalbibliografie; detaillierte bibliografi-
    sche Daten sind im Internet über
    http://dnb.d-nb.de abrufbar./
Bibliographic data of the German National Library
The German National Library lists this
    publication in the Catalogue of the
    German National Library; detailed
    bibliographic data can be accessed under
    http://dnb.d-nb.de.